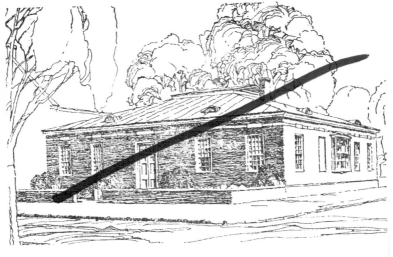

NEW CASTLE LIBRARY

The Road Less Traveled and Beyond

Spiritual Growth in an Age of Anxiety

———— ⚬ ————

M. Scott Peck, M.D.

SIMON & SCHUSTER

SIMON & SCHUSTER
Rockefeller Center
1230 Avenue of the Americas
New York, NY 10020

SIMON & SCHUSTER and colophon are registered trademarks
of Simon & Schuster Inc.

Designed by Irving Perkins Associates

Manufactured in the United States of America

1   3   5   7   9   10   8   6   4   2

Library of Congress Cataloging-in-Publication Data
Peck, M. Scott (Morgan Scott), date.
The road less traveled and beyond : spiritual growth
in an age of anxiety / M. Scott Peck.
p.   cm.
Includes bibliographical references.
1. Spiritual life. 2. Peck, M. Scott (Morgan Scott), 1936–   .
I. Title.
BL624.P43   1997
158—dc20   96-43391
CIP

ISBN 0-684-81314-9

I acknowledge with gratitude the cooperation of all my publishers, including
Bantam Books, HarperSanFrancisco, Harmony Books, Hyperion Books,
Simon & Schuster, and Turner Publishing, for citations and quotations from
my various books. Lyrics for "Can't Keep It In," by Cat Stevens, are reprinted
by permission of Salafa Limited/Sony/ATV Music Publishing.

to my fellow travelers

Contents

�֍

Introduction

❖

I AM SIXTY YEARS OF AGE. That statistic means different things for different people. For me, since I am not in the best of health and feel I've lived enough for three lifetimes, being sixty means that it is time I should start setting my affairs in order, as they say. It seems proper for me these days to be about the business of tying up loose ends of my life insofar as it is in my power to do so. I write this book in that endeavor.

I wrote *The Road Less Traveled* at the vigorous age of forty. It was as if a spigot had been opened, and other books have come pouring out ever since: nine, to be exact, not counting this one. Each time people have asked me what I hoped to achieve by a particular book, as if I generally had a grand strategy in mind. The truth is I wrote them not out of strategy, but simply because each book has said, "Write me." However hard she might be to define, there is such a thing as a muse, and I have always and only operated under her orders.

So it is now, but I believe a more complex explanation is in order. One of those works, a collection of my edited lectures, is entitled *Further Along the Road Less Traveled,* as is the series of audiotapes from which it was developed. The title of this one makes it sound like "The Road Less Traveled III." I worry the sound may be misleading. The fact is that my muse won't allow me to write the same book over and again no matter how commercially smart it might be to do so.

All of my books are quite different from each other. Yet not totally different. With the perspective of age I've come to realize that in their own unique ways they have all been attempts to work out the same complex set of hidden themes. Looking backward, recently I discerned that I have been wrestling with these themes as far back as I can remember. At the time it felt as if *The Road Less Traveled* arose de novo when I was forty. Now I can see how I'd begun work on it and my other books before I'd even entered adolescence. Perhaps I was born working on these themes. Or perhaps I was born *to* work on them. I don't know.

What I do know is that the work was already in progress of a sort two decades before the publication of *The Road Less Traveled*. In late 1957 and early 1958, at the age of twenty-one, I wrote a college senior thesis with the egregious title of "Anxiety, Modern Science, and the Epistemological Problem." Epistemology is that branch of philosophy which addresses the question: "How do we know what we think we know? How do we know anything?" The epistemological problem is that philosophers have never succeeded in answering the question. Many in the nineteenth century thought the answer lay in science. We could know things for certain through the scientific method. As my thesis pointed out, however, perhaps the single most important discovery of modern science has been that there are limits to scientific inquiry. With a few ifs, ands, and buts, there is no more real certainty to be found in science than in theology. Yet uncertainty breeds anxiety. It is scary when our best minds are those who best know that they don't know. This is why W. H. Auden referred to our century as the Age of Anxiety—a time when the Age of Reason has proved to be just as unsettling a period as the Age of Faith.

My college thesis provided no answers, only questions, and one way or another those same questions are echoed in each and every one of my books. A major theme of all of them is the encouragement of the greatest possible range of thought in our search for their answers. Thus the third of the four sections of *The Road Less Traveled* concludes: "But just as it is essential that our sight not be crippled by scientific tunnel vision, so also it is essential that our critical faculties and capacity for skepticism not be blinded by the brilliant beauty of the spiritual realm."

Once I put that college thesis behind me (or so I thought), I got on with the business of real life: medical school, marriage, children, specialty training in psychiatry, military and government service, and eventually private practice. Yet, without knowing that one—much less many—books would eventuate, I was beginning, almost unconsciously, to develop some cautious, tentative answers to my own questions. When enough such answers had accumulated, it came to me twenty years later to write *The Road Less Traveled*. And, as they continued to accumulate, I went on to write what I thought were very different works.

They *are* very different. Yet whether for adults or children, whether focused upon the individual or society, whether fiction or nonfiction, they all may be looked upon in part as elaborations of one or more of the key concepts in *The Road Less Traveled*. As elaborations they carry those concepts further; they look deeper; they go *beyond*. This book is entitled *The Road Less Traveled and Beyond* because it ties together many of the ways in which I have been pushed—often stumbling—to move beyond my first book in both my public writing and my personal journey over the past twenty years.

Some may consider this book a compilation, a compendium, or a summary of all my published work, but those words are inadequate. In writing the book, I found that I had to be quite selective. "Synthesis" would be a more adequate description, but still fails to capture the "beyondness" of the book. For in addition to tying up loose ends, I wanted to break new ground as well. I have been powerfully assisted in doing so by a quote attributed to Justice Oliver Wendell Holmes, Jr., who once said: "I don't give a fig for the simplicity of this side of complexity, but I would die for the simplicity on the other side."* His profound sentiment has led me to organize this work into three sections.

---

*The exact origin of the quote of the quote is unknown, but I am grateful to Max DuPree for passing it on to me in his book, *The Art of Leadership*.

In Part I, "Crusade Against Simplism," I decry the primitive and effortless simplistic thinking that lies at the root of so much individual and societal sickness.

In Part II, "Wrestling with the Complexity of Everyday Life," I describe the complex choices we must continually make and remake if we are to live well.

And in Part III, "The Other Side of Complexity," I describe where we can arrive when we have been willing to pay all our proper intellectual and emotional dues.

Although the phrase "the Other Side" rings with possible intimations of heaven, I am not so bold as to suggest that we can reach heaven this side of the grave. What I do suggest, however, is that we can indeed come to exist in a closer relationship to the Holy. And that on the other side of complexity there is a kind of simplicity where we can know with humility that in the end all things point to God.

Editor's Preface

※

I FIRST MET M. SCOTT PECK in the summer of 1995. I had written him a letter to thank him for his book, *In Search of Stones*, and to tell him of its profound effect on my life. I had also read two of his earlier books, *The Road Less Traveled* and *People of the Lie*, which had become, as I wrote in my letter, companions—intellectual and spiritual—on my own journey of personal growth.

Three weeks later, I received a letter from Dr. Peck in which he wrote that he was in search of an editor for his new book and asked if I would like to explore the possibility of undertaking the job. I was both flattered and surprised. We spoke on the phone, later met, and then, after several long and probing conversations, we began our work together. Over the course of the next ten months, it was a challenge and an exhilarating experience to have a part in the evolution of *The Road Less Traveled and Beyond*.

Many readers of this book will be familiar with Dr. Peck's earlier works, although that is not necessary for a full comprehension of *The Road Less Traveled and Beyond*. Nevertheless, it may be useful here to mention those books and comment briefly on their major themes.

The Road Less Traveled (New York: Simon & Schuster, 1978) was Dr. Peck's first book. Breaking new ground—as reflected in its subtitle, "A New Psychology of Love, Traditional Values and Spiritual Growth"—the book stemmed from Dr. Peck's work as a psychotherapist with patients struggling to avoid or to gain greater levels of maturity. An enormously popular and influential book, *The Road Less Traveled* helped bridge the gap between psychology and religion. In it, Dr. Peck wrote that he made little distinction between the mind and the spirit and, therefore, little distinction between the process of achieving emotional maturity and spiritual growth.

In the Italian edition, the title of *The Road Less Traveled* was translated as *Volo di Bene,* which means "The Good Path," because there is a tradition in Italy to compare the "good path" to the "bad path." So it was not coincidental that Dr. Peck, having written a book about the good path, followed it with one about the bad path. In *People of the Lie* (New York: Simon & Schuster, 1983), he probed in depth the essence of human evil. Writing that people who are evil place themselves in direct opposition to the truth and harm others instead of facing their own failures and limitations, he dramatically demonstrated how they seek to avoid undertaking the difficult task of personal growth. Again, presenting cases encountered in his psychiatric practice, he described vivid incidents of evil in everyday life and their ramifications, as well as offering thoughts about the possibilities for healing human evil.

Dr. Peck's next book, *What Return Can I Make? Dimensions of the Christian Experience* (New York: Simon & Schuster, 1985) was coauthored with Marilyn von Waldner, O.C.D., and Patricia Kay. Accompanied by the spiritual music of von Waldner and the abstract drawings of Kay, the book was dedicated to the "glory of God." In it, Dr. Peck reflected on themes related to his own journey of spiritual growth into Christianity. Although it is his most evangelical work, it does not exclude those not identified as Christians. It is about the discovery of God and the mystery of faith. The book, without the art and sheet music but with the audiotape of songs by von Waldner, was republished and retitled *Gifts for the Journey: Treasures of the Christian Life* (San Francisco: HarperSanFrancisco, 1995).

In 1984, Dr. Peck, his wife, Lily, and nine others started the Foundation for Community Encouragement (FCE), a nonprofit organization for promoting the experience of community as a means of improving human relationships among individuals, small groups, and nations. As a direct consequence of his work with FCE, Dr. Peck wrote *The Different Drum* (New York: Simon & Schuster, 1987) in which he challenged readers to take another journey in self-awareness to achieve a new level of "connectedness" through the creative experience of community.

In a departure from nonfiction, Dr. Peck's next book was a psychological thriller, *A Bed by the Window* (New York: Bantam Books, 1990), subtitled *A Novel of Mystery and Redemption*. Superficially an account of sex, love, and death set in a nursing home, it is, as its subtitle suggests, more than a mystery story; it is an exploration of the nature of mystery itself on multiple levels.

The Friendly Snowflake (Atlanta: Turner Publishing, Inc., 1992), illustrated by Peck's son, Christopher Peck, was also a work of fiction, a story about a young girl's voyage into spiritual awareness. The book's main concerns are life, love, faith, and family.

Dr. Peck's next book, *A World Waiting to Be Born: Civility Rediscovered* (New York: Bantam Books, 1993) explored the role of civility in personal relationships and in society as a whole. Challenging us to recognize the cultural consequences of incivility, Dr. Peck wrote of the many morally disruptive patterns of behavior—both subtle and blatant—that seem ingrained in human relationships, and proposed changes that can be effected to achieve both personal and societal well-being.

Further Along the Road Less Traveled: The Unending Journey Toward Spiritual Growth (New York: Simon & Schuster, 1993) elaborated on themes and concepts first explored in *The Road Less Traveled* and was a revised and edited collection of Dr. Peck's lectures.

Dr. Peck's next work was *In Search of Stones* (New York: Hyperion Books, 1995), an integration of themes related to history, travel, and autobiography. Subtitled *A Pilgrimage of Faith, Reason and Discovery*, it was the story of a three-week trip through the countryside of Wales, England, and Scotland that becomes an adventure of the spirit and an exploration of the complexities of our journey through life.

Dr. Peck returned to fiction with *In Heaven as on Earth* (New York: Hyperion, 1996), a story whose characters inhabit an afterlife where they must confront and attempt to resolve the conflicts and complexities of their lives on earth.

And finally, Dr. Peck is now at work on a new book entitled *Denial of the Soul: Spiritual and Medical Perspectives on Euthanasia* (scheduled for publication in 1997 by Harmony Books).

Collectively, Dr. Peck's books have been a demonstration of both his unfolding consciousness and the ever-increasing courage of his thoughts. There is something in each that we may find helpful, and can emulate, as we strive to develop our own spiritual lives. This book, I feel, will provide profound new insights to guide us on this continuing journey. In its unique way—like the author and each of his books—it has a spirit of its own.

Fannie LeFlore

PART I

Crusade Against Simplism

CHAPTER 1

Thinking

❄

IN IRELAND, THE MIDDLE EAST, SOMALIA, Sri Lanka, and countless other war-torn areas around the world, prejudice, religious intolerance, greed, and fear have erupted into violence that has taken the lives of millions. In America, the damage caused by institutionalized racism is perhaps more subtle but no less devastating to the social fabric. Rich versus poor, black versus white, pro-life versus pro-choice, straight versus gay—all are social, political, and economic conflicts fought under the banner of some ideology or deeply held belief. But given the divisive and destructive results, are these ideologies and beliefs rational, or mere rationalizations for otherwise unreasonable acts? How often, in fact, do we stop to think about what we believe? One of the major dilemmas we face both as individuals and as a society is simplistic thinking—or the failure to think at all. It isn't just *a* problem, it is *the* problem.

Given the imperfections of our society and the apparent downward spiral of spiritual and moral values in recent years, thinking has become a grave issue. It is more urgent now—perhaps more urgent than anything else—because it is the means by which we consider, decide, and act upon everything in our increasingly complex world. If we don't begin to think well, it's highly likely that we may end up killing ourselves.

In one way or another, each of my books has been—symbolically and substantively—a crusade against simplistic thinking. I began *The Road Less Traveled* with the assertion that "life is difficult." In *Further Along the Road Less Traveled,* I added that "life is complex." Here, it can further be said that "there are no easy answers." And although I believe the route to finding answers is primarily through better thinking, even this is not as simple as it may seem.

Thinking is difficult. Thinking is complex. And thinking is—more than anything else—a process, with a course or direction, a lapse of time, and a series of steps or stages that lead to some result. To think well is a laborious, often painstaking process until one becomes accustomed to being "thoughtful." Since it is a process, the course or direction may not always be clear-cut. Not all the steps or stages are linear, nor are they always in the same sequence. Some are circular and overlap with others. Not everyone seeks to achieve the same result. Given all this, if we are to think well, we must be on guard against simplistic thinking in our approach to analyzing crucial issues and solving the problems of life.

Although people are different, an all-too-common flaw is that most tend to believe they somehow instinctively know how to think and to communicate. In reality, they usually do neither well because they are either too self-satisfied to examine their assumptions about thinking or too self-absorbed to invest the time and energy to do so. As a result, it is impossible to tell why they think as they do or how they make their decisions. And when challenged, they show very little awareness of—or become easily frustrated by—the dynamics involved in truly thinking and communicating well.

Twice during my career as a lecturer, I gave an all-day seminar on thinking. At the beginning of each, I pointed out that most people think they already know how to think. At the conclusion of each, during a feedback session, someone said in sheer exasperation, "The subject is simply too large." Indeed, thinking isn't a topic that anyone can digest thoroughly in one sitting. Whole books can be (and have been) written about it. It is no surprise that many people resist the arduous efforts involved in continually monitoring and revising their thinking. And no surprise that by the end of the seminars most of the participants felt so overwhelmed by all that is really involved in thinking that they were either numbed or horrified. Needless to say, these were not among my more popular engagements. Yet if all the energy required to think seems troublesome, the lack of thinking causes far more trouble and conflict for ourselves as individuals and for the society in which we live.

ᵛ   Hamlet's often quoted "To be or not to be?" is one of life's ultimate existential questions. Another question gets to the heart of how we interpret that existence. I would paraphrase Shakespeare to ask, "To think or not to think?" That is the ultimate question in combating simplism. And at this point in human evolution, it may be the very equivalent of "To be or not to be?"

From my practice as a psychiatrist and my experiences and observations in general, I have become familiar with the common errors related to the failure to think well. One, of course, is simply not thinking. Another is making assumptions in thinking, through the use of one-dimensional logic, stereotypes, and labeling. Another problem is the belief that thinking and communication don't require much effort. Another is assuming that thinking is a waste of time, which is a particular factor in the quiet rage we experience around the failure to solve many social problems.

Leonard Hodgson wrote: "It is not through trust in our reason that we go wrong, but because through our sinfulness our reason is so imperfectly rational. The remedy is not the substitution of some other form of acquiring knowledge for rational apprehension; it is the education of our reason to be its true self." Although the language is somewhat misleading, since his book dates back over fifty years, Hodgson's words are relevant to the dilemma we face today. For "reason," I would substitute the word "thinking" and all that it implies. By "sinfulness," Hodgson was referring, I believe, to our combined "original" sins of laziness, fear, and pride, which limit us or prevent us from fulfilling the human potential. In referring to "the education of our reason to be its true self," Hodgson suggests that we should allow our true self to be whatever it's capable of, to rise to its fullest capacity. The point is not that we shouldn't trust our brain, specifically our frontal lobes. The point is that we don't use them enough. Because of our sins of laziness, fear, and pride, we don't put our brain to full use. We are faced with the task of educating ourselves to be fully human.

THE POINT OF HAVING A BRAIN

Obvious as this may seem, we've been given a large brain so that we can think. One characteristic that distinguishes human beings from other creatures is the relatively large size of our brain, compared to our overall body weight. (The exceptions are whales and dolphins. They have larger brains in proportion to their bodies than people do, which is one reason many animal rights activists are vehement in their mission to protect these species; they believe whales and dolphins may, in fact, be smarter than we are in some ways.)

Whether in humans or other mammals, the brain consists of three components—the old brain, the midbrain, and the new brain. Each has unique functions in the orchestra of organs that work in unison to keep us alive.

The old brain—which is also called the reptilian brain—looks little different in humans than it does in worms. At the top of our spinal cord, we have an elongated bulge that's called the medulla oblongata. Throughout the brain are collections of nerve cells called neural centers. In the old brain these centers serve the purpose of monitoring physiological needs, such as controlling our respiration, heart rate, sleep, appetite, and other very basic but primitive functions.

The area known as the midbrain is larger and more complex. The neural centers of the midbrain are involved in the governance and in the production of emotions, and neurosurgeons have actually mapped out the locations of these centers. With a human being lying on an operating table under local anesthesia, they can insert electrodes or very fine needles into the brain, from the tip of which they can deliver a millivolt of electrical current and actually produce specific emotions such as anger, euphoria, and even depression.

The new brain consists mostly of our cerebral cortex, which is also involved in primitive activities including instincts and locomotion. The biggest difference between us humans and the other mammals is the size of our new brain, and specifically of that part known as the frontal lobes. The direction of human evolution has been primarily in the growth of the frontal lobes. These lobes are involved in our ability to make judgments, and it is here that the processing of information—thinking—primarily takes place.

Just as our capacity for learning depends on thinking, our capacity for thinking well depends on learning. So another central factor that distinguishes human beings from other creatures is related to our ability to learn. While we have instincts like other animals', they don't always automatically govern our behavior to as great a degree. This factor gives us free will. We've been endowed with the combination of these frontal lobes and freedom, which enables us to learn throughout a lifetime.

Compared to that of other mammals, the period of our childhood dependency is much longer relative to our total life span. Given our relative lack of instincts, we need that time to learn before we are able to branch out on our own. Learning is crucial to our ability to grow in awareness, to think independently, and to master the knowledge necessary for surviving and thriving in life.

When we are young, our dependency on those who raise us shapes our thinking and what we learn. And given our lengthy dependence, we are at risk of developing thinking patterns that may become ingrained, even seemingly irreversible. If we have adults in our young lives who help us learn to think well, we benefit in a multitude of ways. If we have adults in our young lives whose own thinking is suspect, disordered, or otherwise limited, our thinking will be impaired by what we learn and don't learn from them. But it would be nonsense to presume that we are doomed. As adults, we no longer have to depend on others to tell us what to think or do.

There is a distinction between healthy and unhealthy dependency. In *The Road Less Traveled,* I wrote that dependency in physically healthy adults is pathological—it is sick, always a manifestation of a mental illness or defect. It is to be distinguished, however, from what are commonly referred to as dependency needs or feelings. We all—each and every one of us, even if we try to pretend to others and to ourselves that we don't—have dependency needs and feelings. We have desires to be babied, to be nurtured without effort on our part, to be cared for by persons who are stronger than we are and have our interests truly at heart. But for most of us these desires or feelings do not rule our lives; they are not the predominant theme of our existence. When they do rule our lives and dictate the quality of our existence, we are suffering from a psychiatric illness commonly known as passive dependent personality disorder. Such dependency is, at root, a disorder related to thinking—specifically, a resistance to thinking for ourselves.

Just as the myriad of disorders that stem from resistance to thinking are complex, so also is the relationship between these disorders and our complex brain. One particularly exciting area of research has shed some light on aspects of this relationship. In the last twenty years, a major breakthrough came about as a result of split-brain research examining more deeply the well-known fact that the new brain is divided into a right and a left half. A body of fibers or white matter, the corpus callosum, connects these two hemispheres. It is now believed that the left brain is our deductive brain and the right brain is primarily involved in inductive reasoning. These patterns are not total absolutes, but more or less indicate tendencies.

Some people with epilepsy have been treated and a few cured by severing this connection between the two halves of the brain. Later, these "split-brain" patients were scientifically studied, and a very dramatic study showed that if you cover the eye of someone whose brain has been severed so that visual information gets only to the left brain, and you show him, for instance, an electrical heater, his description of the object will be very specific and telling. He'll likely say, "Well, it's a box with a cord and filaments heated up by electricity." And he'll go on to describe various component parts with stunning accuracy. But he won't be able to name the appliance. On the other hand, if you feed information only to the right side of his brain, he will be able to name the appliance but won't be able to explain why it is what it is.

The crux of split-brain research has shown that the left side is the analytical brain, with the ability to take wholes and break them up into pieces, while the right side is the intuitive brain with the ability to take pieces and makes wholes out of them. As human beings, we have the ability to learn both of these two primary types of thinking: concrete and abstract. Concrete thinking deals with particulars in their material form. Abstract thinking deals with particulars in general and theoretical terms.

The results of split-brain research are one reason it has been suggested that gender differences go beyond mere social conditioning. Women seem to be more right-brained and men more left-brained. That's why in matters involving sex and romance, men seem more likely to be interested in parts, such as breasts, legs, and penises. Women tend to be more interested in the whole picture, which might include not only sexual stimuli but also a night out with candlelight dinner. Therefore, in the battle of the sexes, women frequently have difficulty understanding why men are so focused on these silly concrete physical parts and men likewise have difficulty understanding why women might want to waste time with all this romantic candlelight stuff before getting down to the "real business."

The research on split brains represents, I believe, the most formidable advance in the field of epistemology, suggesting that we have at least two ways of knowing, and that obviously we will know things better if we use both left-brain and right-brain thinking. That's why I'm a great proponent of androgynous thinking. Being androgynous does not imply that someone is desexed. Men do not lose their masculinity and women do not lose their femininity if they are androgynous. Rather, they display the characteristics of both sexes. Thinking, in that sense, would imply the ability to use both sides of the brain to integrate concrete and abstract realities.

In *The Friendly Snowflake,* the main character, Jenny, epitomizes someone who is androgynous. She uses these dual aspects of her thinking capabilities as she considers the relevance that the mysterious presence of a friendly snowflake has in her life. Her brother, Dennis, on the other hand, is stereotypically left-brain-oriented. He is very much hooked on analytical and concrete facts and has less taste for mystery, which makes his vision narrower.

The ancient Sumerians, I am told, had a basic rule for guiding their thinking not unlike split-brain theory. With regard to any important decisions to be made (usually about whether or not to go to war with the Babylonians), they literally had to think twice. If the first decision had been arrived at when they were drunk, it had to be reconsidered when they were sober. If, when drunk, they said, "Let's go get those Babylonians," then later, in the clear, cool light of day, it might not look like such a smart decision. Conversely, if they were cold sober when they decided that it would be strategically clever to beat up the Babylonians, they held off and said, "First let's drink some wine." Drunk, they might come to the conclusion that "there's no need to go to war with them. Hell, we love the Babylonians."

For all they lacked in modern technology, the Sumerians had the right approach. And there's no reason why we shouldn't be able to think reasonably in this day and age. Unless there is brain damage as a result of surgery or a tumor or other disease, we have these wonderful frontal lobes at our disposal. But that doesn't mean people will use them, much less use them to their fullest capacity. Indeed, brain damage isn't the only factor contributing to thinking irrationally or not at all. It is the least of the factors. Among others, there are profound ways in which society actually discourages us from using our frontal lobes, promoting one-dimensional, simplistic thinking as the normal way of functioning.

SIMPLISM AND SOCIETY

Everywhere we turn, the evidence is astounding. Simplistic thinking has become so pandemic in society that it is considered normal and conventional wisdom among some segments of the population. Recent examples of this rampant simplism were evident in the comments of two North Carolina politicians. Representative Henry Aldridge of Pitt County made the simple-minded statement that women who are raped don't get pregnant because "the juices don't flow, the body functions don't work" during an attack, as if to whitewash this horrible crime of violation. U.S. Senator Jesse Helms, in arguing why he wanted to reduce federal funding for AIDS research, said that he saw no reason to provide adequate resources because the disease is brought on by the "deliberate, disgusting and revolting conduct" of those who are gay. The reality is that in addition to being sexually transmitted—among both homosexuals and heterosexuals—AIDS has been transmitted through blood transfusions, to newborn babies through mothers infected with the virus, and to health care workers who were accidentally pricked by improperly sterilized needles used on infected patients. Thus, Helms' comment smacks not only of bigotry but of simplism as well.

Various institutions of society, in their failure to teach or demonstrate how to think well, set people up for thinking simplistically. Typically, this failure is found among the most immensely influential institutions of society including, more often than not, the family, the church, and the mass media. Given that they have the greatest impact on our lives, the deceptive messages they impart to us about what's important in life cannot be taken lightly. Because they are our cultural leaders in portraying certain ways of thinking and living as truth, these institutions have the power to fool and manipulate us. They often unwittingly promote half-truths—sometimes even blatant lies—under the guise of cultural ideas that we've taken for granted to be "normal." On the basis of cultural norms, we usually assume that if everyone is thinking this or doing that, it must be normal and correct.

Such norms include not only notions about what should be the good life and what should be acceptable, but also what should be considered bad or inappropriate. There are positive norms, of course, such as those that promote the work ethic and encourage civility in our encounters with each other. But these positive norms are not the problem. The norms that create cultural chaos are the ones we must rethink. I call them negative norms, and frequently, they are dressed up and made to look and sound pretty. But when you go beneath the surface, you'll find they are negative precisely because they discourage our growth. They are based on half-truths and outright lies that serve to manipulate and hold us hostage psychologically and spiritually.

In *People of the Lie,* I indicated that lies create confusion. Because of the difficulty institutions would have if they were to endorse blatant lies, they usually manipulate people by promoting half-truths. It is a more seductive approach, but a half-truth, which usually looks and sounds true but really isn't, is likely to produce even greater confusion. Indeed, as the English poet Alfred, Lord Tennyson wrote: "A lie which is half a truth is ever the blackest of lies."

The biggest lie promoted by various of our social institutions—and this in some ways plays into our human nature and our sin of laziness—is that we're here to be happy all the time. We're bombarded by business, the media, and the church with the lie that we're here to be happy, fulfilled, and comfortable. For motives of profit, the lies of materialism and advertising suggest that if we're not happy, comfortable, and fulfilled, we must be eating the wrong cereal or driving the wrong car. Or that we must not have it right with God. How wicked! The truth is that our finest moments, more often than not, occur precisely when we are uncomfortable, when we're not feeling happy or fulfilled, when we're struggling and searching.

In this bombardment of one-dimensional thinking, we're told in clear but subtle ways about what is expected of us in order to fit into society. We are discouraged from questioning or sorting through, much less confronting, the lies inherent in materialism. If we want to be seen as normal, we are simply expected to go along to get along. But it is not simply a matter of our being dumped on. Frequently, we willingly go along with the lies. Our laziness—our natural idolatry of ease and comfort—makes us co-conspirators with the mass media.

Of course people are different, but many make up their minds—even about important issues—on the basis of very little information except what society tells them is "normal." Given a choice, most opt not to think things through. They take the lazy way out, buying into simplistic assumptions and stereotypes. In the quest to feel they fit in, they fall prey to mass-media lies and manipulations in order to believe they are not that different from their neighbors or so they can feel they're keeping up with the Joneses. They feel compelled to buy the cereals advertisers say will make them healthy and fit, without questioning the validity of such claims. They base their sense of worth primarily on the purchase of luxury cars and other amenities they cannot afford, even though it will put them in financial strain with long-term debt.

Many go along with negative norms even though an inner gnawing tells them something is suspect. It is quite common for those who are circles, so to speak, to attempt to force themselves to fit into the square pegs of cultural patterns. They are unwilling to challenge norms, in part to avoid paying the price of unpopularity, of being viewed as outcasts who are somehow abnormal. They usually live to regret it. Having established a solid career by the age of thirty-five, but still single, Sally is under great social pressure to marry the next man who comes along. Given society's suspicions and criticism of "old maids," she succumbs without thinking about the issues more radically and for herself. But Sally years later may come to know that she should have followed her own hunches about getting married. Laid off in a corporate downsizing when he is fifty-five, a man like Bill may find himself in deep regret that he bypassed the opportunity to pursue the career he always wanted in nursing and instead bought into the company-man image as the norm. Men in our society experience tremendous pressure to prove their masculinity through their income. But Bill lost out by not daring to be different.

Media images are rife with rigid concepts about our humanity. The fiftyish woman who can't relinquish her image as forever thirty will make herself miserable to maintain her alliance with simplism, and in the process circumvent the possibility of finding grace in the aging process. While this may be easily dismissed as being *her* problem, it is important to recognize that this woman is not alone. The negative norm in our advertising directly or indirectly suggests that women are primarily sexual objects who lose their value as they age. The valuable male in our advertising is the one who makes money. In part because of the simplism inherent in sexist thinking, many a man deems his work outside the home exponentially more important than his wife's homemaking skills in order to boost his self-image, despite the tensions it creates to uphold his flawed assumptions. Rather than update their vision, both men and women in our society engage in simplistic thinking in order to conform to negative norms.

We may feel somewhat like hostages in this predicament. We are caught between the demands of conformity on the one hand, while on the other, given our free will, we can decide that it is in our best interest to rise above conventional group-think. We have the ability to think independently about important issues rather than lead many aspects of our lives in accordance with the simplistic tenets of society. Granted, it takes effort to sort through what we should and shouldn't believe. When we deny ourselves autonomy, it is no wonder we become confused and uncomfortable. But when we use simplistic formulas based on the "normal"—or fashionable—thing to do, internal if not external chaos is the usual result.

WHAT'S IN FASHION ISN'T NECESSARILY FASHIONABLE

The extensive influence of fashion in our culture often leads to conformity through simplistic thinking. We are a fashion-obsessed culture, whether the fashion of the day involves what to wear, what kind of music to listen to, or which political ideology to subscribe to at the moment. Our incredible emphasis on fashion discourages people from thinking independently and encourages conventional thinking in accordance with generally accepted views and stereotypes. Such thinking may border on the irrational or cross the line into insanity, as it did for our nation in Vietnam.

We have an obligation to confront our simplistic thinking about what being "normal" should mean: an obligation to use critical thinking. Think, for instance, about our Constitution. For close to a century, it counted a slave as three-fifths of a person. That was fundamentally crazy. There's no such thing as a fifth of a person. Either you're a person or you're not. While it may have been fashionable—a workable political and social compromise at the time—this anomaly wasn't seriously questioned for decades.

To use critical thinking doesn't suggest that everyone must become a walking encyclopedia. It doesn't mean we all have to know everything about the *Dred Scott* decision, for example. But we have an obligation to study, learn, and think about those things that are of high importance. One of the most crucial skills of critical thinking is that of deciding what is essential to think or learn about, and what is nonessential. And we must acknowledge the gaps in our own knowledge, rather than feel compelled to let pride, fear, or laziness lure us into assuming the role of know-it-all.

ASSUMPTIONS, STEREOTYPES, AND LABELING

To assume we know everything, and particularly something we don't really know, is, as the old saying goes, to make an ass out of you and me. The simplism of assumptions is a way of life for some. There are people who assume their way of thinking—whether it's about a woman's right to abortion or about prayer in schools—has to be "always right," despite any evidence to the contrary. When it involves a precarious need to preserve their own false sense of integrity and dignity, their self-image becomes cloaked in assumptions of righteousness. They can't—won't—consider alternatives. Perhaps it would feel almost like death to do so, to let go of their simplism.

Some of the most common—and often destructive—assumptions are based on stereotypes about ourselves and other people. Stereotyping typically involves labeling and categorizing people and things in a simpleminded manner, then making judgments on the basis of the assumptions we attach to these categories. Such assumptions often prove to be misleading. The hero of my novel *In Heaven as on Earth* starts off assuming that there will be no mystery in heaven; everything will be bland, straightforward, and clear-cut. To his surprise, he finds that heaven—like earth—consists of a complex maze of surprises, twists, and turns rather than some simplistic utopia.

Many make judgments about others on the basis of labels—for example, associating liberals with bleeding hearts and conservatives with the righteously rigid. Racial and ethnic labels are rife with often misleading assumptions about the characters of individuals who are identified with these groups. A Jewish person's political disposition may be incorrectly perceived by some on the basis of categories dividing Judaism into Orthodox, Conservative, and Reform camps. Used-car salesmen are judged by some to be sleazy or unscrupulous, thus undermining the reputation of the many hardworking salesmen whose characters are above reproach. And there is a common assumption that anyone who openly calls himself a Christian must be a fundamentalist, or that anyone who calls himself agnostic must not be spiritually mature.

While some stereotypes may have a grain of truth to them, frequently they are too simplistic to capture the subtle differences, as well as the similarities, in making comparisons and judgments. When extreme, they may form the basis of assumptions that are used to bring about or justify potentially destructive actions.

One of the main dynamics of my murder mystery, *A Bed by the Window*, is the stereotypical thinking of a young detective. On the basis of his many assumptions, Lieutenant Petri makes a host of errors in thinking and judgment that lead him to come perilously close to arresting the wrong person. His first assumption leads him to narrow his investigation to one female nurse simply because she had been sexually involved with the murder victim. His second assumption is believing that this woman couldn't possibly have loved the victim because he was so physically deformed, even though she in fact cared deeply for him. And because more people at the nursing home had died during the shift that this nurse worked, Lieutenant Petri assumes she is a mass murderer who kills patients in the name of mercy.

One of the most cynical assumptions espoused by Lieutenant Petri also turns out to be the most blinding. He believes that people in nursing homes who are senile can never think. As a result, he dismisses subtle leads, overlooks significant clues, and neglects important aspects of his experiences in connecting with others during his investigation.

In his generic stereotypes about people in nursing homes, the character is modeled after myself. Initially in my own professional career when I worked with patients in a nursing home, I wore blinders. My assumption was that nursing homes were mere dumping grounds for the living dead. Over time, what I found instead was an environment with varied depths, filled with interesting people, humor, love, and all other aspects of human behavior. As I did through firsthand experience, Lieutenant Petri eventually learns to look beyond the surface. He gradually has his eyes opened to the realization that simplistic thinking often leads us down blind alleys.

We indeed go down blind alleys when we rely strictly on assumptions, labels, and stereotypes and think about people in a simplistic way. To assume, because I write about spirituality, that I do not have human failings would be a simplistic conclusion.

To say that someone who identifies himself as a Christian must therefore automatically be holier than all others would be another simplistic assumption. With religion in particular, there's a tendency for many to use labels and assumptions to validate their spirituality. Some think that the denomination to which they belong must be the one and only route to realizing God. That is mistaken. God doesn't care as much about labels as She does about substance.

Labeling of people and things always has hidden liabilities. For one, it diminishes and depletes their depth. In my opinion, the assumption that someone who is physically beautiful is also kinder and smarter than someone who is physically deformed is only that: an assumption, not a truth. Yet study after study done on this subject shows that most people favor those who are viewed as attractive and most often attribute such benevolent qualities to them.

Many assumptions we draw from labeling keep life at the level of superficiality. We neglect to question our conclusions. It would, however, be just as simplistic to say that there's never any good reason for labeling. Scientists must categorize things to test theories and to replicate results. Teachers must recognize that not every seventh-grader is capable of becoming a great writer. Parents must distinguish between the personal tastes and temperaments of their children if they're going to be perceptive enough to respond to the specific needs of each child. So labeling has its purposes—limited purposes. When it's productive, it serves to help us make quick, sometimes lifesaving decisions. If you're on the street at night and being approached by a menacing stranger with a gun, it would be foolish to say, "Hm, let me analyze this before I flee."

We need to use labels to size up some things. There are times when we must make temporary decisions until we have more information or experience about a situation or person. But for the most part, we tend to label for the wrong reasons. When we use labeling to make assumptions and unjustly discriminate against others—or to make excuses for ourselves—we infer broader qualities about a person or a situation without the information necessary to support our conclusions. Sometimes, the consequences can be destructive not only to others but to ourselves.

COMMON CRIMINAL THINKING

If we're honest with ourselves, most of us must admit that at some time or another we have engaged in criminal thinking, which is but one form of disordered thinking. The bulk of critical theory on criminal thinking has been derived primarily from people who are incarcerated or have otherwise broken the law. But there is often a thin line separating criminals behind bars from the rest of us. The research on criminal thinking underscores the most common patterns of irrational thought that lead to disordered decisions. Most common criminal thinking patterns are not so much convoluted as simplistic and one-dimensional. Then there is a tendency among some to see themselves as always the victim. People who think this way do not take responsibility for their choices. For others still, there is a lack of perspective about time, which results in living primarily in the present, without investing in the future or taking into account the consequences of one's actions.

One aspect of criminal thinking patterns stands out most because of its prevalence among noncriminal segments of the population. It is an attitude of ownership, or what can be referred to as a sense of entitlement. Inherent in this attitude is a cockiness that borders on blatant narcissism. Those with an extreme sense of entitlement are able to justify violating other people or their property without regard to their rights. If their thinking stems from an "inferiority complex," those who feel entitled see themselves as helpless and often as victims. They complain and protest greatly about the lack of opportunities they have had in life because of their ethnic, economic, or family background. They discount their own failure to put in the effort required to improve their lives. Some will choose to steal, manipulate, and otherwise take from others because of their belief that the world owes them. They fail to see their own negligence in considering alternative ways of thinking and living.

In others the sense of entitlement arises out of a "superiority complex." A person may believe he should always have first shot at everything, again usually because of his ethnic, economic, or family background. He thinks those like him are also superior and therefore due anything they desire, even if getting it means taking from others. He feels entitled to the best educational or job opportunities, and is offended by others who want the best for themselves. Desiring the best in life is not the problem. This thinking is problematic when people are willing to violate others by discrimination, exploitation, and oppression, denying them the same rights, opportunities, and access to valued resources.

Of course, all of this is simplistic thinking. It is as apparent among those considered to be otherwise intelligent and successful, who have attended top-notch schools and run major corporations, as it is among the uneducated, underprivileged, and criminal and mentally ill populations. The common denominator is our human tendency of failing to think well.

Thinking Too Little Is Your Problem

One patient I saw in my practice years ago is an example of the problems created by a failure to think well. His prevailing motive, and the specific defect in his thinking, was resistance to change. Given that we live in a world of change, thinking that it was possible not to change, or simply to avoid change, fell somewhere in between an illusion and a delusion. This man came to see me from a country town that was about a twenty-minute drive from my office. He saw me twice a week for four years and went through his life savings for these sessions. This investment of time and money would seem to reflect an interest in change and growth. Such, I discovered, was not the case.

When he first started, I gave him a map for a shortcut he could take when coming to see me, saving both time and money. About six months into therapy, he complained one day about how long it took to drive to his appointments. So I said, "Well, John, try the shortcut." But he replied, "I'm sorry, I lost the map." I gave him another one.

About six months after that, he complained again about how long it took. I asked, "Well, do you take the shortcut?" He said, "No, it's winter and I haven't wanted to chance it on the icy back roads." I then asked whether he had lost the map again, and I ended up giving him another one. Finally, a year or so later—about two years into therapy—he started complaining again, and again I asked, "John, have you tried the shortcut?" He said, "Oh, yeah. I tried it but it didn't save any time." So I said—and this is not typical of analyst behavior—"John, off the couch. Get off the couch. We're going to do an experiment."

I gave him the option of being the recorder or the driver. He decided to be the recorder. We got into my car and drove the route he usually took, and then we drove the shortcut back to my office. The shortcut would have saved him five minutes each way. "John," I said. "I'd like to point out something to you. You have lost ten minutes on every round trip you have made to my office. You have gone out of your way for the last two years, the equivalent of two thousand minutes, or three days. You have wasted three days of your life. Not only that," I added, "you've driven a total of twelve thousand miles out of your way to avoid taking that shortcut. And if that isn't enough, you've lied to protect your neurosis."

It was a year after that—after a total of three years of therapy—when John finally said, "Well, I guess—I suppose—the dominant motive in my life is to avoid any change." That was why he avoided taking the shortcut. It would have meant thinking and doing something different from what he had become accustomed to. The same was true in our work together. But his use of the phrase "I guess" and "I suppose" made it clear that John was still reluctant to own up to the necessity for change. The power of neuroses can be formidable. Less than a successful case, until the very end of our work he continued to set himself up for failure by seeking to avoid the risks involved with

change. Like John, many people run from the change necessary for growth. They aren't willing to face the task of reformu-
lating some of the assumptions and illusions they have accepted
as truth.

When I was in psychiatric training, schizophrenia was labeled a thinking disorder, or a thought disorder. Since that
time, I have come to believe that all psychiatric disorders are
thinking disorders. Individuals at the extremes of mental illness, as in some forms of schizophrenia, are clearly the victims
of disordered thinking and may be so far out of touch with reality that they cannot function well in day-to-day activities. Yet
we have all met narcissists, obsessive-compulsives, and passive-
dependent people in our social and work lives. Their mental
health may be fragile, but they manage to appear "normal"
and get by. The fact, however, is that they, too, are disordered
thinkers. Narcissists cannot think about other people. Obsessive-
compulsives cannot think about the big picture. Passive-
dependent people cannot think for themselves.

In every psychiatric condition I have worked with over the
years, there was some disorder of thinking involved. Most people who go into therapy are suffering from either a neurosis or
character disorder. Among the general population who never
go to see a psychotherapist, these conditions are equally promi-
nent and are, again, the result of disordered thinking. They
are, at root, illusions of responsibility, and as such, they reflect
opposite styles of thinking about and relating to the world and
the problems in life.

The neurotic person is under the illusion that she is responsible for everyone or everything and, as a result, often assumes too much responsibility. When neurotics are in conflict
with the world, they tend to assume automatically that they are
at fault. The person with a character disorder operates under
the illusion that he shouldn't have to be responsible for himself
or anyone else. Thus, he's not likely to take on enough responsibility. When those with character disorders are in conflict with
the world they automatically assume the world is at fault.

Let me point out that all of us have to live with some illusions. These are what psychologists call healthy illusions, which help support us during periods of transition in life and give us hope. Take the illusion of romantic love. People wouldn't get married without it. The illusion that raising children is going to be more fun than pain is healthy, too. Otherwise we wouldn't have children. I thought that my own children would be easier to deal with when they got out of diapers, and then I thought that they would be easier when they started school. Then I thought they would be easier when they got their driver's licenses. Then when they went to college. Then when they got married. Now I have the illusion that my children will be easier to deal with once they're in their forties. Illusions like that keep us going and encourage growth.

So illusions are not totally bad, unless we hold on to them far too long and beyond their usefulness. The problem comes when our illusions consistently interfere with growth. For example, the sixteen-year-old who becomes obsessive in her thinking about her eating habits and appearance may feel she is never thin enough or good enough to measure up to the other girls in her school. In taking this illusion to an extreme, she may starve herself and become anorexic. Or she may outgrow this neurotic dilemma by the time she reaches her twenties and becomes more confident and self-assured. The young man who doesn't excel in sports may find that his intellectual qualities compensate for his lack of athletic skills. If he can learn to value his intellect, it will be more possible to overcome the neurotic inferiority complex he experiences when comparing himself to the jocks at his school. So a mild neurosis or slight character disorder need not be viewed as a lifetime disposition. On the other hand, our persistent neuroses and character disorders are crippling if not dealt with. They can grow and become like boulders that totally block our way.

Carl Jung wrote, "Neurosis is always a substitute for legitimate suffering." But the substitute can become more painful than the legitimate suffering it was designed to avoid. The neurosis itself ultimately becomes the biggest problem. As I wrote in *The Road Less Traveled,* "True to form, many will then attempt to avoid this pain and this problem, in turn, building layer upon layer of neurosis. Fortunately, however, some possess the courage to face their neuroses and begin—usually with the help of psychotherapy—to learn how to experience legitimate suffering. In any case, when we avoid the legitimate suffering that results from dealing with problems, we also avoid the growth that problems demand from us. It is for this reason that in chronic mental illness we stop growing, we become stuck. And without growth, without healing, the human spirit begins to shrivel."

THINKING TOO MUCH IS SOMEBODY ELSE'S PROBLEM

Although often we do damage to ourselves through simplistic thinking, there are other times when people may seek to damage us for daring to think well. If we think a great deal and others don't particularly like it, that is their problem, not ours. If you use your brain, it's bound to create a problem for others if they are seeking to use, abuse, or control you or keep you dependent or fearful. Their hidden motive may be to discourage you from realizing the sense of personal power that is directly related to the ability to exercise good, independent thinking.

Much is invested in having us believe everything we read in newspapers and everything our government tells us. After all, if we're not thinking for ourselves, we are easy targets for control and manipulation. To keep us dependent, we are taught that it's not necessary to think much. My own parents used to routinely tell me, "Scotty, you think too much." How many parents or teachers have told children the same thing: "You think too much." What a terrible thing to say to anybody. The reason we were given a brain is to think. But we live in a culture that places little value on the intellect, the ability to think well, because it is viewed as different—and possibly even dangerous. For anyone who is in control, like parents or employers or our government, it may feel like a threat when someone else thinks independently.

The most common response to all of my writings is not that I've said anything particularly new. It is that I write about the kinds of things that a lot of people have been thinking all along, but were afraid to talk about. They have found the knowledge that they are not alone—not crazy—to be of great solace in a culture that discourages thinking, and often candor. Indeed, it takes courage to be different, to dare to be oneself. If we choose to think for ourselves, we must be braced for backlash. We risk being seen as eccentrics or malcontents. We may be presumed to be on the fringes of mainstream society, regarded as different and abnormal in the worst sense of the word. But if we dare to seek growth, we have to dare to think.

It can take a lifetime for many people to come to terms with the freedom they truly have to think for themselves. But this path to freedom is obstructed by societal myths, one of which would have us believe that once we have completed adolescence, we can't change much. In reality, we are able to change and grow throughout our lifetimes—even in the subtlest ways. But it is a choice. Often it is when we meet the crises of midlife that our thinking takes off in new and independent directions. And for some, independent thinking evolves only when they are about to die. Sadly, of course, for many it never happens.

THE GOOD, THE BAD, AND THE IN-BETWEEN

It is a true saying that you are what you think. You are what you think most about. You are what you don't think about. So in essence, the good, the bad, and everything in between that we think or don't think about tells much about who we are. When we think simplistically about everything, we set ourselves up to always expect simple solutions, obvious answers, and clear results even in complex situations. We need to come to terms with the reality that many situations—such as whether to marry this person or that one, what career to choose, when to buy a house—involve gambles. We need to learn to live with the "in-betweenness" of uncertainty.

A tolerance for uncertainty, as I pointed out in *The Road Less Traveled,* is crucial in the process of questioning our assumptions. And in *A Bed by the Window,* my detective runs off half-cocked—and astray—with his stereotypical thinking in a rush to judgment in large part because he is unwilling to wait through a period of uncertainty. But since we can never be sure we have considered all aspects of a situation, the willingness to think in depth often leads to indecisiveness. There's always a chance we may leave something out, and we must be willing to bear the pain involved in being uncertain. In the face of this uncertainty, we still have to be able to act and make decisions at some point. In weighing our thoughts and feelings, what matters most is whether we are willing to wrestle with the realization that we don't know it all. This means not only being introspective, but also experiencing doubt. Doubt, I believe, is often the beginning of wisdom.

In my practice as a psychotherapist, I discovered that many people hold tenaciously to the certainty of their childhood beliefs, as if they couldn't function as adults without this certainty as a security blanket. Only when they hit the gaping void would doubt and uncertainty emerge, and in confronting crisis, these became a saving grace.

Frequently, about one or two years into therapy, they would become far more depressed than they were when they first came to me. I called the phenomenon therapeutic depression. At this juncture, patients realized that their old way of thinking was no longer working for them. They had come to see some of their thinking patterns as stupid or maladaptive. But new ways of thinking seemed terrifyingly risky and inherently difficult. They couldn't go back and couldn't go forward, and in this "in-betweenness" they became depressed. At such times, they would ask, "Well, why go anyplace? Why should I exert myself?

Why should I risk changing my beliefs? Why shouldn't I just give up and kill myself? Why bother? What's the point of it all?"

For these questions, there are never easy answers. There are no answers in the medical textbooks or books of psychiatry because these are fundamentally existential and spiritual questions. They are questions about meaning in life. And although it was difficult to grapple with, I called this period of depression therapeutic precisely because such spiritual grappling ultimately led to growth for these patients in long-term therapy.

In the introduction to *The Road Less Traveled,* I wrote that I make little distinction between the mind and the spirit, and therefore no distinction between spiritual growth and mental growth. You cannot separate thinking—intellect—from psychological and spiritual growth. When I was in training, it was fashionable to decry intellectual insight. The *only* thing considered important was emotional insight, as if intellectual understanding were worthless. This was simplistic thinking. While I agree that ultimately there has to be emotional insight, most of the time you can't even begin to understand the emotional aspects of an individual case until you have attained intellectual insight.

Let us take the Oedipus complex. An adult with an unresolved Oedipus complex cannot be healed unless he first intellectually knows what an Oedipus complex is—if he can be healed at all.

To become healthy adults we first must resolve the Oedipal dilemma of giving up our sexual feelings for our parents. If the child is a boy, the father is seen as the competition for the mother's attention. If it's a girl, the desire for the father as a sexual or love object means competing with the mother. For the first time in their lives, basically, children experience the tensions of loss. They are forced to give up something important to them that they cannot have. In my experience, people who fail to resolve the Oedipus complex appropriately will thereafter have the most severe, even overwhelming, difficulty in ever renouncing anything since they never made that first renunciation. So it's crucial that they come to terms with not being able to possess the parent in the way that they have fantasized.

A woman who moved from Florida to Connecticut to see me for therapy was a case in point. She was an early fan of *The Road Less Traveled,* and she had the money to make such a move. In hindsight, I should have discouraged her from packing up and moving so far, because there are always local therapists available. It was one of several mistakes I made in this case, and her healing was incomplete. Given the difficulties I encountered with her in therapy, the furthest we got in penetrating the real issue was the day when she first heard herself clearly utter her hidden motives for coming to me for therapy. After leaving a session this particular day, she sat in her car, sobbing and shaking at the steering wheel. "Well, maybe when I get over my Oedipus complex," she said, "then Dr. Peck will marry me." I had become the father figure in her life, a replacement for the father she could not have. Later, she said to me, "Maybe you're right. Maybe I do have an Oedipus complex." But we wouldn't have gotten even that far had I not first intellectually explained to her what an Oedipus complex was.

Another case involved a man who was treated, again unsuccessfully, for the difficulty he had with renunciation. When he came to see me he was tortured. His complaint was that he had three girlfriends and was sleeping with all of them. Complicating matters, he was starting to be attracted to a fourth one. "Dr. Peck," he said, "you don't understand the agony I'm in, just how terrible this is. Do you know what it's like to try and show up at three different Thanksgiving dinners?"

"That does make your life kind of complicated, doesn't it?" I responded. At that time, I was no longer seeing people for therapy, only for consultations. But since I didn't quite know what to make of this man initially, I asked him to come back for a second visit. In between those sessions, I began to wonder whether the reason he couldn't give up any of his girlfriends— couldn't choose one—was perhaps that he hadn't resolved his Oedipus complex. When he came back for the second session, I asked him to tell me about his mother.

He described her as stunningly beautiful and went on and on and on and on about her. He worked for a company in personnel counseling and conducted workshops related to psychology. Despite the significant background he had in psychology, he was emotionally unaware of his own dilemma. When I said to him, "Harry, by the way, do you know what an Oedipus complex is?" his reply was "It's got something to do with people, doesn't it?" This man should have known, at least intellectually, what an Oedipus complex is. Apparently, he just hadn't heard much of what was said about it during his training. The obvious reason, of course, is that it touched on his own neurosis. Having now made the diagnosis, I referred him to another therapist, but I later heard that their sessions were unsuccessful. He was unwilling to change. It is hard to move on when you can't renounce anything.

It's a similar problem in dealing with masochists. The root of their neurosis is the desire to be miserable. And to get well, they have to learn ways to be happy. But their basic motive is to not be happy. This is a setup for self-defeat in therapy with all those who cling hard to something they are simply unwilling or unable at the time to give up, even though it is making them unhappy. It's as if they have a built-in motive for failure. To give up something represents making a change. Like the man who was unwilling to give up his promiscuity, such individuals are unwilling to make the changes that will heal them. That is the sort of price many pay for a thinking disorder.

THINKING AND LISTENING

Given our almost addictive reliance on assumptions—and on the illusions that coexist with them—we often miscommunicate with others, creating great chaos. The polarization along racial lines in the aftermath of the O. J. Simpson verdict is an example. The failure to question our own—white or black—racial assumptions leads to failures in really hearing what is being communicated to us. We remain oblivious to the basics of good communication. It should go without saying you can't truly communicate well if you don't listen well, and you are unable to listen well unless you are thinking well.

An industrial psychologist once pointed out to me that the amount of time we devote to teaching certain subjects to our children in school is inversely proportional to the frequency with which they will make use of them when they grow up. I do not believe it would be a good thing to make what we teach in school exactly proportional to what will be useful after school, but I do think we would be wise to give our children more instruction in the processes of thinking and listening well.

In most public and private schools, there is virtually no formal education on these crucial aspects of communicating. A successful top executive will spend at least three-quarters of her time thinking and listening. She will spend a small fraction speaking and an even smaller fraction writing. Yet the amount of formal education we get in developing these essential skills is inversely proportional to what is required to be an effective executive. The skills are, in fact, essentials in every aspect of our lives.

Many people think that listening is a passive interaction. It is just the opposite. Listening well is an active exercise of our attention and, by necessity, is hard work. It is because they do not realize this or because they are not willing to do the work that most people do not listen well. When we extend ourselves by attempting to listen and communicate well, we take an extra step or walk an extra mile. We do so in opposition to the inertia of laziness or the resistance of fear. It always requires hard work.

Listening well also requires total concentration upon another and is a manifestation of love in the broadest sense of the word. An essential part of listening well is the discipline of bracketing, the temporary giving up or setting aside of your own prejudices, frames of reference, and desires in order to experience as far as possible another's world from the inside, stepping inside his or her shoes. This unification of speaker and listener is actually an extension and enlargement of ourselves, and new knowledge is always gained from it. Moreover, since lis-

tening well involves bracketing, it also involves a temporary total acceptance of the other. Sensing this acceptance, the speaker
will feel less and less vulnerable and more and more inclined to
open up the inner recesses of his or her mind to the listener. As
this happens, speaker and listener begin to understand each
other better and better. True communication is under way and
the duet dance of love has begun. The energy required for the
discipline of bracketing and the focusing of total attention on
another is so great that it can be accomplished only by love,
which I define as the will to extend oneself for mutual growth.

Most of the time we lack this energy. Even though we may
feel in our business dealings or social relationships that we are
listening well, what we are usually doing is listening selectively.
Often, we have a preset agenda in mind and wonder as we listen
how we can achieve certain desired results to get the conversation over with as quickly as possible or redirected in ways more
satisfactory to us. Many of us are far more interested in talking
than in listening, or we simply refuse to listen to what we don't
want to hear.

While it is true that one's capacity to listen well may improve gradually with practice, it never becomes an effortless
process. It wasn't until toward the end of my career as a therapist that I would sometimes ask my patients to go over something they had said because my mind had wandered. The first
few times I did this, I wondered if they might question whether
I had been listening at all and would be resentful. What I
found, to the contrary, was that they seemed to understand in-
tuitively that a vital element of the capacity to listen well is being
alert for those lapses when one is not truly listening. And my acknowledgment that my attention had wandered actually reas-
sured them that most of the time I was listening well.

I have found that the knowledge that one is being truly listened to is frequently, in and of itself, remarkably therapeutic.
In approximately a quarter of the patients I saw, whether they
were adults or children, considerable and even dramatic improvement was shown during the first few months of psychotherapy, before any of the roots of problems had been uncovered

or significant interpretations had been made. There are several reasons for this phenomenon, but chief among them, I believe, was the patient's sense that he or she was being truly listened to, often for the first time in years—and for some, perhaps for the first time ever.

FREEDOM AND THINKING

There is a sharp distinction between disordered and clear thinking. Yet there is a rule in psychiatry that there's no such thing as a bad thought or feeling. It is a useful rule in certain ways. In other ways, it is itself simplistic.

We can make ethical judgments only about actions. If someone thinks about hitting you and then proceeds to bash you over the head with a lamp, that is bad. To just think about doing so isn't. This is the distinction between private thought and "public" action. The latter involves externalizing our thoughts by acting on them. It is virtually impossible to make judgments about a person's thoughts when they are not translated into behavior.

So we arrive at a paradox regarding freedom and thinking. On the one hand, we are free to think anything. To be healed, we have to be free to be ourselves. But that doesn't mean we are free to be our criminal selves and impose our thoughts on others or engage in destructive actions without consequences. Thus, with the freedom to think and feel anything also comes the responsibility to discipline our thoughts and feelings. Some, as I myself had to, need to give ourselves permission to learn to cry. Others who are easily hurt may need to learn not to cry as much. We have to be free to think and feel, but that doesn't mean we should utter every thought aloud or always wear our hearts on our sleeves.

A great peace activist, conservationist, and civil rights leader, Pete Seeger, used to sing an antifascist German song, "Die Gedanken sind frei," which literally translates "Thoughts Are Free." In order to think and feel, we have got to feel free.

But as with everything else, there are qualifiers. Freedom without discipline can get us in trouble. Indeed, the freedom to think anything presents a complex dilemma. There are freedom-limiting rules for good thinking, and not all thinking is good thinking. Poor thinking often leads to poor behavior. Furthermore, as we've seen in the examples of our society's simplistic thinking, there is much reason to be cautious given the preponderance of evidence that a lot of bad and extreme thinking has been interpreted as good simply because it is commonly accepted as normal.

I am reminded of Cat Stevens's lyrics to his song "Can't Keep It In," which ends with: "Say what you mean, mean what you're thinking, think anything." I love the song, yet when he says, "Think anything," I get a little leery. Allowing people the freedom to think anything can be a scary proposition. But we must, I believe, give them that freedom. At the same time, we must recognize that it does not mean all people are going to think well. In acknowledging our freedom to think, we need always to remain aware that we can make both wrong and right choices. And with the freedom to think, we must also learn to tolerate the freedom of being uncertain.

I champion a proposal by a friend of mine who wants to underscore these points in a symbolic way. He believes we should erect a Statute of Responsibility on the West Coast to bring balance to the Statute of Liberty that stands on the East Coast. Indeed, we cannot separate freedom from responsibility. With the freedom that we have to think for ourselves, ultimately we must hold ourselves accountable for how and what we think and whether we are using our capacity for thinking to get the most out of life.

TIME AND EFFICIENCY

Along with the belief most people have that they naturally know how to think is an underlying, correlating assumption that thinking doesn't require much effort or time. While we are for-

tunate to live in a society that allows us to use our time efficiently in everyday living—as when we can pick up dry cleaning
and a meal along the same route on our way home—we have
come to expect results to be as quick as service at a fast-food
restaurant. We are encouraged to use our time efficiently, but
we seldom take the time to think efficiently. Confronted with
real-life problems, we imagine they can be dealt with as quickly
and easily as a thirty-minute television sitcom would portray
them to be.

As a result, many people show little interest in contemplation. The effort involved in truly thinking often takes a back-
seat, and they end up going in circles rather than dealing with
life's various dilemmas efficiently. They wouldn't think of going
on a long automobile trip without consulting a map and deciding which route to take. But in their psychosocial-spiritual journey through life, they rarely stop to think about why they're
going where they're going, where they really want to go, or how
best to plot out and facilitate the journey.

In this simplistic approach, we often overlook various aspects of our lives that are desperate for attention until they become full-blown crises. Or we dismiss new ideas that could further
our growth simply because they do not fit within the general
framework of our preconceived notions and self-concepts. An
enormous amount of time is spent simply reacting. It's as if we
are robots programmed to respond on cue to whatever demands the least time and attention, and disregard anything that
requires putting in extra time and energy to think. We skim
over the surface thoughtlessly. But we must acknowledge that
thinking well is a time-consuming process. We can't expect in-
stant results. We have to slow down a bit and take the time to
contemplate, meditate, even pray. It is the only route to a more
meaningful and efficient existence.

I've said before that I am a born contemplative. This
means that setting aside time to think—and pray—is as natural
to me as brushing my teeth. My routine involves a total of almost two and a half hours a day, in three separate forty-five-
minute intervals. No more than a tenth of that time is spent

talking to God (which is what most people would consider prayer) and another tenth listening for God (a definition of meditation). For the rest of the time, I'm just thinking, sorting out my priorities and weighing options before making decisions. I call it my prayer time because if I simply called it my thinking time, people would view it as less "holy" and feel free to interrupt me. But I'm not being dishonest. In many ways, thinking is akin to prayer.

My favorite definition of prayer—one that doesn't even mention God—comes from Matthew Fox, who described prayer as "a radical response to the mysteries of life." Thus, prayer has everything to do with thinking. Before we can respond radically we first need to think radically. To think well is a radical activity.

It's important to clarify what I mean by the word "radical." It comes from the Latin *radix,* "root." Thus, to be radical is to get down to the root of things, penetrating their essence and not being distracted by superficialities. The closest synonym for "radical" is "fundamental," which means basic or essential. Fundamentals are what is really important. Curiously, the noun "radical" is used to describe a left-wing, bomb-throwing anarchist, while the noun "fundamentalist" is used to describe a ring-wing extremist. I mean to imply neither of those mind-sets in my use of these words. Rather, I mean that anyone who thinks *deeply* about fundamentals will, by definition, be a radical. And the actions that stem from that kind of thinking will also be radical in the sense that they will address and seek to solve life's most important problems. The same holds true for prayer. Prayer is useless unless it is translated into meaningful action.

Radical thinkers are also independent thinkers. But they know that they cannot simply rely on themselves. To think independently does not mean going to an extreme that would exclude information and learning from others. Therefore, while it is proper that we think for ourselves, that does not imply that we act like rebellious children, rejecting all conventional wisdom and dismissing all societal norms. That would be an unnecessary expenditure of energy and an inefficient waste of time. Rather, we can learn much from good leaders and teachers—formally and informally. It is through those who think well that we can find good examples of what it means to be efficient and live life fully.

I consider one (among many) of my identities to be that of an efficiency expert. Both as a psychiatrist and as a writer, I have worked to help people live their lives more efficiently—not necessarily to be happy or comfortable all the time, but rather to learn as much as possible in any given situation and get the most out of life.

When I was still lecturing, people often asked how I managed to do so much—lecturing, writing, being a father and a husband, a community activist and an avid reader. My response was that because I spent at least two hours a day doing nothing—that is, taking the time to think, pray, and organize my priorities—I became more efficient.

When you are efficient, you can accomplish more things in a shorter time. In thinking efficiently, you learn how to give priority to what's important in order to face life's difficulties head-on rather than pretend they are inconsequential. Efficiency necessarily includes discipline. Being disciplined involves an ability to delay gratification as well as a willingness to consider alternatives. On the other hand, thinking simplistically leads you to make undisciplined, knee-jerk responses rather than considering choices that would lead to wise and productive decisions.

Being efficient does not mean we should become control freaks. It would be ludicrous to attempt to plan out every moment of every day of one's life. Efficiency means not only planning but preparing. When emergency situations come up, as they inevitably will, we will be free to respond to the most important needs at the time because we have done our homework. Efficiency involves attentiveness to those things that must be dealt with before they become such overwhelming problems that they cause far more damage than necessary.

Simplism is inefficient and the lazy way out. No progress is possible when illegitimate shortcuts in thinking are taken in order to avoid the legitimate effort and suffering that accompany the discipline of problem-solving. Not only is simplism a means by which to harbor the illusion that there are easy answers, it is a sure path to becoming rigid and stuck. That's why I distinguish between the simplism that involves simpleminded answers, and the efficient simplicity of ordering one's priorities before making choices. The distinction is crucial if we are to think and act with integrity.

PARADOX AND THINKING WITH INTEGRITY

I believe that those who subscribe to the notion that there are easy answers—a single reason for everything—actually promote simplism and intellectual bigotry. I have found, in my wide travels, that wherever I go such bigotry is the norm rather than the exception. If we assume that there is a reason for everything, naturally we go looking for *it*—and dismiss all other possibilities that potentially conflict with *it*—when we should be looking for *them*. I am astonished by the number of well-educated people who offer or seek simple-minded explanations for complicated phenomena ranging from riots, homosexuality, and abortion to poverty, illness, evil, and war. I believe it would often be considerably healthier for us to dare to live without a reason for many things than to live with reasons that are simplistic.

In *In Search of Stones,* I wrote of a conversation I had with a wealthy white stockbroker. While speaking of the riots in Los Angeles following a jury's decision that the police who beat Rodney King were not guilty of a crime, the stockbroker—a highly educated, intelligent, and successful man—told me with assurance that the reason for the riots was "the decline in family values." He deduced this from his observation that virtually all the rioters were young black males. "If they'd been married and working to support their families, they wouldn't have had time to riot," he explained.

I practically exploded. I told him that for two hundred years under slavery we hadn't *allowed* most blacks to marry or have legal families. We made their family values illegal. I gave him several cultural and historical reasons why, on the average, black women are better educated and more employable than black men. I reminded him that the economic recession in California at the time was worse than that of any other state. I spoke of the decline of *government* values in the United States. I talked about the oppression of prejudice and the psychology of despair. "The 'decline' of family values may have been one of the reasons for the riots," I concluded, "but only one of many, of a whole complex of reasons."

I was teaching him about "overdetermination," the concept that everything important has multiple causes. Far from being simplistic, overdetermination demands the integration of multiple dimensions in order to see the whole picture. It is necessary for the understanding of many issues. To think well means to perceive in multidimensional ways. It is the essence of thinking with integrity. The word "integrity" comes from the noun "integer," which signifies wholeness, entirety, completion. To think and ultimately to act with integrity, we have to integrate the multiple reasons and dimensions of our incredibly complex world.

We psychiatrists have a verb for the opposite of "integrate": "compartmentalize." To compartmentalize is to take things that are properly related and stick them in separate, airtight compartments in our minds where they don't have to rub up against each other and cause us any stress or pain, friction or tension. An example I cited in *The Different Drum* and *In Search of Stones* would be that of the man who goes to church on Sunday morning, devoutly believing that he loves God and God's creation, and then on Monday has no trouble with his company's policy of dumping toxic wastes in the local stream. This is, of course, because he has put his religion in one compartment and his business in another. He is what we have come to call a Sunday morning Christian. It is a very comfortable way to operate, but integrity it is not.

To think and act with integrity requires that we fully experience the tensions of competing thoughts and demands. It requires that we ask the crucial question: Has anything been left out? It requires us to look beyond our usually simplistic illusions and assumptions to try to discover what is missing.

Early in my psychiatric training, I was taught that what the patient does *not* say is more important than what he or she does say. This is an excellent guide for getting to the root of what is missing. For instance, during the course of a few psychotherapeutic sessions, healthy patients will talk of their present, past, and future in a well-integrated fashion. Should a patient speak only of the present and future, never mentioning the past, you can be sure that there is at least one unintegrated, unresolved, and important issue in childhood that must be brought to light for full healing. If the patient only speaks of her childhood and her future, the therapist can tell that she has some major difficulty dealing with the here and now—often a difficulty connected with intimacy and risk. And should the patient never make mention of his future, one might properly be led to suspect that he has a problem with fantasy and hope.

If you want to think with integrity, and are willing to bear the pain involved, you will inevitably encounter paradox. The Greek word *para* means "by the side of, beside, alongside, past, beyond." *Doxa* means opinion. Thus, a paradox is "a statement contrary to common belief, or one that seems contradictory, unbelievable, or absurd but may actually be true in fact." If a concept is paradoxical, that in itself should suggest that it smacks of integrity and has the ring of truth. Conversely, if a concept is not in the least paradoxical, you may suspect that it has failed to integrate some aspect of the whole.

The ethic of rugged individualism is an example. Many fall prey to this illusion because they do not or will not think with integrity. For the reality is that we do not exist either by or for ourselves. If I think with integrity at all, I have to recognize immediately that my life is nurtured not only by the earth and the rain and the sun but also by farmers, publishers, and booksellers, as well as by my children, wife, friends, and teachers—

indeed, by the entire fabric of family, society, and creation. I am not solely an individual. I am interdependent, and much of the time I do not even have the right to act "ruggedly."

If no pieces of reality are missing from the picture, if all the dimensions are integrated, you will probably be confronted by a paradox. When you get to the root of things, virtually all truth is paradoxical. The truth is, for example, that I am and I am not an individual. Thus, to seek the truth involves an integration of things that seem to be separate and look like opposites when, in reality, they are intertwined and related in some ways. Reality itself is paradoxical, in that while many things in and about life seem simple on the surface, they are often complex—although not always complicated. There is a difference, just as clear as the difference between simplism and simplicity. There is, in fact, a great simplicity to wholeness.

The Road Less Traveled is filled with paradoxes. I wrote that "life is difficult because the process of confronting and solving problems is a painful one." But when I say that life is difficult, I'm not suggesting that it is never easy or rewarding. To say that life is difficult without qualifying the statement would be to subscribe to the idea that "life is difficult and then we die." It is a simplistic and nihilistic notion. It discounts all beauty, goodness, opportunities for spiritual growth, serenity, and other wonderful aspects of living. Indeed, one of the mysterious and paradoxical realities is that in addition to the pain that life brings, living can be accompanied by an unfathomed joy once we get past the pain.

To understand paradox ultimately means being able to grasp two contradictory concepts in one's mind without going crazy. As a psychiatrist, I do not use the word "crazy" in a flippant way. It can actually make people feel crazy when something they have taken for granted as truth—and the only truth—comes into question. It is certainly a skill of mental acrobatics to be able to juggle opposing ideas in one's mind without automatically negating or rejecting the reality of either idea. But even when the strongest impulse is to want to deny something that one finds hard to digest—such as the fact that evil coexists with good in our world—the ability to understand paradox is necessary in the process of sorting through illusions, half-truths, and outright lies.

Almost all of us have the capacity to think paradoxically. The extent to which we neglect or use this capability varies greatly. It is not so much determined by our IQs as by the depth of practice we put into thinking. To become keen in paradoxical reasoning, you must, as the saying goes, use it or lose it. The more we use our capacity for thinking paradoxically, the more likely we will expand this ability.

It is unquestionable that certain changes are needed in society to encourage better thinking. But at the same time, each individual is responsible for his or her own thinking and how to meet this challenge. Ultimately, if we can teach people to think well, we could heal most of the ills of individuals and most of the ills of society. In the end, however, the benefits of thinking well are worth the effort—and far better than the alternative. This is ultimately a hopeful business. Long ago I heard it said: "Once a mind is truly stretched, it never returns to its former dimensions."

CHAPTER 2

Consciousness

❖

THE POINT OF THINKING WELL IS to become more conscious, which, in turn, is a prerequisite for solving problems well. But what is consciousness? And why is it the point?

Consciousness is among the many things—such as love, prayer, beauty, and community—that are too large, complex, and mysterious to submit to any single adequate definition. In *The Road Less Traveled,* I concluded the section about love with a subsection entitled "The Mystery of Love." Therein, having gone on for a hundred pages as if I knew what love was all about, I raised many issues of love I couldn't even begin to explain.

In *In Search of Stones,* I wrote that art is also hard to define. One of the characteristics of art is its unreasonableness. Other human creations have an obvious reason. They are necessary, useful, and serve a clear function. Few would ponder the purpose of a fork or spoon, a knife or an ax, a house or an office building. But as soon as you carve something into the handle of that fork or the blade of that knife or the molding of that building, you are engaging in the practice of adornment and have entered the not entirely reasonable—or easily definable—realm of art. Whether we use makeup on ourselves, paint on canvas, carve on stones, write poetry, or make music, we are doing something very—and uniquely—human. Therefore, art implies consciousness: not only of self, as the practice of self-adornment demonstrates, but also consciousness of things—and beauty—external to ourselves.

That there is no single adequate definition of consciousness is not surprising. For the most part, we can define only those things that are smaller than we are. I believe that all those things too large for a single, simplistic definition, including consciousness, ultimately have something to do with God. That is why, for example, the Muslims have a prohibition against any image of God: it could not capture or define God, but would only represent a tiny segment of the whole and hence would be, in a sense, a desecration.

THE MYSTERY OF CONSCIOUSNESS

Descartes is most famous for his statement "Cogito, ergo sum"—"I think, therefore I am." I would substitute the word "conscious" and say, "I am conscious [or aware] that I am thinking; therefore I am."

Does this mean that unconscious things don't exist? Hardly. Even if we assume that the trees outside my window do not have consciousness, I very much enjoy their presence and am aware of their existence as entities separate from me. They display definitive signs of life—without provocation from humans. Constantly invigorated by the earth, rain, and sunlight, their leaves change colors as they adjust to the seasons. Indeed, we have no knowledge that the trees or the grass or even the stones aren't conscious. The belief that they have no kind of self-awareness is simply an assumption. They may be aware in some different way than we are. Would that I could read the mind of a deer or a flower or a dolphin and understand its consciousness, but I can't.

So this notion of consciousness, or self-awareness, is not simple. Generally, we tend to think of consciousness as that which distinguishes human beings from other creatures. On the one hand, the whole world is animate with consciousness—alive, aware, growing and changing. At the same time, we are all mired in unconsciousness, and this can be seen quite obviously among humans—given the reality that while some people think in depth, many think very little and some simply fail to think at all.

In *The Road Less Traveled,* I wrote that we have both a conscious mind and an unconscious mind. The conscious mind makes decisions and translates them into action. The unconscious mind resides below the surface; it is the possessor of extraordinary knowledge that we aren't naturally aware of. It knows more than we know—the "we" being defined as our conscious self. How we come to know that which is hidden and unconscious, is mystery—and mysterious. But we do have some hints about what is involved in the development of consciousness.

REVISITING OUR FRONTAL LOBES

In the preceding chapter, I wrote that one of the things that seems to distinguish human beings from the other creatures is our relative lack of instincts. Having few instincts, we are compelled to learn. Since we don't instinctively know many things, we have to be taught how to behave and deal with problems in life.

The most primitive of our limited instincts are called reflexes. An example of a reflex is our response to sudden pain. Put your hand on a hot stove burner accidentally, and you will immediately pull it away, even before you have felt the pain. This is because there are "reflex arcs" in our spinal cord. The incoming pain messages will arc over to nerve fibers going the other way that control movement without the brain itself even being involved. But if the pain is at all severe, the brain will very quickly become aware—conscious—of it and we will experience the agony mentally as well as physically.

Consciousness has no specific site in the brain. Nonetheless, insofar as it can be regionalized, it is more localized in our frontal lobes than anyplace else. Tumors of our frontal lobes will often first manifest themselves in diminished awareness and alertness, and hence a diminished capacity to solve complex problems.

For many years, neuropsychiatrists performed prefrontal lobotomies on certain schizophrenic patients who were in agony as a result of fixed delusions. The surgical procedure is a simple one that severs the connections between the prefrontal lobes (the most highly evolved part of our brain) and the rest of the brain. In other words, with this operation, surgeons rendered dysfunctional the most developed or human part of the brain. They did not do this out of cruelty. Indeed, in my career I have seen several patients with prefrontal lobotomies who reported to me that the operation was the best thing that ever happened in their lives because it had relieved them of years of excruciating misery. But the price they paid was a loss of part of their humanity; these patients demonstrated a loss of fine judgment. The operation had taken away their agony but it left them with a distinctly limited self-awareness and restricted their range of emotional responses.

LESSONS FROM GENESIS 3

The sciences of anthropology and neuroanatomy strongly suggest that the direction of all evolution is toward the development of the frontal lobes and hence the development of consciousness. But the Bible and mythology also have much to teach about the evolution of human consciousness. The great myth of Genesis 3, one of the most complicated and multidimensional myths about our humanity, provides us with another major hint. In it, God forbids Adam and Eve to eat of the fruit of the Tree of the Knowledge of Good and Evil. Instead—urged by a fallen angel, we are told—they give in to temptation. In their disobedience, they hide from God. When God asks why they are hiding, they explain it is because they are naked. "Who told you you were naked?" God asks. And the secret is out.

In other words, the first result of eating of the Tree of the Knowledge of Good and Evil is that Adam and Eve become shy or modest because they are now *self-conscious*. They are aware that they are naked. From this we can also extrapolate that the emotions of guilt and shame are manifestations of consciousness, and although both emotions can be exaggerated to the point of pathology, within limits they are an essential part of our humanity and necessary for our psychological development and functioning. So Genesis 3 is a myth of evolution, and specifically of human evolution into consciousness. Like other myths, it is an embodiment of truth. And among the many truthful things the myth of the Garden of Eden tells us is that it is human to be shy.

I have had the opportunity to meet a great number of wonderful, deep-thinking people, and I have never met such a person who was not basically shy. A few of them had not thought of themselves as shy, but as we talked about it, they came to realize that they were. And the very few people I have met who were not the least bit shy were people who had been seriously damaged in some way, who had lost some of their humanity.

When we humans became self-conscious, we became conscious of ourselves as separate entities. We lost that sense of oneness with nature and the rest of creation. This loss is symbolized by our banishment from Paradise. And inevitably, as Adam and Eve developed a higher level of self-awareness, they arrived at the realization that consequences follow actions, and that their choices would be forever burdensome by virtue of the responsibility choice entailed. All of humanity has inherited this predicament. We have all been thrust out into the desert of maturity.

Thus, our evolution into consciousness has a far more profound implication than just guilt and shame. It is when we are conscious that we have free will. More than anything else, I believe what is meant by God's creating us in His own image is that, through the evolutionary process, He gave us free will. There is no free will when we are operating at a purely reflexive or instinctual level. But let me emphasize the word "free." One can also not be free when a gun is pointed at one's back. God or evolution gave us the freedom to choose what we think or do.

Genesis 3 elucidates our need to continue evolving into greater consciousness. Given that human evolution is a forward-moving phenomenon and that we are creatures with consciousness, we can never go back again to the innocence of not knowing otherwise, however hard we may try to do so. The gate of Eden is forever barred to us by cherubims with a flaming sword. So, in many ways, we are both blessed and cursed by consciousness. With it comes the awareness of the reality of good and evil.

GOOD AND EVIL

The first three chapters of Genesis tell us much about the genesis of good and evil. At the very beginning they suggest that the impulse to do good has something to do with what creativity is all about. God first created the firmament and saw that it was good; then He created the land and the waters, the plants and animals and humans—and saw that they, too, were good creations. In contrast, the impulse to do evil is destructive rather than creative. The choice between good and evil, creativity and destruction, is our own. And ultimately, we must take that responsibility and accept its consequences.

As soon as God (or evolution) gave us free will, He immediately let loose the potential for human evil in the world. If there is no choice, there is no evil. If one is to have free will, then one must have the power to choose between good and evil. And one is as free to choose the evil as the good.

So it strikes me as no accident that the very next thing that happens in the story is an example of evil: in Genesis 4, Cain murders Abel. Is it nothing more than a matter of free will that he chooses to do so? When God asks Cain where Abel is, he replies with a question: "Am I my brother's keeper?" We can recognize this as a gross rationalization; and, as a rationalization, it represents thinking of a sort—defensive thinking. It is extremely shallow, almost reflexive thinking. This gives us a hint that Cain murdered Abel because he chose not to think more deeply. With free will we have the choice to think or to not think, or to think deeply or shallowly.

But why would someone choose not to think deeply? Why would someone choose to think only simplistically, superficially, and reflexively? The answer, again, is that, despite our consciousness, what we have in common with the other creatures is a preference for avoiding pain. Thinking deeply is often more painful than thinking shallowly. When we think with integrity we must bear the tension of all manner of causes and factors pulling against each other in our minds. Just as integrity is never painless, so consciousness is inevitably associated with pain.

Before going more deeply into the matter of evil, let me re-iterate that we are not here simply to experience pain-free living—to be comfortable, happy, or fulfilled all the time. The reality is that painful feelings accompany problem solving, and the process of becoming increasingly conscious is, like life in general, difficult. But it has many benefits, the greatest of which is that we will become more effective in life. We will be aware of a broader array of choices in responding to different situations and the daily dilemmas of life. We will be more aware of the games people play, thus less willing to be manipulated by others into doing things we deem to be against our best interests. We will be in a better position to determine for ourselves what to think and believe, rather than simply fall prey to the dictates of mass media or family and peer influences.

Unfortunately, pain is an inevitable side effect of consciousness. We will also become more aware of the needs, burdens, and sorrows of ourselves and others. We will become more aware of the realities of our mortality and the aging process working in every cell of our bodies. We will become conscious of our own sins and imperfections and, inevitably, more aware of the sins and evils of society.

The choice of whether or not to think deeply is, therefore, the choice of whether or not to accept that pain is associated with consciousness. This choice is so crucial that the first chapter of *The Road Less Traveled* focuses on how problems cause us pain and how, because we are pain-avoiding creatures, we try to run away from our problems rather than face them and deal with the pain. Similarly, the first chapter of *Further Along the Road Less Traveled* is entitled "Consciousness and the Problem of Pain."

The pain involved may not make consciousness seem worthwhile or good—until you consider some of the prices we pay for failing to grow in consciousness or to think with integrity. There is much evil in the world—unnecessary individual suffering, tremendous damage to human relations, and social chaos—due to our failure to think and grow in consciousness.

EVIL, SIN, AND OTHER DISTINCTIONS

While important distinctions are to be made between evil and insanity, illness and sin, I wrote in *People of the Lie* that to name something correctly gives us a certain amount of power over it. I believe that evil can be defined as a specific form of mental illness and should be subject to at least the same intensity of scientific investigation that we would devote to some other major psychiatric disease. Yet evil is still evil. Auschwitz and My Lai and Jonestown and the Oklahoma City bombing are facts. Evil is not a figment of the imagination of some primitive religious mind attempting to explain the unknown. And it is more than just a "sickness."

Given the state of world affairs, it's impossible to overlook the reality of evil if you are thinking with integrity. But there is widespread denial in our country. Many downplay evil or hesitate to see it for what it truly is, in part because they don't want to appear to be acting arrogant or holier-than-thou. Indeed, it is quite common to read newspaper articles that describe those who commit a range of human atrocities as simply "sick." As a psychiatrist, I believe the word "sick" is more appropriately applied to those who are afflicted with something for which treatment or a cure is possible—and also *desired*. Although the evil are operating from a "sick" perspective, the difference is that many of those who are "sick" deal with their venom internally, turning it painfully upon themselves if they choose not to seek help. Those who are evil go another way. They fail to suffer. Because they lash out at others and use them as scapegoats, it is the people around them who must suffer. Think of the ill effects caused by those who are addicted to a high opinion of themselves, to complacency and self-righteousness or far worse.

Because it is so destructive, evil is the ultimate illness. But a thinking disorder does not absolve someone of responsibility for his actions. We have the choice to think or not to think, and while evil should be considered a psychiatric diagnosis, that doesn't mean people shouldn't go to jail when they have committed a crime. I'm in full agreement with the law, which most *infrequently* absolves people of a crime on the grounds of insanity. The reality is that whenever we have a choice, we should be held accountable.

In *People of the Lie,* I boldly asserted that certain people are evil. Who are they? It is important that we make distinctions between evil people and ordinary criminals and between evil people and ordinary sinners. During my career as a psychiatrist, I spent some time working in prisons with convicted criminals. While many think that the problem of evil is confined to those who are locked up, seldom have I experienced inmates as truly evil people. Obviously they are destructive, and usually repeatedly so. But there is a kind of randomness to their destructiveness. Moreover, although they generally deny responsibility for their evil deeds, there is still a quality of openness to their wickedness. They themselves are quick to point this out, claiming they have been caught precisely because they are the "honest criminals." The truly evil, they will tell you, always reside outside of jail. Clearly, such proclamations are self-justifying. They are also, I believe, generally accurate.

Indeed, most people who commit evil are usually seen as ordinary citizens. They live down the street—on any street.

They may be rich or poor, educated or uneducated. Most are not designated "criminals." More often than not, they are "solid citizens" who fit in well with society, who do and say most of the right things on the surface. They may be active leaders in the community, Sunday school teachers, policemen or bankers, students or parents.

The case of Bobby and his parents, described in *People of the Lie,* is a compelling example of the kind of major evil that can be committed by so-called normal people in everyday life. After his older brother, Stuart, committed suicide by shooting himself in the head with a .22 rifle, fifteen-year-old Bobby recalled all manner of little incidents and began to feel guilty for having called his brother names or having hit or kicked him during a fight. To some degree, he felt responsible for Stuart's death. Consequently, he began judging *himself* as evil. That was not surprising. If someone close to us commits suicide, our first response after the initial shock—if we are normally human, with a normal human conscience—will be to wonder what we did wrong.

Had Bobby lived in a healthy family environment, his stable, blue-collar parents would have talked to him about his brother's death and attempted to reassure him that Stuart must have been suffering from a mental illness and that it was not Bobby's fault. But his parents did not do so. And without this reassurance, Bobby became visibly depressed. His grades plummeted and the school advised his parents to take him to a therapist. They did not do this either.

What they did do at Christmas, although he had not asked for it, was to give Bobby a .22 rifle—*the* rifle—as his "big present." The message this sent was chilling. Given Bobby's obvious depression and lack of sufficient maturity to understand his parents' motives in giving him this "gift," the message he received was in essence: "Take your brother's suicide weapon and do likewise. You deserve to die." When confronted with the horrific nature of this gesture, his parents responded in a way typical of the denial and self-deception inherent in evil. "It was better than any other present we could afford," his parents told me. "We're just *working* people. We're not sophisticated, smart, and educated people like you. We can't be expected to think about these kind of things."

Of course, an evil deed does not an evil person make. Otherwise, we would all be designated evil, because we all do evil things. But I believe it would be a mistake to think of sin or evil as simply a matter of degree. Sinning is most broadly defined as "missing the mark," which means we sin every time we fail to hit the bull's-eye. Sin is nothing less than a failure to be continually perfect. And because it is impossible for us to be continually perfect, we are all sinners. We routinely fail to do the very best of which we are capable, and with each failure we commit a crime of sorts—against ourselves or others.

Of course, there are crimes of greater or lesser magnitude. It may seem less odious to cheat the rich than to cheat the poor, but it is still cheating. There are differences before the law in defrauding a business, claiming a false deduction on your income tax, telling your wife that you have to work late when you are being unfaithful, or telling your husband you didn't have time to pick up his clothes at the cleaner when you spent an hour on the phone with a friend. Surely some of these deeds are more excusable than others—and perhaps all the more so under certain circumstances—but the fact remains that they are all lies and betrayals.

The reality is that we do betray ourselves and others routinely. The worst of us do it blatantly, even compulsively. The noblest of us do it subtly and self-centeredly, even when we think we are trying not to do it. Whether it is done consciously or unconsciously is of no matter; the betrayal occurs. If you imagine you are sufficiently scrupulous never to have done any such thing, then ask yourself whether there is any way in which you have lied to yourself. Or have kidded yourself. Be perfectly honest with yourself and you will realize that you sin. If you do not realize it, then you are not perfectly honest with yourself, which is itself a sin.

Thus, we are all sinners to one degree or another. But those who are evil cannot be strictly defined by the magnitude of their sins or the illegality of their deeds. It is not their sins per se that characterize them; rather it is the subtlety and persistence and consistency of their sins. And underlying this consistency, what distinguishes those who are evil, like Bobby's parents, is the extremes that they will go to in order to avoid the consciousness of their own evil.

THE SHADOW

Carl Jung ascribed the root of human evil to "the refusal to meet the Shadow." By "the Shadow," Jung meant the part of our mind containing those things that we would rather not own up to, that we are continually trying to hide from ourselves and others and sweep under the rug of our consciousness.

Most of us, when pushed up against the wall by evidence of our own sins, failures, or imperfections, will acknowledge our Shadow. But by his use of the word "refusal," Jung was implying something far more active. Those who have crossed over the line that separates sin from evil are characterized most by their absolute refusal to tolerate a sense of their own sinfulness. This is because their central defect is not that they have no conscience but that they refuse to bear its pain. In other words, it is not so much the sin itself but the refusal to acknowledge it that makes it evil.

In fact, the evil are often highly intelligent people, who may be quite conscious in most respects but have a very specific unwillingness to acknowledge their Shadow. The briefest definition of evil I know is that it is "militant ignorance." But evil is not general ignorance; more specifically, it is militant ignorance of the Shadow. Those who are evil refuse to bear the pain of guilt or to allow the Shadow into consciousness and "meet" it. Instead, they will set about—often at great effort—militantly trying to destroy the evidence of their sin or anyone who speaks of it or represents it. And in this act of destruction, their evil is committed.

I have written that guilt—although often viewed as a "downer"—is in many ways a blessing. Having a genuine awareness of one's own shortcomings is what I call a sense of personal sin. It is not pleasant to be aware of oneself as a naturally lazy, ignorant, self-centered being that rather routinely betrays its Creator, its fellow creatures, and even its own best interests. Yet this unpleasant sense of personal failure and inadequacy is, paradoxically, the greatest blessing a human being can possess. Unpleasant though it may be, the gift of appropriate guilt is precisely what keeps our sins from getting out of hand. It is our most effective safeguard against our own proclivity for evil.

Among the reasons for becoming more conscious is to avoid becoming evil. Fortunately, the truly evil represent only a minority of the human population. Yet lesser forms of psychological illness abound. And although not evil, they too can reflect an unwillingness to meet our Shadow. Sigmund Freud and his daughter, Anna, compellingly demonstrated that there is often "sinister" stuff lurking in the depths of the unconscious mind. Traditional Freudian psychology has taught us that the causes of most psychological disorders stem from hidden feelings—anger, unacknowledged sexual desire, and so on. Because of this, psychological illness has been localized in the unconscious realm by most thinkers, as if the unconscious were the seat of psychopathology, and symptoms were like subterranean demons that surface to torment the individual. My own view is the opposite.

As I wrote in *The Road Less Traveled,* I believe that all psychological disorders are basically disorders of consciousness. They are not rooted in the unconscious but in a conscious mind that refuses to think and is unwilling to deal with certain issues, bear certain feelings, or tolerate pain. These issues, feelings, or desires are in the unconscious only because a pain-avoiding conscious mind has thrust them there.

Of course, no one walking around is so unhealthy that he is not at least slightly conscious. And no one is so healthy that she is *totally* conscious. There are innumerable degrees of consciousness, given that some people exert themselves more or less than others. But the degree of consciousness is inherently hard to measure. Even with the tools for gauging mental health through standard psychological testing, it is difficult to determine anyone's true level of consciousness. We can speculate from his or her behavior. But perhaps the best measure of someone's degree of consciousness can be found in the consistency of his or her general approach to thinking. For example, a person who is oriented more toward thinking simplistically has a lesser degree of consciousness than a person who thinks with integrity.

In this way, thinking and consciousness are inextricably locked together in a parallel relationship. Consciousness is the foundation of all thinking, and thinking is the foundation of all consciousness. Anytime there is a failure in thinking, there is corresponding deficit in a person's level of consciousness. Thus, all human behavior—the good, the bad, and the indifferent—is determined by the extent, or lack thereof, of the quality of thinking and consciousness involved.

People have frequently asked me, "Dr. Peck, since we all have neuroses of one sort or another—since no one can be completely conscious—how do you know when to go into therapy?"

My answer to them is: "When you're *stuck.* There's no need for therapy when you're clearly growing well without it. But when we're not growing, when we're stuck and spinning our wheels, we're obviously in a condition of inefficiency. And whenever there's a lack of efficiency there is a potentially unnecessary lack of competence." So there is yet another reason to seek greater consciousness. It is the foundation of mental and spiritual growth. And it is through this growth that we become ever more competent.

CONSCIOUSNESS AND COMPETENCE

Although we can pinpoint various capabilities and talents that allow us to meet the demands of life or to develop deftness in problem-solving skills, general competence is a much more complex capability. In relation to the development of consciousness, it is broader than just attaining adequacy in basic survival skills, learning how to organize, or having an excellent memory. True competence is more about growing in wisdom than accumulating mere knowledge. It entails striving toward a psychological and spiritual maturity that results in real personal power.

Many people can cook without recipes or work on car engines without a manual, or have brilliant memories that enable them to recall quick, formulaic ways of responding to situations. But, because of an inability or unwillingness to think in broader ways or to handle different situations creatively, they may fail in dealing with situations that do not fit within expected patterns. The man who can easily fix a garbage disposal without much help from a manual may feel totally incompetent when faced with handling more complex or detailed situations involving the discipline of his children or communication with his wife.

The reality is that even when people are competent in some aspects of their lives, their competence in other areas varies. Heather, one of the main characters in *A Bed by the Window*, is very skilled and conscientious in her work as a nurse—so competent and well-rounded as a caregiver that she is one of the most appreciated staff members at the nursing home. Her personal life is another matter altogether. She is less competent in making decisions about mates, and often finds herself in compromising—even abusive—situations as a result of her poor judgment about men. As a superb nurse on the one hand but a lousy girlfriend on the other, Heather is a glaring example of what psychologists refer to as someone with a combination of both "conflict-free areas of the ego" and extremely conflicted ones, someone who is fully conscious in certain areas but, because of neurotic conflict, utterly unconscious in others.

Many people find themselves confused by the uneven nature of their consciousness. As did Heather, they may go into therapy seeking an end to their torment. Although some relief usually comes quickly with the realization that they are not crazy, and major growth may come more slowly, they will find that even therapy does not offer a panacea for the pain of developing consciousness.

In my practice as a psychotherapist, I would routinely tell my patients, "Psychotherapy is not about happiness; it is about power. If you go the whole route here, I cannot guarantee you that you will leave one jot happier. What I can guarantee you is that you will leave more competent." I would go on to say, "But there is a vacuum of competence in the world, and so as soon as people become more competent, God or life will give them bigger things to do. Consequently, you may well leave here worrying about far bigger problems than when you first came. Nonetheless, a certain kind of joy and peace of mind do come from knowing that you're worrying about big things and no longer getting bent out of shape about the little ones."

Once, when asked the purpose of psychotherapy, Freud commented, "To make the unconscious conscious." This, of course, is what has been said all along. Therapy's purpose is to help people become more aware so that they can think more clearly and live their lives more effectively and efficiently.

Another way of talking about this progression of awareness or consciousness is in terms of what is known as ego development, which is very much a development of consciousness. In *A World Waiting to Be Born*, I wrote that the ego is the governing part of our personality and that its development—the maturation of this governor—can be delineated in three overall stages. The first stage, that of early childhood, is one of an absolute or almost absolute lack of self-consciousness. Here the ego is totally down at the level of the emotions and enmeshed with them. It is this lack of self-consciousness that can make young children so frequently charming and seemingly innocuous. When they are joyful, they are one hundred percent joyful. They are marvelously spontaneous and innocent. But it is this same lack of self-consciousness that can so often make them difficult. For when children are sad, they are also one hundred percent sad, sometimes to the point of being inconsolable. And when they are angry, their anger will erupt in temper tantrums and sometimes violent or vicious behavior.

There are glimmerings of self-consciousness by the age of nine months, and the capacity for self-awareness very gradually increases throughout childhood. In adolescence, however, it undergoes a dramatic growth spurt. For the first time young people have a quite obvious "observing ego." Now they can observe themselves being joyful or sad or angry while they are feeling so. This means the ego is no longer wholly confined to the level of the emotions. Now a part of it—the observing ego—is detached from the emotions, above them looking on. There is a certain resulting loss of spontaneity.

The observing ego is still not fully developed in adolescence. Thus, adolescents are frequently spontaneous, sometimes dangerously so. At other times, however, they seem to be nothing but a mass of affectations as they self-consciously try on one new identity after another by wearing bizarre hairstyles and clothes and behaving outrageously. Constantly comparing themselves with peers and parents, these seemingly flamboyant creatures are often painfully shy and suffer innumerable spasms of excruciating embarrassment and self-deprecation.

Since self-consciousness often becomes painful at this stage of psychosocial and spiritual development, many people move into adulthood forsaking rather than continuing its development. Because they fail to further develop their observing egos once they enter adulthood, their self-observing capacity becomes modulated (and less painful), but this often occurs only because of an actual shrinkage of consciousness. When, unwittingly, the majority settle for a limited—even diminished—awareness of their own feelings and imperfections, they have stopped short on the journey of personal growth, thereby failing to fulfill their human potential or grow into true psychospiritual power.

But a fortunate minority, for reasons both mysterious and graceful, continue the journey, ever strengthening their observing egos rather than allowing them to atrophy. One of the reasons that psychoanalytically oriented psychotherapy may be profoundly effective is that it is a vehicle for the exercise of the observing ego. What the patient is doing as he lies on the analyst's couch is not merely talking about himself but observing himself talking about himself and observing his feelings as he does so.

The exercise of the observing ego is crucial because if it becomes strong enough, the individual is then in a position where she can proceed to the next stage and develop what I call a transcendent ego. With a transcendent ego, we become more aware of our broader dimensions, better prepared to decide realistically when, where, and why to express the essence of who we are. In becoming more conscious of the full range of our thoughts and feelings, we inevitably become less threatened by the knowledge of our flaws and can more readily integrate and appreciate the whole of who we are—the good and the bad. We may develop the capacity to live with, perhaps even laugh at, our limitations. When we can acknowledge our imperfections, we find ourselves in a better position to work on those areas within our power to change and to accept those things we cannot.

It's a given that the very existence of a significant observing ego implies a certain loss of spontaneity. Since the development of a transcendent ego is based on the prior foundation of an observing ego, a fully conscious person knows he is often not free to do everything he simply feels like doing. On the other hand, he has the psychological flexibility to consciously decide when he can be spontaneous and to know when the situation calls for caution.

I was attempting to explain the concept of transcendent ego to a patient one afternoon. This particular patient was seeing me because of a problem expressing his anger. He had some years before been high in the administration of a university at a time of student riots. "Aha!" he suddenly exclaimed. "Now I understand what you're talking about." He recounted how at the height of the riots, the president of the university re-

signed and a new president was immediately brought in to re-
place him:

> We went from meeting to meeting to meeting. More
> often than not, the discussions were very heated. The
> new man mostly just listened. Occasionally he would
> very calmly comment that university policy was proba-
> bly such and such, but he wasn't sure because he was
> still learning the ropes. I admired how he kept his
> cool. But I also began to wonder if he wasn't being too
> passive, possibly even ineffective. Finally, we were at a
> huge meeting in the amphitheater, open to the entire
> faculty. The issue was particularly critical. A very
> young faculty member went into a long diatribe about
> how the entire administration was nothing but a col-
> lection of insensitive and unresponsive fascist pigs.
> When he was finished the new man stood up and
> strode to the lectern. "I have been with you for three
> weeks now," he said with his usual calm, steady voice,
> "and you have not yet had the occasion to see your
> new president get angry. Today you are going to have
> that opportunity." Then he proceeded to utterly blast
> the arrogant young fool away. It was very impressive.
> Maybe that's an example of what you mean by a tran-
> scendent ego at work.

While there is a small loss of freedom associated with consciousness and constant self-examination, those who have become accustomed to it have found that, on balance, it makes
for a way of life that can be profoundly liberating. That is because underlying a high degree of consciousness is a degree of
self-control—in other words, psychological competence.

Having a transcendent ego is analogous to being an orchestra conductor. Like the university president, an individual
with a transcendent ego has become so aware of her emotions
that she can actually orchestrate them. She may be feeling some
sadness, but she is in command of herself, so she can say in

essence, "This is not the time for sadness or violins; it is a time for joy. So hush now, violins. And come on, horns, blow forth." What defines her competence here—her personal power—is that she does not repress or deny her sadness any more than an orchestra conductor would smash the violins. She simply sets aside her sadness, or brackets it. Similarly, with the emotional and intellectual competence of a transcendent ego, she would be able to address the joyful part of herself: "I love you, horns, but this is not a situation for joyful expression. It is one that calls for anger. So beat the drums."

Yet once again, in the interest of realism, we must remember that all blessings are potential curses, and that both consciousness and competence are inextricably interwoven with pain. As I wrote in *The Road Less Traveled,* "Perhaps the best measure of a person's greatness is the capacity for suffering." This point is underscored in the aptly titled book *The Price of Greatness,* by Arnold Ludwig, a professor of psychiatry at the University of Kentucky College of Medicine. Ludwig's book is based on ten years of research that examined the lives of 1,004 eminent figures of the twentieth century who represented various disciplines including artists, writers, inventors, and other creative individuals. In exploring the relationship between genius and mental health, Ludwig wrote that among the great geniuses of our times, all showed a readiness to discard prevalent views, an irreverence toward established authority, a strong capacity for solitude, and a "psychological unease," which could cause mental trouble such as depression, anxiety, or alcoholism. But if these qualities were not too incapacitating, they actually contributed to the individual's ability to achieve significant creativity, blaze new trails, propose radical solutions, and promote new schools of thought.

Another aspect of the pain of being gifted and highly conscious has to do with the struggle to come to terms with one's superiority. As I wrote in *A World Waiting to Be Born,* many who are truly superior will struggle against their genuine call to personal and civic power because they fear exercising authority. Usually, they are reluctant to consider themselves "better than" or "above" others, in large part because of a sense of humility that accompanies their personal and spiritual power.

A woman named Jane was a case in point. She was a brilliant and beautiful young student in the second year of business school who had come to see me because of irritability. Her dates were dull. Her professors seemed pompous. Her fellow students, even the women, struck her as remarkably limited and unimaginative. She had no idea what the problem was, but she was smart enough to know that something was wrong about living in a state of constant annoyance.

After several sessions going over the same old ground, she exclaimed in exasperation, "I feel that all I'm doing here is whining. I don't want to be a whiner."

"Then you'll need to learn how to accept your superiority," I retorted.

"My what? What do you mean?" Jane was dumbfounded. "I'm not superior."

"All your complaints—your whining, if you will—center around your probably accurate assessment that your dates aren't as smart as you, your professors aren't as humble as you, and your fellow students aren't as interesting as you," I pointed out. "In other words, all your unhappiness relates to the fact that you feel—and probably are—superior to most people."

"But I don't feel superior," she exclaimed with a touch of desperation. "That's the point. I shouldn't feel superior. Everyone's equal."

"Are they?" I arched my eyebrows. "If you believe everyone is as smart as you, then you're bound to be chronically irritated when people prove themselves not to be as smart. You're going to be constantly disappointed with them when they don't live up to your expectations."

The weeks that followed were ones of excruciatingly hard work for Jane, although tinged with the excitement of grudgingly sensing that she was on the right track. It was so much easier being ordinary. It was so safe. How could she accept her superiority and not succumb to arrogance? Not become mired in self-righteousness? If she really was superior, was she not then doomed to a life of loneliness? And if she was not ordinary—if she was, in fact, extraordinary—why? Why her? Why was she singled out, chosen or cursed? Of course, I could never answer these questions for her. But it was reassuring for her that I acknowledged that they were very real and very important questions. Gradually, she came to accept that she was not ordinary, that she was both chosen and cursed, blessed and burdened.

Yet another painful burden that comes with increased consciousness and competence is the loneliness of transcending traditional culture. Throughout the ages, only a few among millions—a Socrates, a Jesus—have obviously risen above the rigid culture and simplistic thinking of their times. Now, as a result of mass communications, psychotherapy, and grace, I would estimate that there are hundreds of thousands of adults in our country who are on this cutting edge. These individuals think well enough to challenge conventional and irrational thinking. They question blind national and tribal loyalties—and the limitations imposed by their culture—in order to grow. They no longer believe everything they read in the newspapers. They seek truth and challenge the illusions about "normalcy" as promoted by society and the mass media. They show the courage to no longer be sucked into the simplistic thinking around them. They have redefined "family" to include not only blood relatives but the meaningful relations they establish with others who share common interests and a common—and growth-oriented—approach to life.

In the process of becoming increasingly conscious, many experience a sense of freedom and liberation in striving toward becoming true to—and truly—themselves. Their awareness is becoming rooted in the eternal, and the evolution of consciousness is the very essence of spiritual growth. But they pay a price as well, because theirs can be a lonely journey. Deep thinkers are often misunderstood by the masses who continue to view life and the world simplistically. Since many who are conscious do not readily buy into the "go along to get along" mentality that is prevalent in society, they find it hard to fit neatly into the mainstream. They find that others have difficulty understanding and communicating with them. They pay the price of feeling at least partially alienated from families and isolated from old friends and cultural rituals.

These intellectually and spiritually "elite" come from a variety of backgrounds. They may be rich or poor, of any race, gender, or level of education. But because consciousness requires great internal strength to cope, many with the potential to rise above their lot—a certain mentality they were raised with—instead choose what seems the easier path, of stagnation over growth.

For example, a number of black servicemen whom I evaluated while working as a psychiatrist in the Army during the Vietnam era chose to play "dumb" even though it was clear they were intelligent enough to answer complex questions. Many didn't want to rock the boat; others wanted to avoid the responsibility that comes with being competent and the demands it would place on them. For the same reason, a large number of people shun consciousness to a lesser or greater extent because they find it a more comfortable way to live. Even if they give lip service to the importance of awareness and growing, their actions do not always correspond to their words.

In fact, it is common for consciousness to be treated almost as if it were a common cold, contagious or potentially deadly if one spreads deep thinking too much to those in one's environment. As I wrote in Chapter 1, it is quite common for contemplatives to be told by others that they "think too much." Being aware is often greeted with suspicion and trepidation, as if thinking deeply and well can be equated with a bad drug that one can become addicted to and overdose on.

THE CONSCIOUSNESS OF DEATH

There is still another pain of consciousness so great and so important that it warrants even deeper consideration. I refer to our consciousness of death and dying. Assuming that we are more conscious than other animals, one of the things most frequently said about the human condition is that "man is the only creature to be aware of his mortality." Some have labeled this not only the human condition but the human dilemma because people tend to find this awareness excruciatingly painful.

Consequently, most people, one way or another, attempt to flee from directly facing their mortality. Rather than meeting our mortality head-on—doing so as early as possible and doing so on a regular basis—many of us fail to prepare in any significant way. In our death-denying and youth-worshiping culture, we go to great lengths to avoid facing even the smallest reminders of death. As Ernest Becker pointed out in his now classic work, *The Denial of Death,* this, too, may lead us to evil in a variety of subtle ways (as in scapegoating or actual human sacrifice to propitiate the gods so that they won't get us).

Naturally associated with our reluctance to deal with death is our reluctance to deal with old age. I wrote in *In Search of Stones* that it would be unnatural to actually welcome aging because it is a process of stripping away—eventually a stripping away of everything. In the later days of my practice, I was consulted by four remarkably similar women in their late sixties or early seventies who came to me with the same chief complaint: depression at growing old. Each was secular-minded. Each had either made money or married money. All their children had turned out golden. It was as if life had gone according to a script.

But now they were getting cataracts, requiring hearing aids or dentures, and facing hip replacements. This wasn't the way they would have written the script, and they were angry and depressed. I saw no way to help them without converting them to a vision of old age as something more than a meaningless time of watching themselves simply rot away. I tried to help them "buy it" as a spiritual period in their lives, a time of preparation. It was not an easy sell. In attempting it, I kept saying to each of them in every possible way, "Look, you're not the scriptwriter; it's just not entirely your show." Two of them soon left, preferring to be depressed rather than come to terms with the fact that life was not solely their own show.

Although she was even more depressed, I had a much easier time of it with an elderly woman who had a distinctly religious, Christian mind-set. In her mid-sixties, she had suffered a detached retina in each eye. Ninety percent blind, she was incensed at her fate and furious at the ophthalmologist who had been unsuccessful in healing her condition with the most advanced laser treatment. A theme soon emerged during our sessions. "I just hate it when they have to take hold of my arm to help me out of the pew or walk me down the steps at church," she ranted. "I hate being stuck at home. I know that lots of people volunteer to take me places, but I can't be asking friends to drive me around all the time."

It was clear to me, I told her, that she had taken a lot of pride in her independence. "You've been a very successful person, and I think you needed that pride for your many accomplishments. But you know, it's a journey from here to heaven, and it's a good rule of journeying to travel light. I'm not sure how successful you're going to be in getting to heaven, carrying around all this pride," I said. "You see your blindness as a curse, and I don't blame you. Conceivably, however, you might look at it as a blessing designed to relieve you of the no longer necessary burden of your pride. Except for your eyes, you're in pretty good health. You've probably got at least a dozen more years to live. It's up to you whether you'd rather live those years with a curse or a blessing."

Whether someone can make the transition and learn to discern a blessing where once they only saw a curse seems to have something to do with whether they can view old age as a time of preparation. Preparation for what? Obviously, an afterlife. In my book *In Heaven as on Earth,* one of the major subjects is that of purgatory, which I describe—I believe quite properly—as a very elegant, well-appointed psychiatric hospital with the most modern techniques for as-painless-as-possible learning. Nonetheless, I make it indelibly clear that the amount of time we must spend in purgatory, if any, is directly proportional to the effort we have made to avoid dealing with the important issues in our lives (including our Shadow and our old age) and our failure to prepare for death. Whether in an afterlife or on earth, we must do the work of purgatory or remain forever in limbo, separated from God. Why not get on with it?

Some people manage to get on with it more courageously than others. The elderly woman I previously mentioned rapidly began working through her turmoil. Her depression of four years' duration began to lift by our third session. But most situations do not change so easily or become resolved permanently. In the struggle to face aging and ultimately death, some even kill themselves because they do not want to go deeper into what they perceive as the indignity of dying; many cannot bear to endure all the losses that come with the stripping-away process.

The stripping away of health and physical agility is not as painful for me, and I suspect for others, as the psychological stripping away. The loss of heroes, mentors, and even interests can leave us feeling empty. The stripping away of illusions—hundreds of them—may be all for the good, but it still hurts and may leave many distrustful, cynical, and embittered. I'm not sure I will be as graceful as the blind woman I described. But I am utterly certain that I will not be able to deal decently with my aging without relying on my relationship with God. It's not solely a matter of faith in an afterlife that is my true home, and faith that aging is a process of preparation for it. I need something even more personal, including my wife Lily and God, to complain to about the indignity of the stripping-away process. And I need God upon occasion to answer in Her peculiar way, sometimes seemingly through spirits and angels of a sort, to help me along. What I've come to realize is that the stripping-away process of old age is not partial. It is not just physical; it is total. The reality is that God doesn't just want part of us. God wants all of us.

The path of health and healing is the opposite from that of the denial of death. The best book I have read on the subject is *Living Our Dying* by Joseph Sharp. He believes, as I do, that death is not a taker away of meaning but a giver of meaning. Whether we are young or old, a deep consciousness of death ultimately leads us on a path to seeking meaning. People may grab upon some simplistic secondhand faith out of fear, in order to avoid thinking about their deaths. But while such religions may keep us warm for a bit, like hand-me-down clothes they are just trappings. A fully mature religion, however, begins with an active struggle with the mystery of death and in a personal search for meaning in its face. You cannot let anyone else do the struggling for you. Thus the saying "God has no grandchildren." You cannot be related to God through your parents. You must find your meaning as a "child of God" in a direct relationship with the cycle of birth, death, and rebirth.

Inherent in this is that we must come to terms with the reality of change, which requires continual adjustments in the way we think and behave—and particularly when we have become the most comfortable with where we are. And change often feels like dying, like death. In *The Road Less Traveled*, I quoted Seneca as saying two thousand years ago, "Throughout the whole of life one must continue to learn to live, and what will amaze you even more, throughout life one must learn to die." Among other things this includes the fearsome learning of how to consciously give up control of our lives when it is appropriate to do so—and ultimately hand ourselves over to God.

TRAVELING WITH GOD

I have suggested many reasons to grow in consciousness, but we can always ask more radical questions. If one reason is to find meaning, what meaning are we seeking? We need to become conscious to become good and save ourselves from evil, but why? Why be good? The more we can become conscious, the more we will grow in power and competence, but to what purpose? Granted that the whole thrust of evolution is in the direction of consciousness, where are we evolving toward?

Nothing ever will remove all mystery. But I believe at least part of the answer to these questions can be found in the Latin derivation of the very word "conscious," *con-scire*, which literally means "to know with." What a strange derivation! To know with? To know with what? I suggest that the answer is to know with God. I have said that psychological disorders primarily have their root in consciousness rather than in our unconscious, that "nasty" material is contained in our unconscious only because our conscious mind refuses to deal with it. If we can deal with this unpleasant stuff, then our unconscious mind offers an absolute garden of delights through which we are connected to God. In other words, I believe that God reveals Herself to us through our unconscious if we are willing to be open to it and become conscious of its wisdom.

In *Gifts for the Journey*, one of Sister Marilyn's "wisdom" songs begins with "Wisdom is a spirit." Its refrain is "And I say: ask and you will receive. Seek and you will find. Knock and it will be open to you. And I say: the Lord will give you His mind, the Lord will show you the way, the Lord will make you his light." The Lord will actually give us His mind. If we become conscious enough, we can actually begin to think with the mind of God. The development of consciousness is thus, among other things, a process of the conscious mind opening itself to the unconscious in order to be congruent with the mind of God. When we become aware of a new truth, it is because we consciously *re-cognize* it to be true; we re-know that which we knew all along in our unconscious mind. We come to know the wisdom that God shares with us.

In *The Road Less Traveled*, I suggested that God actually speaks to us in a whole variety of ways, and I gave some examples. One is through Her "still, small voice." Of this still, small voice I gave another example in *Gifts for the Journey*, where I told of a woman in her late thirties who had traveled remarkably far on the spiritual journey but was still deeply engaged in confronting her general fearfulness and lack of faith.

A friend of mine, she recounted an experience she had had a few mornings before as she was putting on her lipstick just before going out the door to work. A "still, small voice" inside her head said, "Go running." She shook her head as if to shake away the voice, but it came back stronger. "That's ridiculous," she replied, half to herself, half to the voice. "I don't go running in the mornings. I only run in the evenings. Besides, I'm on my way to work."

"Nonetheless, go running now," the voice insisted, and as she thought about it, she realized it made no difference if she got to her office at ten that morning instead of nine. So, in obedience to the voice, she undressed and got into her jogging outfit. After she had run a mile and a half in a nearby park, she began feeling quite awkward; she was not enjoying it and she didn't even know why she was running in the first place. At that point the voice spoke again. "Close your eyes," it commanded.

"That's crazy," she countered. "You don't close your eyes when you're running." Finally again in obedience, she closed her eyes. After two strides she opened them in panic. But she was still on the path. The woods hadn't moved and the sky hadn't fallen. The voice told her to close her eyes again. Eventually, she was able to take up to twenty strides with her eyes closed, never running off the path or into trouble. At which point the voice said, "That's enough for today. You can go home now."

As she finished telling me this story, my friend's eyes filled with tears. "To think," she exclaimed with joy, "that the Creator of the whole universe would take the time out to go running with me."

As my running friend's experience demonstrates, the Holy Spirit often speaks to us when we least expect it. But She can be heard and obeyed only when Her voice falls upon a soul that is open to Her and prepared to listen. And that still doesn't make it all easy or simple. I also suggested in *The Road Less Traveled* that God can reveal Herself to us through our dreams. They are gifts from the unconscious. But we may not want to become conscious of our dreams or have much taste for discerning revelations.

I myself had a dream that proved to be a revelation. It was around a time in my life when I was just beginning to learn the real meaning of what is involved in truly surrendering to God. *The Road Less Traveled* had just been accepted for publication and I felt I deserved a vacation, but I didn't want to sit on a beach someplace. So I went off for two weeks to a convent, my first "retreat," something I knew would be a totally different experience.

I had a number of agenda items for this retreat, but my largest item was to decide what to do if by some dim chance *The Road Less Traveled* became a popular best-seller. Should I give up my privacy and go out on the lecture circuit, or should I retire into the woods like J. D. Salinger and get an unlisted phone number? I didn't know which way I wanted to go. And I didn't know which way God wanted me to go. The stakes seemed high, so at the top of my agenda was the hope that in the quietness of the retreat and the holiness of the atmosphere, I might get a revelation from God about how to deal with this dilemma. I recounted my experience in *Further Along the Road Less Traveled.* The dream—although initially obscure—was to give me a whole new perspective on life.

> I was an onlooker in a distinctly middle-class home. In this two-car family there was a seventeen-year-old boy who was the kind of son every mother and father would love to have. He was president of the senior class in high school, he was going to be valedictorian at graduation time, he was captain of the high school football team, he was good-looking, he worked hard after school at a part-time job, and if all that wasn't enough, he had a girlfriend who was sweet and demure. Moreover, the boy had his driver's license, and was an unusually responsible, mature driver for his age. Only his father wouldn't let him drive. Instead, the father insisted on driving this boy wherever he had to go—football practice, job, dates, proms. And to add insult to injury, the father insisted that the boy pay him five dollars a week out of his hard-earned after-school earnings for the privilege of being driven around, which he was quite capable of doing himself.

I awoke from this dream with a sense of absolute fury and outrage at what an autocratic creep the father was. I didn't know what to make of the dream. It didn't seem to make any sense at all. But three days after I had written it down, when I was rereading what I had written, I noticed that I had capitalized the "F" in "father." So I said to myself, "You don't happen to suppose that the father in this dream is God the Father, do you? And if that's the case, you don't suppose that I might be that seventeen-year-old boy?" And then I finally realized that I had gotten a revelation. God was saying to me, "Hey, Scotty, you just pay your dues and leave the driving to me."

It is interesting that I had always thought of God as being the ultimate good guy. Yet in my dream I had cast Him in the role of autocratic, overcontrolling villain, or at least I was responding to Him as such, with fury and outrage and hatred. The problem, of course, was that this wasn't the revelation I had hoped for. It wasn't what I wanted to hear. I wanted some little bit of advice from God such as I might get from my lawyer or accountant, which I would be free to accept or reject. I didn't want a *big* revelation, particularly not one in which God said, "Leave the driving to me." Many years later I am still trying to live up to this revelation, to abandon myself to God by learning the surrender that welcomes His or Her being in the driver's seat of my still-adolescent life.

CHAPTER 3

Learning and Growth

⁂

IF, AS I HAVE SAID OVER and again, we are not here to necessarily be happy, fulfilled, or comfortable all the time, then what are we here for? What is the meaning of life?

I believe the reason we are here is to learn, which is to say, to evolve. By "evolve" I mean to progress. When people learn, they are in a position to pro-gress (move forward) as opposed to re-gress (move backward). And I defy you in your imagination to construct a more ideal environment for human learning than this life. It is a life filled with vicissitudes, uncertainty, and hard lessons. In our gloomier moments, life may seem like some sort of a celestial boot camp. But in Benjamin Franklin's words, quoted in *The Road Less Traveled,* "Those things that hurt, instruct." Learning is a process inextricably interwoven with thinking and consciousness. And like both thinking and consciousness, the business of learning is neither simple nor entirely straightforward. It, too, is filled with mystery.

My primary identity is that of a scientist, and we scientists are empiricists, who believe that the best route to knowledge is through experience. In other words, experience is deemed the best way to learn, although it is clearly not the only route. So we scientists conduct experiments, or controlled experiences, to gain new knowledge and find truth in the world.

By the same token, I am a spiritual person. I know of God not only because of faith, but also on the basis of evidence, namely my experiences of grace. I gave examples of these experiences in *The Road Less Traveled* and *In Search of Stones*. And I have previously talked about grace as much as possible in terms of statistical methods of proof. One of the most useful ways to establish something scientifically is to apply what are called the statistics of improbability. That means that the lower the mathematically calculated probability, the greater the improbability, and the safer we feel concluding that an event was not the result of chance alone. Thus, we may conclude that something occurred because of a significant reason, even if it may or may not be explainable.

That is why I have commonly spoken about grace in terms of a "pattern of highly improbable events with a beneficial outcome." It is also why I have concluded that in such patterns we can see the fingerprints—if not the actual hand—of God. So I am very much like Carl Jung who, toward the end of his life, was interviewed on film. The climax of that film, for me, came at its conclusion when the interviewer asked Jung, "Do you believe in God?" Jung, who was about eighty-three at the time, puffed on his pipe and replied, if I remember correctly, "Believe in God? We use the word 'believe' when we think of something as true but for which we do not yet have a substantial body of evidence. No, no, I don't believe in God. I *know* there is a God."

THE ROLE OF THE SOUL

My assertion that this world is an ideal environment for human learning suggests the possibility that it might have been constructed by God for that purpose, which immediately brings us to a discussion about the notion of the soul. In *People of the Lie*, I quoted Keats as referring to this world as "the vale of soul-making," which means we're here to learn and be prepared. This belief is one that Christianity and other religions have in common with reincarnation theory, which suggests that we're here to get rid of "bad karma" and to learn lessons that are necessary so that we can eventually make the transition beyond this world of rebirth.

Given that we're here to continually learn on the journey of life, it seems that the ultimate goal of learning is the perfection of our souls. To propose the idea of becoming perfected is not the same as saying that we humans can be perfect, or that we should try to be perfect in everything. It only means that we are capable of learning, changing, and growing throughout the span of our earthly life.

I cannot prove the existence of the soul, any more than I can prove the existence of God to a diehard secularist. I can offer many hints that suggest its existence, and have done so in all of my books. But that doesn't mean that everyone is open to the same sort of evidence that impressed Jung or led Keats to his conclusion. Thus my latest book, on the subject of euthanasia, is entitled *Denial of the Soul*. And I would not have used the word "denial" unless I had the sense that many secularists are not only ignorant of the evidence of the existence of the soul but, for one reason or another, are strongly immune or closed to it.

But what is the soul? Once again, we find ourselves involved with something that is actually much larger than we are, and therefore cannot be submitted to any single, adequate, or simplistic definition. That doesn't mean, however, that we can't use an operating definition, imperfect though it might be. I believe such a definition can at the very least facilitate our progress in looking at the equally mysterious subject of learning.

I define the soul as "a God-created, God-nurtured, unique, developable, immortal human spirit." Each of these modifiers is crucial, but for the moment let me focus upon three. I have already suggested that this world is such an ideal environment for human learning that it has actually been designed for that purpose. Now I am saying that we are created by God, and further suggest that we are created to learn. By "God-nurtured" I mean that not only did God create us from the moment of our conception but also that God, through grace, continues to nurture us throughout our lives. There would be no purpose in

Her doing so unless She wanted something from us. What does She want? She wants us to learn—and most of grace seems to be devoted to that end.

The other key word for the moment is "developable." There would be no point in God's wanting us to learn unless we *could* learn, unless we were capable of development. We are evolving creatures, not only as an entire race but as individuals. As physical beings, we have bodies that stop developing and inevitably decay. But our psychospiritual development can continue until the moment we die (and, I suspect, long, long afterward). For this psychospiritual development, I will frequently use the word "growth," and growth is inextricably dependent upon learning.

I have repeatedly said that we have a choice of whether to grow or not, whether to learn or not to learn. One of the greatest psychologists of this century, Abraham Maslow, coined the term "self-actualization," by which he meant human beings' capacity to grow and evolve into higher levels of psychosocial and spiritual functioning, autonomy, and personal power. Once people have achieved the means to meet basic needs of survival, they can move on to higher levels of awareness, Maslow suggested.

Much as I am indebted to Maslow, I take issue with the term "self-actualization." I do not believe that we can actualize ourselves any more than we can create ourselves. I can no more create myself than I can an iris or another flower. What I can do is steward the flower garden that God has made it possible for us to enjoy. What this means is that while we cannot create our own souls, we can steward them well or badly. In the choice we make to grow, we can become cocreators of ourselves, whereas whenever we resist growth, we are rejecting the role of being cocreator with God.

Therefore, I believe that what Maslow called self-actualization should be viewed instead as perceiving life as a series of opportunities for learning and making choices, and opting to choose growth most of the time. Typically, the hard work of cocreating (or coactualizing) ourselves with God's guidance is an ongoing process of unfolding, development, and blooming. But the deliberate choice to learn and grow is primarily one that we make or fail to make as adults. During our childhood, most of our learning is "passive." In other words, for the most part it just happens.

PASSIVE LEARNING

Scientists do not fully understand how we learn, any more than they fully understand thinking or consciousness. Back when I was a psychology major in college, we had to study a very important (and for me, somewhat difficult) subject, learning theory. At that time, most of learning theory had to do with the process of conditioning, which had been recognized and studied by Pavlov with his experimental dogs. It was thought that we learned primarily through reward and punishment, just as rats may be taught to run a maze by either punishment (electric shocks) or reward (food pellets).

It was further assumed that the way children learned language was through this "behaviorist" process of conditioning. But then the great thinker Arthur Koestler, in his book *The Ghost in the Machine,* totally demolished the behaviorist theory of how we learn language, asking dozens of questions about language acquisition that behaviorism in no way could answer. Koestler himself made little attempt to explain how we learn language, but he did prove that we know hardly anything about the subject. To this day, how children learn to speak their language remains mostly a mystery.

One fact we do know is that one's ability to learn is not necessarily fully dependent on having all of one's five senses active. Helen Keller, for example, was deaf and blind, yet learned not only language but also astonishing wisdom. On the other hand, we have learned that deprivation of sensory needs can severely interfere with a child's learning. Infants raised without meaningful human contact or play in a German orphanage in the 1920s taught us that we need a certain foundation of sensory relations with others (through touch we feel connected, for example) to thrive physically or achieve any mental growth whatsoever. Furthermore, there are critical periods in children's development, when deprivation or neglect of some areas of need can limit their advancement if no appropriate intervention takes place. That's why Head Start programs work so well. As part of children's early learning, such programs provide consistent stimulation to help develop the social and mental competence of children.

But like the learning of language, most learning in childhood seems to be a fairly passive affair. For instance, even before children learn language, they learn what psychologists call their ego boundaries. There is reason to believe that the newborn infant cannot distinguish himself from the world. But somehow, during the first nine months of life, the child learns that his arm is his and that it is different from Mommy's arm, and his fingers are distinguishable from Daddy's fingers. He learns that when he has a stomachache, that doesn't mean the whole world must have a stomachache, too. Such learning does not seem to be a matter of choice, which is why I call it passive.

But there may be a good deal of activity involved as the infant tries out its arms and fingers. In a very real sense, this learning of ego boundaries is a development of consciousness, because it is by the age of about nine months that we see the first evidence of self-consciousness. Up until that time, when a stranger comes into the room, the infant will lie in its crib peacefully exploring its ego boundaries as if nothing had happened. But suddenly, around nine months of age, when a stranger comes into its room, the child will start screaming in terror or otherwise become agitated. It has developed what psychologists call stranger anxiety. Why? We can deduce from this that the child has now become aware of itself as a *separate* entity, one that is terribly small, relatively helpless, and extremely vulnerable. From this demonstration of the terror of vulnerability, we can deduce that the child has developed the first rudiments of self-consciousness. One's awareness of self is accompanied by a sense of reality that allows us to perceive ourselves as separate and different from others.

The passive learning of language and ego boundaries seems to be a painless sort of affair. This does not mean that all passive learning is so painless. Perhaps no time is more painful in the life of a young human being than the terrible twos. By the time a child completes its second year, he has learned his ego boundaries very well. But he has not yet learned the boundaries of his power. Consequently, the child assumes that this is the best of all possible worlds and that he has all the power. Thus, you will see a child just short of two bossing around his parents, his siblings, and the family dog and cat as if they were all little minions in his own private royal army. But then what happens, now that he is able to walk and throw things and pull the books off the shelves, is that his mother and father will say, "No. No. No, you can't do that, Johnny. No. No, you can't do that either. No, you're not the boss. No. No. We love you very much. You're very important. But no, you're not the boss. Mommy and Daddy are the bosses. No. No. No."

What essentially happens is that in the course of no more than twelve months or so the child is psychologically demoted from a four-star general to a private. No wonder it is a time of depression and temper tantrums! Yet painful though the terrible twos are, they are a very important period of learning. And if the child is not burdened with an excess of humiliation by the end of his third year, he will have taken his first giant step out of "infantile narcissism." It is a time that has laid the entire foundation for what Erich Fromm called socialization, which he defined it as the process of "learning to like to do what you have to do."

As childhood continues, the child may work in certain ways at learning, but generally only because of outside pressure in the form of homework assignments, tests, grades, and expectations at home. Otherwise, most of a child's learning continues to be passive. An example of this is Jenny, my eight-year-old heroine in *The Friendly Snowflake*. She lives in a healthy family, and her left and right brains operate in sync; one can see her learning like crazy. But she is not working at it. She is not deliberately interpreting things. She is just doing what comes naturally, thinking away a mile a minute.

Perhaps the most important learning of childhood is that which comes from our role models. In an intact family, the primary role models will automatically be the parents. The child has a natural tendency to assume that the way parents do things is the way they should be done. This is particularly true in the matter of self-discipline. If the child sees her parents behaving with self-discipline, she will be likely at an early age to simply, unconsciously choose to become self-disciplined herself. On the other hand, if the mother and father behave with a lack of self-discipline, the child will think that this is the way to behave and will likely fail to learn to develop significant self-discipline. That is particularly the case if he or she has "Do as I say, not as I do" parents. Although it is passive, learning during childhood is extremely important. It is also the time when, if we are fortunate, we will begin to gain emotional as well as intellectual intelligence.

Many have steadfastly bought into the notion that intelligence can only be gauged by numerical measures. That is perhaps true of analytical intelligence. But as a result, other aspects of intelligence have tended to be overlooked or downplayed, particularly those involving intangible factors such as self-awareness, empathy, and social consciousness. There is now growing debate over the long-standing tests used to determine the so-called intelligence quotient. Although IQ tests are helpful and have positive aspects, they also have limitations. One problem is their tendency to be culturally biased, which has resulted in many students being academically mislabeled and has led to the misapplication of some standardized tests.

Thus, I find quite promising some new research suggesting that how someone handles emotions is as accurate—and important—an indication of human intelligence as intellectual skills. The skills that make up emotional intelligence are complex and multifaceted. One example of emotional intelligence cited in this research is the ability to delay gratification, which I myself wrote about in *The Road Less Traveled*. There I described it as a process of scheduling the pain and pleasure of life in such a way as to enhance the pleasure by meeting and experiencing the pain first and getting it over with.

Time magazine devoted a lengthy article to this most recent research. Not surprisingly, the research also found that a cornerstone of emotional intelligence, on which most other emotional skills depend, is a sense of self-awareness. For example, in relation to self-awareness, psychologists refer to the importance of "metamood," or the ability to pull back and recognize what one is feeling—whether the emotion is anger, shame, or sorrow—before taking action. This is equivalent to what I described in the previous chapter as having an observing and transcendent ego. Once an emotional response comes into awareness, the chances of handling it appropriately improve if one is emotionally astute. The self-awareness that accompanies such intelligence is most crucial of all, because it is the very thing that allows us to exercise more self-control.

The impediments to developing emotional intelligence are formidable in a culture that emphasizes left-brain (intellectual) over right-brain (intuitive) reasoning. It is no wonder that we find the beginnings of emotional numbness in childhood, when children learn to repress feelings or shut off completely. Adults who are uncomfortable with emotions may constantly criticize children about feelings or scold them to "not feel that way," resulting in the repression of emotional awareness.

An inability to handle frustration or recognize distressing feelings has led many children on the path of destructive behavior—including eating disorders and bullying or other antisocial behavior—because they lacked guidance from mature adults about managing their emotions. I believe it would be more helpful if teachers and parents began teaching children that it is okay to feel how they feel. (This does not mean children can—or should—act on everything they think and feel.)

Vital though the passive learning of childhood is—both emotionally and intellectually—the active learning of adulthood, if it occurs at all, is ultimately even more important. Among some psychologists, there has been a tendency to think that by adolescence "the damage has been done" and that, for better or for ill, the personality is set. While this is quite frequently the case, it is not necessarily so. And, if we have the will, it is in the last 75 percent of our lives that we can make the greatest changes and leaps of growth. Among other things it is possible that, as Jonathan Swift said, "the latter part of a man's life is taken up in curing all of the follies, prejudices and false opinions he has contracted in the former part." The active learning of adulthood is not only possible but infinitely desirable.

GROWTH AND WILL

In some ways we understand much more clearly how people can learn in adulthood by active, deliberate choice. What we do not understand is *why*. We are now confronted with the extraordinary mystery of the human will.

As I have written, certain people (for instance, all the members of my immediate family) seem to have been born with a strong will while others seem to be relatively weak-willed. The subject, however, has never been studied scientifically. We do not actually know whether there are differences in the strength of will or whether they are genetic or to what extent they are developed or learned. It is an extremely mysterious matter and represents a wide-open frontier for psychological research.

In any case, I believe that a strong will is one of the two greatest blessings that can be bestowed upon a human being. I believe this not because a strong will necessarily guarantees success—it may backfire and create a Hitler, for example—but because a weak will pretty much guarantees failure. For instance, it is strong-willed people—those with the mysterious will to grow—who do well in psychotherapy no matter what their childhood or background was like, no matter what the odds.

On the other hand, other people who seem to lack this mysterious will to grow may possess all manner of assets—great ideas and talents—and yet sit on their duffs, getting noplace. Still, as I continually point out, all blessings are potential curses, and one downside of a strong will is a bad temper. It is strong-willed people who wrap golf clubs around trees because that damn little ball won't go where they *want* it to go. Strong-willed people have a lot of learning to do to effectively manage their anger.

In *Further Along the Road Less Traveled,* I wrote that I used to explain to my patients that having a weak will is like having a little donkey in your backyard. It can't hurt you very much; about the worst it can do is chomp on your tulips. But it can't help you that much either, and you could end up with a life of regrets for not doing things you thought you should do. Having a strong will, on the other hand, is like having a dozen Clydesdales in your backyard. Those horses are massive and extremely strong, and if they are not properly trained, disciplined, and harnessed, they will knock your house down. On the other hand, if they are properly trained, disciplined, and harnessed, then with them you can literally move mountains. Thus the distinction between the harnessed and unharnessed will is important. But to what is the will to be harnessed? Your will cannot be harnessed simply to yourself. It has to be harnessed to a power higher than yourself.

In his book *Will and Spirit,* the first chapter of which is entitled "Willingness and Willfulness," Gerald May writes that willfulness characterizes the unharnessed human will, whereas willingness identifies the strong will of a person who is willing to go where he or she is called or led by a higher power. Furthermore, given the relationship between willingness and a higher power, it is no coincidence that I wrote in *The Road Less Traveled* that the will to grow is in essence the same phenomenon as love. I defined love as the will to extend oneself for one's own spiritual growth or another's. Genuinely loving people are, by definition, growing people. I have spoken about how the capacity to love is nurtured in one by loving parents, but I have also noted that parental nurturing alone fails to account for the existence of this capacity in all people. Thus, I have come to believe that people's capacity to love, hence their will to grow, is nurtured not only during childhood by loving parents but also throughout their lives by grace, or God's love.

Yet we are left with the question of why only some people continue to show a will to grow throughout life, while many shun not only growth but the responsibility that comes with learning. Mysterious though it is, the choice to actively learn as an adult and devote one's will consciously to growth and learning is the most crucial decision one ever makes in life. But when is this choice made? Again, the issue has not been scientifically studied the way it should be. As I have suggested, there is no evidence that the choice is made in childhood. But it can be made as early as mid-adolescence. I have received letters from people as young as fifteen and sixteen in response to my books who clearly have already made that choice.

My daughters had made the decision by the time they entered college and chose to major in the hard sciences and mathematics, even though they found those subjects quite difficult. Agonizing over their difficulty, I asked them why they didn't major in the humanities, subjects at which they were good and to which they took like ducks to water. Both answered, "But, Dad, what's the point of majoring in something that's easy for you?" It is clear to me that they were, in some ways at least, more advanced in their will to learn than I was at their same age.

But while the choice to be a learner may be made as early as adolescence, this does not necessarily mean that it is made then. I have known people whose critical moments of making that choice seemed to come in their thirties, forties, fifties, or sixties, or even in the month or two preceding their death. I also don't mean to imply that it is a single choice. Some seem to make the choice but do so only halfheartedly and not be remarkably active learners for the rest of their lives. Others who make the choice in midlife may become the most fervent of learners. Sometimes it comes during periods of taking stock, as in a midlife crisis. In most cases, as far as I can discern, the choice is made repeatedly. The decision then becomes stronger and stronger as it is remade and remade. Certainly that has been my own pattern. I cannot remember any one particular moment when I first chose to become an active learner, but I can recall many moments when I chose to cement that choice.

My own personal style has been, for most of my life, learning from experience, and particularly through the contemplation of my own life experiences. That's why I describe the contemplative as someone who takes a little bit of experience and milks it for all it's worth. It's not simply a matter of how much experience you have in life but what you do with it. We all know people who have accomplished many tasks, or done this and that which seem to amount to a broad range of experiences, but who seem as naive or confused as ever. Just going around having different experiences is worthless if one does not learn something about oneself and the rest of the world from those experiences. That's why it's important to be alert not only to external but to internal experiences that serve our spiritual growth. Thus a large part of the willingness to learn must include learning by looking within. Specific to the point is a quote from the philosopher Søren Kierkegaard, who said: "A man may perform astonishing feats and comprehend a vast amount of knowledge, and yet have no understanding of himself. But suffering directs a man to look within. If it succeeds, then there, within him, is the beginning of his learning."

Ultimately, someone whose will has become devoted to learning and growth is someone whose will is clearly in alignment with God's purpose. That does not mean, however, that such a person is conscious of this fact, or that he sees himself as being "in harmony with an unseen order of things." He may consider himself to be agnostic. Yet even many who do not identify God as their higher power may show a willingness to submit themselves to something they consider greater than themselves—perhaps the ideals of love, light, and truth. In the end, of course, all these qualities have something to do with God. Nonetheless, it is my impression that as such people continue over the years and decades to devote their will to learning and growth, they almost inevitably will fall into the hands of the living God, and their soul will be in a personal relationship with its creator and nurturer.

OUT OF NARCISSISM

We have all heard about people so self-centered that they wonder how the world would manage to survive without them. For others, narcissism may not run that deep. But for each of us one of the most difficult—and most important—things to learn and come to terms with is that the world does not simply revolve around any one of us.

I have previously spoken of narcissism as a thinking disorder. In *In Search of Stones,* I wrote that the primary reason Lily and I have unlisted phone numbers and other elaborate security devices is to protect us from the narcissists of the world. Before we acquired these protections a dozen years ago, it was becoming increasingly common for the phone to ring at 2:00 A.M. The caller would be a stranger wanting to discuss with me some fine point of what I had written. "But it's two o'clock in the morning," I would protest. "Well, it's only eleven out here in California," the voice at the other end of the line would explain, "and besides, the rates are cheaper now."

Narcissists cannot or will not think about other people. I believe that we are all born narcissists. Healthy people grow out of their natural narcissism, a growth that can be accomplished only as they become more conscious and learn to consider others, and think about them more. This learning builds on itself because the more we learn, the more conscious we become.

I have already suggested that the terrible twos are a time when children take their first giant step out of infantile narcissism. We do not know what causes people to fail to grow out of narcissism, but I have strong reasons to suspect that the failure begins in this vulnerable period of life, the terrible twos, which is an inevitably humiliating time. It is the task of parents to be gentle with a child in that humiliation as much as realistically possible. Not all parents do this, however. There are parents who, during the terrible twos and throughout a childhood, will do everything that they can to humiliate their children beyond what is necessary for them to become humble. I have an inkling that the failure to grow out of narcissism may be rooted in such excessive humiliation.

I suspect that children who have been so deeply humiliated tend to begin clinging desperately to a self-centered worldview. One reason for this is that they may literally feel as if they're holding on to dear life. Narcissism is the only thing that provides a sense of security in an otherwise tumultuous period. Since they have been shamed in such a way that their egos become incredibly fragile, they begin to equate their very survival with viewing life through a narcissistic frame of reference.

While it is during the terrible twos that we take our first giant step out of infantile narcissism, that doesn't suggest by any means that it is the only or the final step. Indeed, a flare-up of narcissism can commonly be seen in adolescence—for example, when the adolescent never even stops to think that any other member of the family might possibly need the car. Nonetheless, it may also be in adolescence that we take our next giant step. I recount an example in *A World Waiting to Be Born* of a turning point in my own life during early adolescence.

One morning, at the age of fifteen, I was walking down a road at my boarding school and spied a classmate fifty yards away. He was strolling toward me, and when we came abreast, we spoke to each other for five minutes and then went our separate ways. Fifty yards farther down the road, by God's grace, I was struck by a revelation. I suddenly realized that for the entire ten-minute period from when I had first seen my acquaintance until that very moment, I had been totally self-preoccupied. For the two or three minutes before we met, all I was thinking about was the clever things I might say that would impress him. During our five minutes together, I was listening to what he had to say only so that I might turn it into a clever rejoinder. I watched him only so that I might see what effect my remarks were having upon him. And for the two or three minutes after we separated, my sole thought was of those things I could have said that might have impressed him even more.

I had not cared a whit for my classmate. I had not concerned myself with what his joys or sorrows might have been or what I could have said that might have made his life a little less burdensome. I had cared about him only as a foil for my wit and a mirror for my glory. By the grace of God, it was not only revealed to me how self-centered and self-absorbed I was, but also how, if I continued with that kind of consciousness, it would inevitably lead me into a fearful, empty and lonely "maturity." So at the age of fifteen I began to do battle with my narcissism.

But that was just the beginning. Given the tenaciousness of our narcissism, its tentacles can be subtle and penetrating. We must continue to hack away at them day by day, week after week, month after month, and year after year. And there are all manner of pitfalls on the journey, such as being proud of how humble you have become. As I've grown in consciousness, naturally I'm learning to be less narcissistic and more empathetic toward other people. But in looking back, one of my regrets is how unempathetic I was with my own parents as they were aging. It took my own personal struggles with the aging process to better understand what my own parents must have endured, and now I feel a greater sense of kinship with them than ever before.

Learning my way out of narcissism has been the single greatest theme of my life and, again looking back, marriage has been my greatest teacher. In *A World Waiting to Be Born,* I wrote that because of my own narcissism early in our relationship, it began to dawn on me only after two years of marriage that Lily might be something more than my appendage, something more than my "it." It was the friction in our relationship that opened my eyes. I found myself repeatedly annoyed at her for being away from home, shopping, at times when I needed her and equally annoyed at her for "pestering" me at home when I felt in need of solitude. Gradually I began to realize that most of my irritation was the result of a bizarre assumption in my mind. I assumed that Lily should somehow be there for me whenever I wanted her, and not be there whenever her presence was inconvenient. Furthermore, I assumed that she should somehow not only know which time was which but also know it without my having to tell her. It was perhaps another decade before I was able to fully cure myself of that particular insanity.

But that was only the beginning. One of the reasons my marriage to Lily has survived is that we both, in our own way, are deeply considerate people. At first, however, our consideration was rather primitive and had more to do with our self-image than anything else. We wanted to think of ourselves as good people, so we tried to be good. Being good meant being considerate, and we knew the great rule of goodness or consideration was "Do unto others as you would have them do unto you." So we tried very hard to treat each other the way we wanted to be treated. Only it didn't work out very well because the reality is that Lily and I, like many couples, entered marriage as relatively mild narcissists. We were not like the 2:00 A.M. phone callers. We were exquisitely polite—but not yet wise, because we were operating under the narcissistic assumption that the other was just like us or else misguided.

What we eventually learned was that the Golden Rule is just the beginning. To grow, we had to learn to recognize and respect the *otherness* of each other. Indeed, this is the advanced course of marriage, which teaches: Do unto others as you would have them do unto you if you were in their particular, unique, and different shoes. It is not easy learning. After more than six decades of living, Lily and I are still learning it and sometimes feel like beginners. We are learning that our differences create the spice of our marriage as well as the *wisdom* of it. The expression "Two heads are better than one" would be meaningless if both heads were exactly the same. Because Lily's and my heads are so different, when we put them together—as we've done in child-raising, money management, the planning of vacations, and the like—the outcome is invariably wiser than if either of us had acted alone. So growing out of narcissism allows for the process known as collaboration, in which people labor together with wits as well as brawn.

NARCISSISM VERSUS SELF-LOVE

Yet we are confronted with a paradox. While growing out of narcissism—our self-centeredness and often excessive sense of importance—is more than anything else what life is about, it is equally vital that we also simultaneously learn to come to terms with just how important and valuable we are.

Humility means having true knowledge of oneself as one is. In my opinion, it is critical for us to be realistic about ourselves as we are, and be able to recognize both the good and bad parts of ourselves. But that does not mean—as many falsely conclude—that we should give more emphasis to the negative parts of who we are and downplay or altogether dismiss the good parts as secondary. Yet many do so, trying to display a pseudo-humility that may extend to an inability to receive compliments or assert oneself when appropriate to do so.

Further, there is a distinction to be made between self-love (which I propose is always a good thing) and self-esteem (which I propose can often be questionable). As I wrote in *Further Along the Road Less Traveled,* the two are often confused because we do not have a rich enough vocabulary to cover these phenomena. I hope that eventually the problem will be resolved by developing new words that are more adequate, but for the moment we are stuck with the old ones.

For example, there are times when we act in ways that are unbecoming. If we deny that our behavior is "bad" and fail to seek ways to correct it or redeem ourselves by learning from what we have done wrong, then we are primarily concerned with self-esteem. On the other hand, if we are operating from a sense of self-love, the healthier thing to do would be to acknowledge our mistakes and chastise ourselves if we must—as well as have the ability to discern that our failure at any given moment does not totally define our worth or who we are as a person. We need moments when we realize that we do not have it all together and that we are not perfect. Such moments are crucial to our growth because loving ourselves requires the capacity to recognize that there is something about us we need to work on.

So there is a difference between insisting that we always feel good about ourselves (which is narcissistic and synonymous with constantly preserving our self-esteem) and insisting that we regard ourselves as important or valuable (which is healthy self-love). Understanding and making this distinction is a prerequisite for mature mental health. In order to be good, healthy people, we have to pay the price of setting aside our self-esteem once in a while and not always feeling good about ourselves. But we should always be able to love and value ourselves, even if we shouldn't always esteem ourselves.

About twenty years ago, I saw a seventeen-year-old patient who had been on his own since the age of fourteen. He had had atrocious parenting, and I told him during one session, "Jack, your biggest problem is that you don't love yourself, that you don't value yourself." That same night I had to drive from Connecticut to New York in the middle of a terrible storm. Sheets of rain were sweeping across the highway, and the visibility was so poor that I couldn't even see the side of the road or the yellow line. I had to keep my attention absolutely glued on the road, even though I was very tired. If I had lost my concentration for even a second, I would have gone off the road. And the only way I was able to make the ninety-mile trip in that terrible storm was to keep saying to myself, over and over again, "This little Volkswagen is carrying extremely valuable cargo. It is extremely important that this valuable cargo get to New York safely." And so it did.

Three days later, back in Connecticut, I saw Jack again and learned that in the same rainstorm, not nearly as tired as I was and on a much shorter journey, he had driven his car off the road. Fortunately, he hadn't been seriously hurt. I do not believe he had done this because he was covertly suicidal—although the lack of self-love can lead to suicide—but simply because he was not able to convince himself that his little Volkswagen was carrying extremely valuable cargo.

Another example involves a woman I began treating shortly after *The Road Less Traveled* was published. She had to travel from central New Jersey to where I lived in Connecticut. She was a woman who had spent all of her life in the Christian church; she had been raised in the church and had even married a clergyman. We worked together once a week for the first year and got absolutely nowhere, made no progress at all. And then one day she opened the session by saying, "You know, driving up here this morning, I suddenly realized that what is most important is the development of my own soul." I broke out in a roar of joyful laughter at the fact that she had finally gotten it, but also laughter at the irony of the fact that I had assumed that this woman—who had come to see me because she liked my book, who was willing to make a six-hour round trip once a week to see me, and who had spent the entirety of her life in the church—already knew that what was most important was the development of her own soul. But she didn't, and I suspect many fail to identify how central this is to their lives. Once she realized it, however, her progress in therapy was like lightning.

If we value ourselves, we are likely to believe that we are worth whatever effort we need to make for ourselves. The decision to go into therapy to get unstuck and help our progress, or to take the time to practice safety in certain situations that are within our control—these are among the measures of whether we truly value ourselves. And, as I wrote in *The Road Less Traveled,* the primary determinant of whether we consider ourselves valuable and important is whether our parents treated us as if we were truly valuable and important. This determines so much of how we regard ourselves from then on, because those young and impressionable years are crucial to our sense of worth.

Nonetheless, eighteen years after writing that book, I believe I was unduly pessimistic when I described the problem of someone who enters adulthood with a deep-seated lack of self-value. I had said it was close to impossible for such a person ever to develop a healthy sense of worth. But I now know there are at least two ways that a significant number who never learned to value themselves when they were children can learn to do so. One is long-term psychotherapy, during which the therapist can, and often does, become a substitute parent of sorts and heals by persistently demonstrating her or his sense of the patient's value. Certainly the most common response I have received from my own patients at the conclusion of a lengthy course of psychotherapy—when successful—was "You know, Dr. Peck, you treated me as if I was more important than I thought I was."

There is also another way: sometimes God actually seems to directly intervene in people's lives to give them a message of their value. Because of the power of such an experience, its beneficiaries remain puzzled and awed by it. Although appreciative and humbled, they often continue to ask, "Why me?" years after the fact, because they still wonder what they had done to deserve such a blessing. It is indeed an experience of overwhelming grace when one who for very long has devalued himself is granted a divine revelation that he does indeed matter after all.

Although I have not described such events in my works of nonfiction, I have former patients and friends who have recalled such radical changes in their sense of self-worth. Sometimes these revelations occurred in the context of a horrendous life experience, and for some—like a woman who decided she valued herself enough to leave a physically abusive relationship—when their very lives were at risk. I have written about such events in both my novels. In *A Bed by the Window*, Mrs. Simonton, a sixty-year-old nursing home administrator, receives just such a learning message. As does Tish in purgatory, as described in *In Heaven as on Earth*. While both accounts are fictional, they reflect the reality of actual people whom I have met and who have told me of such experiences.

NARCISSISM, DEATH, AND THE LEARNING OF DYING

Our inborn narcissism is an extraordinarily complex phenomenon, because some of it is necessary as the psychological side of our survival instinct. But unbridled narcissism is the principal precursor of psychospiritual illness. The healthy spiritual life consists of progressively growing out of narcissism. The failure to grow out of narcissism, although extremely common, is also extremely destructive.

The prospect of our death and the process of our dying physically can be one of the greatest stimuli to such healthy growth. They may even be the greatest such stimulus. When psychiatrists talk about injuries to pride, we call them narcissistic injuries. And on any scale of narcissistic injuries, death is the ultimate. We suffer little narcissistic injuries all the time: a classmate calls us stupid, for example; we're the last to be chosen for someone's volleyball team; colleges turn us down; employers criticize us; we get fired; our children reject us. As a result of these narcissistic injuries, we either become embittered or we grow. But death is the big one. Nothing threatens our narcissistic attachment to ourselves and our self-conceit more than our impending obliteration.

So it is utterly natural that we should fear death and everything that begins to become a reminder of death. There are two ways to deal with that fear: the common way and the smart way. The common way is to put it out of our mind, limit our awareness of it, try not to think about it. The smart way is to face death as early as possible. In doing so, we can realize something really rather simple. That is, insofar as we can overcome our narcissism we can overcome our fear of death. For people who learn to do this, the prospect of death becomes a magnificent stimulus for their psychological and spiritual growth. "Since I am going to die anyway," they think, "what's the point of preserving this attachment I have to my silly old self?" And so they set forth on a journey toward selflessness.

It is not an easy journey, but what a worthwhile journey it is. Because the further we proceed in diminishing our narcissism, our self-centeredness and sense of self-importance, the more we discover ourselves becoming not only less fearful of death but also less fearful of life. And this is the basis for learning to become more loving. No longer burdened by the need to constantly protect and defend ourselves, we are able to lift our eyes off ourselves and truly recognize others. And we begin to experience a sustained, underlying sense of happiness that we have never experienced before as we become progressively more self-forgetful and hence more able to remember God and notice Her in the details of life.

Again and again all of the great religions tell us that the path away from narcissism is the path toward meaning in life. And this is their central message: Learn how to die. Buddhists and Hindus speak of this in terms of the necessity for self-detachment; indeed, for them even the notion of the self is an illusion. Jesus spoke of it in similar terms: "Whosoever will save his life [that is, whosoever will hold on to his narcissism] shall lose it: and whosoever will lose his life for my sake shall find it."

In her classic *On Death and Dying,* Elisabeth Kübler-Ross was the first scientific person who ever dared to ask people what they were experiencing as they faced their physical death. Doing so, she discerned that five emotional stages are involved in the process of dying. And she found that people went through these stages in this order: denial, anger, bargaining, depression, and finally acceptance.

In the first stage, denial, they might say, "The lab must have gotten my tests mixed up with somebody else's. It can't be me, it can't be happening to me." But denying doesn't work for very long. So they get angry. They get angry at the doctors, angry at the nurses, angry at the hospital, angry at their relatives, angry at God. When anger doesn't get them anywhere, they start to bargain. They say, "Maybe if I go back to church and start praying again, my cancer will go away." Or, "Maybe if I start being nicer to my children for a change, my kidneys will improve." And when that doesn't get results, they begin to realize the jig is up and they're really going to die. At that point, they become depressed.

If they can hang in there and do what we therapists call the work of depression, they can emerge at the other end and enter the fifth stage, acceptance. This is a stage of great spiritual calm and tranquillity, and even of light for many. People who have accepted death have a light in them. It's almost as if they had already died and were resurrected in some psychospiritual sense. It's a beautiful thing to see, but it is not very common. Most people do not die in this stage of acceptance. They die still denying, still angry, still bargaining, or still depressed. The reason is that the work of depression is so painful and difficult that when they hit it most people retreat into denial or anger or bargaining.

These stages are not always gone through in exactly the way Kübler-Ross described, but they are nonetheless not only generally applicable to the emotional pain that is involved in dying but generally equally valid (although she did not realize it at the time) to all manner of life's learnings where unlearning is involved.

UNLEARNING AND FLEXIBILITY

I have written about an experience with my daughter in which such unlearning was necessary for my growth. One night I decided to spend some free time building a happier and closer relationship with my daughter, who was fourteen at the time. For several weeks she had been urging me to play chess with her, so I suggested a game and she eagerly accepted. We settled down to a most even and challenging match. It was a school night, however, and at nine o'clock my daughter asked if I could hurry my moves because she needed to go to bed; she had to get up at six in the morning. I knew her to be rigidly disciplined in her sleeping habits, and it seemed to me that she ought to be able to give up some of this rigidity. I told her, "Come on, you can go to bed a little later for once. You shouldn't start games that you can't finish. We're having fun."

We played on for another fifteen minutes, during which

time she became visibly discomfited. Finally, she pleaded, "Please, Daddy, please hurry your moves." "No, goddammit," I replied. "Chess is a serious game. If you're going to play it well, you're going to play it slowly. If you don't want to play it seriously, you might as well not play it at all." And so, with her feeling miserable, we continued for another ten minutes, until suddenly my daughter burst into tears, yelled that she conceded the stupid game, and ran weeping up the stairs.

My first reaction was one of denial. Nothing was seriously wrong. My daughter was just in a fragile mood. Certainly, it had nothing to do with me. But that didn't really work. The fact of the matter was that the evening had turned out exactly opposite from what I had intended. So my next reaction was to become angry. I became angry at my daughter for her rigidity and the fact that *she* couldn't give up a little sleep time to work on our relationship as well. It was her fault. But that didn't work either. The fact is that I, too, was rigid in my sleeping habits. So I thought I might run upstairs, knock on her door, and say, "I'm sorry, honey. Please forgive me for being rigid. Have a good night's sleep." Yet I had some sense at this point that I was bargaining. It would be a "cheap apology." Finally, it began to dawn on me that I had seriously goofed. I had started the evening wanting to have a happy time with my daughter. Ninety minutes later, she was in tears and so angry at me she could hardly speak. What had gone wrong? I became depressed.

Fortunately, albeit reluctantly, I was able to hang in there and do the work of depression. I began to face the fact that I had botched the evening by allowing my desire to win a chess game become more important than my desire to build a relationship with my daughter. I was depressed in earnest then. How had I gotten so out of balance? Gradually I began to accept that my desire to win was too great and that I needed to give up some of this desire. Yet even this little giving up seemed impossible. All my life my desire to win had served me in good stead, for I had won many things. How was it possible to play chess without wanting to win? I had never been comfortable doing things unenthusiastically. How could I conceivably play chess enthusiastically but not seriously? Yet somehow I had to change, for I knew that my competitiveness and my seriousness were part of a behavior pattern that was working and would continue to work toward alienating my children from me. And if I was not able to modify this pattern, there would be other times of unnecessary tears and bitterness.

Since I have given up part of my desire to win at games, that little depression is long over. I killed the desire to win at games with my desire to win at parenting. When I was a child my desire to win at games served me well. As a parent, I recognized that it got in my way. I had to give it up. I do not miss it, even though I thought I would.

Mature mental health demands the ability to be flexible. We must be able to continually strike—and restrike—a delicate balance among conflicting needs, goals, duties, and responsibilities. The essence of this discipline of balancing is unlearning and "giving up" something in ourselves in order to consider new information. While it may seem strange to choose stagnation over flexibility in order to avoid the pain of giving up parts of the self, it is understandable given the depth of emotional pain that may be involved in doing so. In its major forms, giving up is the most painful of human experiences. When giving up parts of ourselves entails giving up personality traits, well-established and learned patterns of behavior, ideologies, and even whole lifestyles, the pain can be excruciating. Yet these major forms of giving up are required if one is to travel very far on the journey of life toward ever-increasing maturity and spiritual growth. As with any giving up, the biggest fear is that one will be left totally empty. This is the existential fear of nothingness, of being nothing. But while any change from one way to another represents a death of the old way, it also makes room for the birth of a new one.

I cannot emphasize how important these stages of dying are to the process of unlearning and new learning. They are routinely gone through not only by individuals but also by groups and even entire nations. Consider, for instance, the behavior of the United States in Vietnam. When evidence first began to accumulate in 1963 and 1964 that our policies in Vietnam were not working, what was our nation's first reaction? Denial. Nothing was really wrong. All we needed was a few more Special Forces troops and a few more millions of dollars. Then, in 1966 and 1967, as evidence continued to accumulate that our policies were not working and obviously seriously flawed, what was the government's reaction? Anger. The day of the body count began. And My Lai. And torture. And bombing such that we were going to turn North Vietnam into an American parking lot. By 1969 and 1970, when the evidence was now massive that our policies in Vietnam were a failure, our next response was to attempt to "bargain" our way out of Vietnam. We selectively stopped bombing here as a carrot and started bombing there as a stick, thinking that we could somehow bring North Vietnam to the negotiating table. But it continued to fail.

Although some of us as individuals at the time went through a significant depression over the war, our government led the majority of Americans to believe that somehow we succeeded in bargaining our way out of Vietnam. We did not bargain our way out of Vietnam. We were defeated. We fled with over half a million men. Because, as a nation, we generally failed at the time to do the work of depression involved in this tragedy, there was little evidence that we learned any lesson as a result. Only recently, twenty-five years after the fact, does it look as if we may have done some portion of the work of that depression and come to a modicum of humility in our international relations.

To learn something new, we so often have to empty ourselves of the old. This can be both an individual and a group process, and in *The Different Drum* I describe it in some depth as "emptiness," one of the stages of community making. There, I wrote that a group going through the stage of emptiness—the most critical stage of its learning—seems for all the world like an organism going through its death throes. This period can be excruciatingly painful. It is also the period when the group commits itself to learning—which is also to commit itself to unlearning that which is obstructive and outdated and unworkable.

When we are going through pain individually or collectively, we often feel as if the pain will last forever. But in the cycle of life, there is always opportunity for renewal. Hope is the foundation of the rebirthing that may follow death and change. So when it is worked through, the stage of depression is inevitably followed by the stage of acceptance. Someone in an audience once asked me whether long-term marriages go through these stages, and I said they do indeed. Initially, as differences between partners emerge, our first tendency is to try to deny those differences and deny that we have fallen out of love. When we can no longer deny that, we get angry at our spouse for being different from us. When that eventually doesn't get us anywhere and our spouse doesn't change, we try to bargain in some manner or another—"I'll change in this way if you'll change in that way." When that doesn't work, then we tend to become depressed and the marriage looks very doubtful.

But if we can hang in there—often for a period of many years, and in the case of my marriage to Lily it was close to twenty years—we can finally learn how to accept our spouse and can come, as Lily and I have done, to a relationship that is better than romantic love and even seems to partake of glory. But many people seem to believe a marriage that experiences these stages is not a good one at all, as if long-term relationships must be totally smooth sailing. In fact, this is one of the primary illusions we must overcome. I am reminded of a woman who remarked, "Scotty, I very much liked *In Search of Stones,* but it was so sad." I wasn't sure what she meant by "sad," but I imagine she thought it was sad because she believed that a marriage shouldn't go through all of the downers I wrote about there. Yet I believe that *In Search of Stones* is ultimately a triumphant book. Indeed, despite all the ups and downs—through the death of illusions and the rebirths of trust and acceptance—that Lily and I experienced, we have emerged with a greater degree of understanding than either of us could have ever envisioned.

So the stage of dying is followed by the stage of rebirth, which initially may be as painful as the dying. In Chapter 1, I recounted how many of my patients went through a "therapeutic depression" when the old way was no longer tenable and the new ways seemed impossibly difficult, when they could not go backward but were unwilling to go forward because the new way seemed so incredibly risky. I describe this risk in *A Bed by the Window*, where, in the course of therapy, Heather makes the terrifying decision to finally discard her "old tapes" or maladaptive ways of relating to men and experiment with "new tapes." These two processes are inextricable, but experimenting with a new tape is just as terrifying as discarding an old one. Although an old tape may be demonstratively ineffective, it may still feel comfortable, fitting like an old shoe. The new tape—which may require us to do things in ways totally different from those that were initially comfortable, and that our parents taught us, and, indeed, that our whole culture has endorsed—may seem incredibly dangerous.

But learning is an adventure. We must have a taste for it to some extent, since all adventure is going into the unknown. If we always know exactly where we're going, how to get there, and what we'll see or experience along the way, it isn't an adventure. It is human—and smart—to be afraid of the unknown, to be at least a tiny bit scared when embarking on an adventure. But it is only from adventures that we learn much of significance, where we can be exposed to the new and unexpected.

LEARNING AS ADVENTURE

Entering psychotherapy is often one of the greatest adventures in life. For one woman I'll call Tammy, it was a bout with life-threatening depression in her mid-twenties that compelled her to seek help. The source of her depression and the dynamics of her case were a classic example of an individual operating under the illusion of perfectionism. For much of her young life,

Tammy had unknowingly developed self-imposed, unrealistic standards and tried to live up to exaggerated expectations she thought others had of her.

The seeds of perfectionism had been planted early—and were costly. As is typical of many such patients, Tammy had grown up in an alcoholic family. As a child, she was in many ways forced to take on adult responsibilities, because of the emotional absence of her mother, who was incapacitated by depression and a serious drinking problem, and because her father was mostly absent. In the attempt to rise to the occasion, she was required to help raise her younger siblings. This meant, of course, that she didn't have much of a life of her own in elementary school and her early high school years. Given the confusion of home life, school became the place where Tammy felt most competent. It was also the one place she received nurturing as the child she truly was, rather than being required to provide it to others. This led to her excelling academically; ultimately, she became the first in her family to graduate from college.

Although it was an unspoken assumption, Tammy interpreted living up to a self-image that entailed perfectionism as requiring that she "have it all together." It seemed to her that her family's expectation was that she not only have it together, but have it together at all times. It was an incredibly stressful standard to live up to, and in many ways an oppressive one. Deep within, on some level, Tammy knew she couldn't possibly meet the standards of perfectionism. But in attempting to maintain this illusion, she simultaneously found it difficult to acknowledge the reality of her limitations. The pressure, both external and internal, eventually led not only to physical symptoms of distress but to tremendous anxiety over several years. At one point Tammy contemplated suicide, although she never acted on it.

During long-term therapy, she learned that the primary source of her depression was her attempt to live up to a standard too high to meet and her lack of her own true identity. Although on the surface she seemed self-assured and independent to most who met her, her self-image had been centered primarily around what other people thought or expected of her.

Initially, much of Tammy's conversation during therapy revolved around her perception of herself as a victim. She gave a litany of complaints about what others had done to her or not done for her. After a couple of months going back and forth about this, she finally began to consider what her own role in her victimization had been. In doing so, she experienced a dramatic turning point. She realized she had a choice after all. This was accompanied by a decision to acknowledge that she had some limitations, even if others wanted to continue placing her on a pedestal because she was the first in her family to go to college. As she stopped talking so much about "them" and started owning her own feelings, using "I" statements, she felt a sense of personal power she had never known. Once, as hard as it was to admit, she said she realized that a former boyfriend had taken advantage of her kindness not simply and only because he was a jerk, but also in large part because she kept giving much more than she received in the relationship.

As Tammy got more in touch with the ways she had been socialized since childhood to take on the role of family rescuer and martyr, she became clearer about how as an adult she had continually based her self-image on this role. Even more surprising—and humbling—was her discovery that she somewhat enjoyed the psychological payoff. It enhanced her ego to be the family savior and the girlfriend who tried to be "good" all the time. Still, the price she paid was too great.

In hindsight, Tammy was able to discern that she had at least passively complied with her own predicament. Then she faced the fact that she had felt used, and became angry at her family, friends, and previous boyfriends for the demands they placed on her. Complicating matters, however, was the guilt she felt at times: after all, it seemed that her problems were irrelevant and minor in comparison to the problems of poverty and poor education that beset most in her family. Even most of her boyfriends up to that point had not achieved as much as she had.

As her process of healing continued, Tammy decided to re-define what expectations she should realistically have for her-self. "I came to the realization that making mistakes only made me human, not a total disgrace. I've learned that not being per-fect doesn't mean that I am totally imperfect, either. It is not a black or white matter, but has many shades of gray. I know I can be okay even when I make mistakes. I can still value myself, strengths, warts, and all," she said, then chuckled.

As humbling as the "bad stuff" she learned about herself was, it was equally uplifting to her—and surprising—to realize her real strengths, the "good stuff" she learned in the process of therapy. For one thing, as she loosened the grip of perfec-tionism, Tammy became less harsh and less strict about judging herself. She experienced a cathartic moment when, asked dur-ing therapy to picture herself as a child, she cried when she felt empathy toward herself. She learned to give herself credit for having survived a difficult childhood and for having thrived in spite of it.

An even greater breakthrough came as she realized that the unhealthy need of perfectionism had gotten in the way of admitting her needs for affection and support from others. "Maybe it hasn't simply been a matter of my friends and family not being willing to help me. Perhaps I didn't allow them to do so since I seemed to have it all together," she said. So she made a goal to practice assertiveness by asking for help from others periodically, and to work on her difficulty with receiving since she had become so accustomed to giving. She was elated to re-port that one day, when someone told her he thought she was both smart and pretty, she was able to respond with a gracious thank-you rather than recite reasons to dismiss the compli-ment.

Although she first entered therapy when she felt she had no other choice—"I was lost, I was broken," she said—Tammy found the process quite rewarding, even spiritually renewing. "As I became conscious of my own limitations, I no longer held high expectations for me to meet in every area of life. Now I'm more likely to give my best in those things that are important to me, and let other people pull their own weight so I won't feel responsible for the whole world," she said. "When I think about it, how arrogant it was of me to think I had to be involved in everything for it to turn out right. Now I've learned to sit in the background more and not feel I have to take care of everything and everybody. It's very liberating. In a very real sense, I feel I've been able to gradually restore my humanity, as odd as that may sound."

The Spirituality of Imperfection, by Ernest Kurtz and Katherine Ketcham, speaks directly to the journey of those like Tammy who are recovering from perfectionism. Such individuals, in facing the truth of their limitations, become more spiritually aware—if they are open to it—through the humility of coming clean and getting real.

Sometimes it's hard to distinguish whether it is courage or desperation (the urgency that comes from hitting rock bottom) that leads someone to embark on the adventure of psychotherapy. I am reminded of something said by the greatest teacher I know of next to Jesus: Jalal ad-Din ar-Rumi, a thirteenth-century Muslim mystic. Rumi said: "Organs evolve in response to necessity. Therefore, increase your necessity." So I believe that the acceptance of necessity is an act of courage itself. Thus, even when necessity—or feeling desperate—seems the consuming motivation, it still takes courage to enter therapy because it is truly a step into the unknown. One is exposing oneself to the therapist and has no idea what challenges one will receive. When people enter therapy, opening themselves to challenge, they do not know what they are going to learn about themselves, but they are generally certain that they are going to discover some "bad things." In my experience with patients, just as it is true that in the course of therapy they learn unanticipated "bad things," they also virtually always learn unanticipated "good things" about themselves.

One thing that never ceases to amaze me is how relatively few people understand what courage is. Most people think it is the absence of fear. The absence of fear is not courage; the absence of fear is some kind of brain damage. Courage is the capacity to go ahead in spite of fear, or in spite of pain. When you do that, you will find that overcoming the fear will not only make you stronger but will be a big step forward toward maturity.

When I wrote *The Road Less Traveled,* I never gave a definition of maturity, but I did describe in the book a number of immature people. It seems to me that what most characterizes immature people is that they sit around complaining that life doesn't meet their demands. On the other hand, what characterizes those relative few who are fully mature is that they regard it as their responsibility—even as an opportunity—to meet life's demands. Indeed, when we realize that everything that happens to us has been designed to teach us what we need to know on our journey of life, we begin to see life from an entirely different perspective.

A unique—and mature—perspective is definitely necessary for facing life's ultimate adventure. There is only one adventure I know of greater than that of entering serious psychotherapy: the final adventure of death. No matter what our belief system, we do not know for certain where or how we shall find ourselves when the adventure of death is completed. What a going into the unknown it is!

Since death and dying make up the greatest of all life's adventures, it is no accident that this time is not only our final opportunity for learning but our greatest one. As a psychotherapist, I have found that my most fulfilling opportunity has been working with dying patients. This may seem paradoxical until it is realized that those who are clearly dying may be aware that they do not have much time left. I say "may" because the awareness is a choice. As I have already indicated, most choose to deny their dying, and hence deny themselves the learning involved. But when they choose to accept that they are dying—that they have very little time left—they may make the most extraordinary leaps of growth within their final days or weeks on earth. We have all heard tales not only of deathbed confessions and conversions, but also of dramatic repentance, forgiveness, and reconciliation. We hear these tales because they are true. Dying may be the time of our greatest glory.

Indeed, this subject is so important that I will return to it in the next chapter, "Personal Life Choices." Let it simply be said here that the choice to die well can be made only by those who have made the choice for learning, who have developed the attitude that learning is central—even as essential as shelter—to living. Choosing to die well is an inherent part of choosing to learn how to live well.

VALUES AND LEARNING CHOICES /

Three factors play central roles in our learning: attitude, temperament, and values. Although interrelated, insofar as they can be separated, each is a valuable and separate component in learning in and of itself.

Because attitude is one's acquired disposition or general approach to viewing things, it undoubtedly affects one's ability to learn. An atheist has an "attitude" about religion that will affect his perception of things. An alcoholic man who is superficially religious may still have a negative attitude toward AA in general because the notion "to become powerless" is anathema to him.

To what extent an attitude is learned or inborn is hard to determine, but there is reason to believe that much of it is nurtured by our environment. Everybody has an "attitude" problem in those areas where he doesn't think well or is mostly negative. We tend to learn better in areas where we have a positive attitude. For example, the more frightened you are—if you feel you're always having to defend or protect yourself—the less likely you are to be open to learning about a particular subject or experience. Thus, part of learning is becoming conscious of our attitudes and calling them into question. Of course, we can't do this all the time. But just as a patient will set aside time for therapy, we can set aside time to question and think about our own attitudes with impunity in an atmosphere of safety.

Temperament refers to the biological part of our personality. It's in our genes. That's why, even when children are very young, parents and others who spend a great deal of time with them can make fairly accurate assessments and predictions about how an individual child may respond to certain situations. Whether temperaments are irretrievably established by a certain age or set in stone at birth is a matter of debate.

Values are those qualities we deem important. And those that we deem more important than others affect the choices we make and the options we perceive in life. Since we cannot learn everything there is to know, we are faced with the ongoing problem of making choices based primarily on what we value the most. Consequently, throughout life we must make choices about what we are going to learn—if we have made the decision to learn at all. As the Sufi Muslim Idries Shah said (and I paraphrase him), "It is not enough to study. First one must determine what to study and what not to study. When to study and when not to study. And who to study with and who not to study under."

This applies not only to focused, academic learning but also to life experiences and to choices about what to give our time and attention to. In part, Idries Shah was referring to a matter of priorities, and nowhere do I spend more of my prayer time than trying to sort out my priorities. Some of those priorities have to do with what to study and what not to study. But probably my most important choice has been that of discerning my values. For instance, the value of integrity has come to be very high on my list of priorities. From *The Road Less Traveled,* it can be discerned that another two of my primary values are dedication to reality or truth and the acceptance of appropriate responsibility. Critical to this issue of accepting responsibility has been the decision to accept the pain involved in learning.

The dedication to truth is one part of my being a scientist. What we call the scientific method is nothing more than a series of conventions and procedures that we have adopted over the centuries in order to combat our very human tendency to want to deceive ourselves. We practice this method out of a dedication to something higher than our immediate intellectual or emotional comfort: namely, the truth. Science, therefore, is an activity submitted to a higher power (except, of course, in those instances when the egos of scientists get in the way of their search for truth). Since I believe God is the epitome of our higher power—God is light, God is love, God is truth—anything that seeks these values is holy. Thus, while it cannot answer all questions, science, in its proper place, is a very holy activity.

Hunter Lewis's book *A Question of Values* demonstrates that people have quite different primary values upon which they base their decisions and through which they interpret the world. He lists those values as experience, science, reason, authority, and intuition. Lewis is unclear about when we make our choice of a primary value. Perhaps it is not a choice at all but is something genetic. In any case, if it is a choice, it seems to be made both unconsciously and passively, during childhood. Nevertheless, we have it within our power during adulthood to continually reassess our values and priorities.

As an empiricist, I primarily value experience as the best route to knowledge and understanding. But Lewis goes on to talk about "hybrid value systems," and here, to me, is the importance of his book. If we can become aware of our primary values, then, in adulthood, we can deliberately go about nurturing other values. For instance, the "authority of the Scriptures" was not a great value for me during my childhood. Even today, I do not consider the Scriptures to be "perfect" in their authority, but I delight in studying them, learning them, and putting them to use. It is also in adulthood that I have deliberately chosen to learn from Lily her intuitive skills, which I did not possess when I was younger. Just as I extolled using both the right brain and the left brain, since there is more than one way that we can learn, so I extoll using multiple values by developing as complex a hybrid value system as possible.

So we are back to the subject of integrity and wholeness. Unlike children, adults can practice integrity by conscious choice. Some people find they're good at learning information or content skills (which tends to be a masculine inclination) and others feel more adept at relational skills (which tends to be a feminine inclination). When we're good at one thing and not so good at another, we tend to avoid the one that is difficult, or to neglect aspects of ourselves that we find uncomfortable because they are unfamiliar or seem threatening. Many men tend to run from their feminine side, and many women tend to avoid exercising their masculine qualities.

In learning wholeness, we must be open to androgyny, to encompassing both feminine and masculine components. We are called to be whole people. The words "health," "wholeness," and "holiness" all have the same root. It is both our psychological and our spiritual task—particularly during the second half of our life—to work toward the fullest expression of our potential as human beings, to become the best that we can be. Becoming whole involves using our latent talents, which can be learned or developed, but usually only with a great deal of practice and often only with the maturity required for the humility to work on our weak sides.

I have told the story of my learning experience as a tennis player. I had become quite a decent tennis player by early adolescence. I had a reasonably good serve, and while my backhand was very weak, I had an extraordinarily powerful forehand. What I did, then, was develop a pattern of "running around" my backhand. I would stand to the left of the court and take every possible shot I could with my forehand. In this fashion I was able to wipe 95 percent of my opponents off the court. The only problem was the other 5 percent. They would immediately realize my weakness and hit to my backhand, pulling me farther and farther to the left, then hit cross-court out of reach of my forehand and wipe *me* off the court. At the age of thirty-two, I realized that if I was ever going to fulfill my potential as a tennis player—to be the best that I could be in the game—I was going to have to work on my backhand. It was a humbling business.

It meant that I had to do what had become profoundly unnatural: stand to the right of the center of the baseline and take every possible shot I could on my backhand. It meant losing repeatedly to inferior players. And it meant that onlookers who had come down to the courts to see me play tennis watched me hit balls two courts down, over the fence, or dribble them into the net. But within three months I had a decent backhand for the first time in my life and, with a whole tennis game, I became the best player in the little island community where I then lived. At which point, I took up golf. That was really humbling.

For me, golf is so humiliating (or humbling) that I can neither play it nor enjoy it unless I regard it as a learning opportunity. I have, in fact, learned an extraordinary amount about myself, such as the outrageousness of my own perfectionism and the depths of self-hatred I indulge in when I fail to be perfect. Through golf, I am slowly healing myself of my perfectionism and my many other imperfections. And I don't think there can be any healthier—or more important—way to become whole persons than working on our weak sides.

LEARNING FROM ROLE MODELS

Our relations with others—and learning from them—can be one of life's gifts. As a blessing, role models help prevent us from having to learn everything from scratch, so to speak, since if we are good listeners and observers we can avoid some of the pitfalls someone else has found on the path we are heading. But we must choose wisely whom we emulate, because role models may be detrimental at times. In childhood, one of the routes for learning, for better or for worse, is through our parents as primary role models. In adulthood, we have the opportunity to make a deliberate choice of role models; we can not only decide on good role models but even use negative role models appropriately, as examples of what not to do.

A big part of my learning came about through a negative role model I had in my early professional years. I'll call him Dr.

Bumbles. Dr. Bumbles was a supervising psychiatrist and a nice enough man. But all his psychiatric instincts were wrong. I was in training at the time, and the first couple of months of my residency were terribly confusing until I realized that Dr. Bumbles was usually wrong. As soon as I discovered that, he became very useful to me as a negative role model—an example of what not to do.

Usually, I could tell what was the right thing to do by comparing my professional judgments to Dr. Bumbles's thinking. If I went to him and said, "Well, this man is diagnosed as schizophrenic and he kind of looks schizophrenic, but he doesn't quite act like a schizophrenic . . . " and Dr. Bumbles said, "Oh, definitely—a classic case of schizophrenia," I knew I was right to doubt the diagnosis. Or if I said, "This patient doesn't look schizophrenic, but I wonder if he may be, because of how he acts," and Dr. Bumbles responded, "Oh, no question, he is not schizophrenic," I knew then I was right to suspect schizophrenia.

So in learning from others, one must keenly perceive the nuances that allow us to distinguish between good and bad teachers. Because they fail to make such distinctions, many people develop neuroses when they have had bad role models but feel they must behave the same way as their parents or other influential adults did. From some elderly patients, for example, I have learned a great deal about what I don't want for myself. To me, one of the saddest sights in the world is old people still trying to live life as usual and control their affairs when they're no longer competent to do so. Usually these people have in no way prepared for serious aging and death. They have become stuck. Many will continue to try to maintain a house without much help. They will have paperwork strewn all over the place, and their affairs will be in total disorder.

Almost paradoxically, it was these patients, who could not give up control, whom I often had to send into nursing homes against their will. It was a terribly painful thing to have to do. Had these patients been willing to sit back and learn to let others do for them, they could have enjoyed their last years at home. But it was precisely because they refused to learn how to give up any control that their lives became such shambles. I and their families had to wrest control from them and place them in institutional settings where they would be taken care of whether they liked it or not.

It is from these poor souls, as negative role models, that I have learned to pray almost daily that when my time comes I will be better prepared and able to give up whatever control I need to. In fact, I have already begun to learn to do so. I only worry that this learning will not continue.

GROUP LEARNING

Continuing to learn is a matter of great importance not only for individuals but also for groups. I have spoken of the "emptiness" involved in group learning, and the death throes that entire groups will go through in the process of "unlearning." It is a phenomenon I have witnessed many times. For the past dozen years, the greatest adventure of my professional life—and learning—has come from working with others in the Foundation for Community Encouragement (FCE). It is the mission of FCE to teach the principles of community, by which we mean the principles of healthy communication within and between groups. FCE teaches groups how to be healthy and "whole"—even "holy."

When groups are healthy, their individual members are in an environment where they can learn more effectively and efficiently—about themselves and other people—than in any other place. The group itself also learns. Although it takes a great deal of work, including the work of unlearning, a group can develop a consciousness of its own which is wiser and greater than the sum of its individual members. Such groups can become extraordinarily effective decision-making bodies.

Because healthy groups can be so extraordinarily productive in addressing extremely complex issues, FCE is working more and more in businesses and other organizations. We have learned to build temporary communities in such organizations for the purpose of collaborative decision making. Indeed, we have learned to do this very well. What we are struggling with now is learning how to help these organizations develop the capacity to maintain the ingredients of community on their own *after* FCE's intervention—to be what we call a sustainable community, so that such decision making and healthy group functioning can and will continue to occur routinely.

Our work at FCE has dovetailed with that of Peter Senge at the Organizational Learning Center of the Massachusetts Institute of Technology. In his book, *The Fifth Discipline,* Senge coined the term "learning organization," which is synonymous with what we at FCE call sustainable community. A learning organization must be a community. A sustainable community will be a learning organization. The key issue, however, is this matter of continuing learning. It is comparatively easy to help organizations learn temporarily, when they are facing some kind of crisis. What is not so easy is to teach them how to learn continually. We believe that groups can begin to integrate a new perspective about learning when it is seen as an opportunity for individual and collective growth, not simply as a burden to be tolerated such as the equivalent of enrolling in mandatory classes once a year. We have gained glimpses of how to teach this, but only glimpses; the field is a true frontier.

There is great reason to believe that the matter of group health is even more significant than that of individual health. Just as individuals must continue to learn in order to survive well, so must our organizations and institutions. The survival of our civilization may well depend upon whether our institutions can evolve into sustainable communities and hence become ongoing learning organizations.

PART II

Wrestling with the Complexity of Everyday Life

CHAPTER 4

Personal Life Choices

❖

PART OF THE COMPLEXITY OF LIFE is that at one and the same time we are individuals, members of family and work organizations, and members of society. Indeed, it is almost arbitrary to separate these categories. But it is sometimes necessary to make such arbitrary distinctions in order to talk about anything in detail and depth. Therefore, let me focus first upon what I believe to be the most critical of the many choices that we make as individuals in our hearts and minds.

As always, consciousness precedes choice; without it, there is no choice. Thus, the single most important personal choice that we can make in our lives is the choice for ever-increasing consciousness. Consciousness, however, does not make choices easy. To the contrary, it multiplies the options.

To give an example of the complexity of choices, consider how we might deal with our anger. In the midbrain, there are collections of nerve cells or centers that not only govern but actually produce our powerful emotions. One of these is an anger center. In *Further Along the Road Less Traveled,* I wrote that the anger center in humans works in exactly the same way as it does in other creatures. It is basically a territorial mechanism, firing off when any other creature impinges upon our territory. We are no different from a dog fighting another dog that wanders into its territory, except that for human beings definitions of territory—or boundaries—are so complex and multifaceted. Not only do we have a geographical territory and become angry when someone comes uninvited onto our property and starts picking our flowers, but we also have a psychological territory, and we become angry whenever anyone criticizes us. We also have a theological or an ideological territory, and we tend to become angry whenever anyone casts aspersions on our belief systems, even when the critic is a stranger to us and speaking into a microphone thousands of miles away.

Since our anger center is firing much of the time, and often very inappropriately—sometimes on the basis of perceived, rather than actual, infringements—we need to be flexible in dealing with situations that easily provoke our wrath. We must learn a whole complex set of ways of dealing with anger. Sometimes we need to think, "My anger is silly and immature. It's my fault." Or sometimes we should conclude, "This person did impinge upon my territory, but it was an accident and there's no reason to get angry about it." Or, "Well, he did violate my territory a little bit, but it's no big deal. It's not worth blowing up about." But every once in a while, after we think about it for a couple of days, we may discern that someone really did seriously violate our territory. Then it may be necessary to go to that person and say, "Listen, I've got a real bone to pick with you." And sometimes it might even be necessary to get angry immediately and blast that person right on the spot.

So there are at least five different ways to respond when we're angry. And not only do we need to know them, we also have to learn which response is appropriate in any given situation. This requires extraordinary consciousness of what is going on both inside and outside of ourselves. It is no wonder that very few people learn how to deal well with their anger before they are into their thirties or forties, and many never learn to do so constructively.

In fact, it is the ability to learn how to deal with all the problems and challenges of life in a constructive manner that defines psychospiritual progress. Conversely, that which refuses progress is in opposition to our growth and ultimately self-destructive.

THE PATH OF SMART SELFISHNESS VERSUS THE PATH OF STUPID SELFISHNESS

To grow, we must learn to discern between that which is self-destructive and that which is self-constructive. When I was in practice, I would no longer allow any of my patients to use the word "unselfish" after about five sessions. I would tell them that I was a totally selfish human being who had never done anything for anyone or anything else. When I watered my flowers, I did not say to them, "Oh, look, flowers, what I'm doing for you. You ought to be grateful to me." I was doing it because I liked pretty flowers. Similarly, when I extended myself for one of my children it was because I liked to have an image of myself in my mind as a reasonably decent father and a reasonably honest man. In order to maintain those two images side by side with any integrity, every so often I had to extend myself beyond what I might normally feel like doing. Besides, I also like pretty children.

The truth is that we rarely do anything without some gain or benefit to ourselves, however small or subtle. Making a donation to charity helps me feel good. Someone who claims to be "sacrificing" a well-paying job right out of undergraduate school in order to go on to law school so she can "better serve society" is also better serving herself. A woman who "sacrifices" by staying at home to raise her children rather than going out to work may do so because she "believes in family," but she also personally benefits from this decision. We can look at monks and nuns and think, "God, how unselfish they are. Look at all that they have sacrificed: sex, family life, personal property ownership, and, in some ways, even autonomy over their own lives." But they are in it for the same selfish reason as anyone else. They have decided that for them that is the best path toward joy.

So selfishness isn't always a simple matter. What I would do was ask of my patients that they distinguish between the path of smart selfishness and the path of stupid selfishness. The path of stupid selfishness is trying to avoid all pain. The path of smart selfishness is trying to discern which pain or suffering, particularly emotional suffering, is constructive and which is unconstructive. Because I write a great deal about pain and suffering and discipline, a lot of people think I am some kind of pain freak. I am not a pain freak, I am a joy freak. I see no value whatsoever is unconstructive suffering. If I have an ordinary headache the very first thing I am going to do is get myself two super-strength uncapsulized acetaminophens. There is no virtue inherent in that headache, either per se or to me. I see absolutely no value in such unconstructive suffering. On the other hand, there are types of suffering in this life from which we have many constructive things to learn.

My preferred words for "constructive" and "unconstructive" are, respectively, "existential" and "neurotic." Existential suffering is an inherent part of existence and cannot be legitimately avoided—for example, the suffering involved in growing up and learning to be independent; the suffering involved in learning how to become interdependent and even dependent again; the suffering that is associated with loss and giving up; the suffering of old age and dying. From all these kinds of suffering we have a great deal to learn. Neurotic suffering, on the other hand, is that emotional suffering which is not an inherent part of existence. It is unconstructive and unnecessary, and rather than enhancing our existence impedes it. What we need to do with neurotic suffering is get rid of it just as quickly as possible because it is like carrying ninety-eight golf clubs around the course when all you need is ten or twelve to play a perfectly good game. It is just so much excess baggage.

Fifty years ago, when Freud's theories first filtered down to the intelligentsia (and were misinterpreted, as so often happens), there were a large number of avant-garde parents who, having learned that guilt feelings could have something to do with neuroses, resolved that they were going to raise guilt-free children. What an awful thing to do to a child. Our jails are filled with people who are there precisely because they do not have any guilt, or do not have enough of it. We need a certain amount of guilt in order to exist in society, and that's what I call existential guilt. I hasten to stress, however, that too much guilt, rather than enhancing our existence, hinders it. Neurotic guilt is unnecessary and depletes our lives of joy and serenity.

Take another painful feeling: anxiety. Although it may be painful, we need a certain amount of anxiety to function well. For instance, if I had to give a speech in New York City, I might be anxious about how to get there, and my anxiety would propel me to look at a map. If I had no anxiety, I might just take off and end up in Quebec. Meanwhile, there are a thousand people waiting to hear me give a talk in New York City. So we need a certain amount of anxiety in order to exist well—the kind of existential anxiety that propels us to consult maps.

But once again, there can be an amount of anxiety above and beyond that, which, rather than enhancing our existence, impedes it. So I could think to myself, "Supposing I had a flat tire or got into an accident. They drive awfully fast on the roads near New York City. And even if I do manage to get to the place I was supposed to lecture, I probably won't be able to find a parking place. I'm sorry, people in New York, but it's beyond me." This kind of phobic anxiety, rather than enhancing my existence, limits it and is clearly neurotic.

We are naturally pain-avoiding creatures. But just as it would be stupid to welcome all suffering, so it is stupid to try to avoid all suffering. One of the basic choices we make in life is whether to follow the path of smart selfishness or try to avoid all problems and take the path of stupid selfishness. To do so, we must learn how to make this distinction between neurotic and existential suffering.

As I wrote in *The Road Less Traveled,* life is difficult because it is a series of problems, and the process of confronting and solving problems is a painful one. Problems, depending on their nature, evoke in us many uncomfortable feelings: frustration, grief, sadness, loneliness, guilt, regret, anger, fear, anxiety, anguish, or despair. These feelings are often as painful as any kind of physical suffering. Indeed, it is *because* of the pain that events or conflicts engender in us that we call them problems.

Yet it is in this whole process of meeting and solving problems that life finds its meaning. Problems call forth our courage and wisdom; indeed, they create our courage and our wisdom. Problems are the cutting edge that distinguishes between success and failure. It is only because of problems that we grow mentally and spiritually.

The alternative—not to meet the demands of life on life's terms—means we will end up losing more often than not. Most people attempt to skirt problems rather than meet them head-on. We attempt to get out of them rather than suffer through them. Indeed, the tendency to avoid problems and the emotional suffering inherent in them is the primary basis of all psychological illness. And since most of us have this tendency to a greater or lesser degree, most of us lack complete mental health. Those who are most healthy learn not to dread but actually to welcome problems. Although triumph isn't guaranteed each time we face a problem in life, those who are wise are aware that it is only through the pain of confronting and resolving problems that we learn and grow.

CHOICES OF RESPONSIBILITY

Most people who come to see a psychotherapist are suffering from either a neurosis or what is called a character disorder. As indicated in *The Road Less Traveled,* these conditions are at root disorders of responsibility: the neurotic assumes too much responsibility and the person with a character disorder not enough. As such, they are opposite styles of relating to the world and its problems. When neurotics are in conflict with the world, they automatically assume that they are at fault. When those with character disorders are in conflict with the world, they automatically assume that the world is at fault.

Even the speech patterns of neurotics and of those with character disorders are different. The speech of the neurotic is notable for such expressions as "I ought to," "I should," and "I shouldn't," indicating, to some extent, a self-image of an inferior person who believes he or she is always falling short of the mark, always making the wrong choices. The speech of a person with a character disorder, however, relies heavily on "I can't," "I couldn't," "I have to," and "I had to," demonstrating a self-image of a being who believes he or she has no power of choice, and whose behavior is completely directed by external forces totally beyond his or her control.

Before 1950, the term "character disorder" didn't exist as a separate diagnosis or category. Most psychiatric disorders were called neuroses, and neuroses were generally divided into two categories: ego-alien and ego-syntonic. An ego-alien neurosis was one in which the person's ego fought against a problematic condition. Since the individual didn't want to have the condition, he was willing to work toward alleviating it. An ego-syntonic neurosis, on the other hand, involves a condition a person's ego doesn't even want to identify, much less see as problematic in his life.

While I was an Army psychiatrist on the island of Okinawa, I met two women, both of whom had strong fears of snakes. Many people have a fear of snakes, so this wasn't unusual in itself. What made their fear problematic—and phobic—was the degree of incapacitation caused by it. To say the least, when daily routines are interrupted or neglected because of fear, it creates difficulties in many aspects of the person's life.

Okinawa was a natural place to see such phobias because of the dreaded habu, a snake unique to the island. It's poisonous, and its size falls somewhere between that of a large rattler and a small python. It also sleeps only during the day, which means that it does its roaming at night. There were about 100,000 Americans at Okinawa at the time; only about once in two years was one bitten by a habu, and half of those bitten had been walking out in the jungle at night, not around the Army housing sections. Adequate information was dispensed. All Americans were told about the snake, and all the hospitals had the necessary antitoxins to treat bites. Overall, not one American had actually been killed by a snake for years.

The first woman, who was in her early thirties, came to see

me at my office. "I've got this fear of snakes and I know it's ridiculous," she said. "But I won't go out at night. I can't take my children out to the movies at night and I won't go to a club with my husband at night. It's really silly of me, because I know that hardly anyone gets bitten. I feel so stupid." As her language suggested, her phobia was ego-alien: it didn't fit with her self-image and was therefore conflictual to her. Although she was housebound most of the time and especially fearful of going out at night, she was willing to acknowledge that this was a problem in her life, and she wanted to find ways to lessen her fear so that it would not interfere with all her activities.

Freud first pointed out that phobias are often displacements from a real fear. What we found in therapy was that this woman had never faced up to existential issues involving her fear of death and fear of evil. Once she started dealing with such issues, although she still remained timid, she was able to go out at night with her husband and children. Thanks to treatment, by the time she was preparing to leave Okinawa, she was on the path of growth.

I learned about the second woman's fear of snakes only when I began talking to her toward the end of a dinner party she hosted. She was in her forties and the wife of an executive. In talking with her, I learned that she had become a recluse. She mentioned with enthusiasm how much she looked forward to going back to the United States, since she was housebound in Okinawa. "I can't go out because of those horrible snakes," she said. She knew that other people managed to go out at night, but said, "If they want to be stupid, that's their problem." Moreover, she blamed the American government and the island for her problem because "they should be doing more about those horrible snakes." As is typical of those with phobias that are ego-syntonic, she didn't see the fear as being *her* problem. She never sought out treatment even though the crippling consequences of her fear were evident. She had allowed her phobia to totally get in the way of living a fuller life. She refused to attend any social gatherings away from home—even those that were important to her husband's job—and she didn't seem to consider how this might jeopardize his career.

As these two cases demonstrate, neurotics are relatively easy to work with in psychotherapy because they assume responsibility for their difficulties and therefore see themselves as having problems. Those with character disorders are much more difficult to work with, because they don't see themselves as the source of their problems; they see the world rather than themselves as being in need of change, and therefore fail to recognize the necessity for self-examination.

Thus, a significant part of the existential suffering of life is the suffering involved in constantly discerning—or choosing— what we are responsible for and what we are not responsible for and maintaining a healthy balance. Obviously, the character-disordered person avoids that existential suffering. What may not be so obvious is that the neurotic also does. By simply assuming that everything is her responsibility, she will ultimately suffer more through neurotic suffering—even though she does avoid the existential suffering of having to make choices, the kind of suffering that may be involved in saying to people, "No! I'm drawing a line."

The problem of distinguishing what we are and are not responsible for in this life is one of the continuing challenges of human existence. It is never completely resolved for all time. We must continually assess and reassess where our responsibilities lie in the ever-changing course of events that shape our lives. There is no formula for how to do it. Each situation is new and we must discern all over again the choice of what we are and are not responsible for. It is one that we must make thousands upon thousands of times, almost up until the very day we die.

CHOICES OF SUBMISSION

Discipline is the means for solving life's problems. All discipline is a form of submission. The discipline to discern what we are or are not responsible for is most crucial, since we must go through the existential suffering of choosing when and what to submit to and what not to submit to, whether that is our own ego, love, God, or even the forces of evil.

For instance, when we are young, we more or less have to submit to our parents or other caretakers. But as we grow into adulthood, we have to make decisions about when and how to submit to our parents and when and how not to—and particularly to their values. Not all submission is good. To totally submit to one's parents in adulthood would be destructive, every bit as destructive as to submit to a cult. We must figure out to what extent we are going to submit to society and to what extent we are going to disagree with society, just as we must choose our values every step of the way. Ultimately, we have to choose whether or not to submit to God and, indeed, even choose the kind of God that we are going to submit to.

The term "higher power" first appeared in, or at least was initially popularized by, the Twelve Steps of Alcoholics Anonymous. In *A World Waiting to Be Born,* I wrote that the term implies that there is something "higher" than us as individuals and that it is appropriate to submit ourselves to that something higher, be it love, light, truth, or God. "Thy will, not mine, be done" is a glorious expression of desire for such submission, and the key word is "will." Submission implies an effective submission of the human will to something higher than itself. "God is light, God is love, God is truth." People need not be believers in God, but if they are to be healthy, they must submit themselves to these attributes of God.

Submission to the light might be defined as submission to the choice of consciousness and hence, sight—both external sight and, particularly, insight. Then there is the choice of whether to submit to love or not—that is, the decision whether to extend or not extend oneself. This is not simplistic. Love is often very subtle and mysterious. In *The Road Less Traveled,* I defined love as the will to extend oneself for the purpose of nurturing one's own or another's spiritual growth. This definition is an acknowledgment that love is far broader than romance, marriage, or parenting. Monks and nuns, for example, don't have those, but many are great lovers in the true sense of the word.

There are numerous paradoxes related to love that test the myths and common thinking in our culture. In the section on love in *The Road Less Traveled,* I found I had to begin by speaking of all the things that genuine love is *not* (such as romance) in order to combat our cultural stereotypes. For instance, we have all been told that it's better to give than to receive. I believe it would be more appropriate to say that it's just as good to receive as it is to give. Yet many have neurotic guilt over this issue and feel compelled to live up to cultural or religious ideals about charity that potentially promote more bitterness and friction than love in the true sense.

One reason people have a hard time receiving is that they feel manipulated, as if they will forever owe someone. In the earlier years of our marriage Lily and I maintained what we came to call a guilt bank. Whenever I did something for Lily, that meant I had money in the guilt bank. When she did something for me, my account (my worth) dropped. Like many couples, it took us years to learn ourselves out of this silliness. For some people, it's even obligatory to discount any compliments or good news due to upbringing and culture. The inability to receive love is almost as destructive as the inability to give it.

We have also been taught that "love is gentle, love is kind"— and yet there are times when we must display what is called tough love. Love is often ambiguous; sometimes it requires tenderness and sometimes it requires being stern. The reality is that we cannot love well if we are constantly extending ourselves to others and not nurturing ourselves. Submission to love does not mean being a doormat. Just as throughout our lives we must choose what is and what is not our responsibility, so we must also choose, even if we are submitted to love, when to love others and when to love ourselves.

I believe the key of loving is to work on oneself. We can't begin to love others well until we lovingly work on ourselves. In many relationships, you will find people trying to heal and convert each other in the name of love. Our attempts to heal and convert another are usually selfish, controlling, and nonloving despite all the ways we might think otherwise. Again, over the years of our own marriage, Lily and I had to work quite hard on healing ourselves of our need to change each other to arrive at that kind of love which combines acceptance and understanding.

Because of cultural indoctrination, many people equate love with doing: they feel they have to do something simply because of their own or others' expectations. The paradox is that many times just doing nothing—just being who you are rather than constantly focusing on what you do—is the more loving approach. For example, nothing is more fun for me than discussing theology, but one of the loving things I did was refrain from talking to my children much about theology because it would have been preaching to them in a way that was intrusive. In my novel *The Friendly Snowflake,* the preteen Jenny asks her father if he believes in an afterlife. His reply is "There are certain questions so important that people ought to figure out the answer for themselves." In this case, his withholding of his opinion was a very loving and respectful act toward his daughter.

And then there is the matter of submission to truth, which is far more complex and demanding than merely accepting scientifically proven facts or following the scientific method in a laboratory. In *The Road Less Traveled,* I listed dedication to reality—to the truth—as one of the four basic disciplines of living well. Speaking of this discipline, I noted that occasionally withholding a portion of the truth may be the loving thing to do. But even this tiny bit of "fudging" with the truth is so potentially dangerous that I felt compelled to offer stringent criteria for those relatively few times when the telling of little white lies might be permissible. The fact is that withholding a key piece of truth from others is often at least as deceptive as an outright black lie. Such lying is not just unloving; it is ultimately hateful. Every instance of it adds to the darkness and confusion in the world. Conversely, speaking the truth—particularly when it requires some risk to do so—is an act of love. It diminishes the darkness and confusion, increasing the light the world so desperately needs.

When we lie, we are usually attempting to avoid responsibility for our actions and what we imagine to be their painful consequences. I am forever grateful to my parents for teaching me during childhood a most pithy and powerful expression: "face the music." Meaning, face up to the consequences; don't cover up; don't lie; live in the light. While the meaning is clear, it only occurs to me now that it is a somewhat strange expression. Why "music"? Why should facing up to something potentially painful be called facing music when we normally think of music as pleasurable and lovely? I don't know. I don't know how the expression originated. But perhaps the choice of word is deep and mystically appropriate. For when we do submit ourselves to the dictates of honesty, we are in harmony with reality, and our lives, although never painless, will become increasingly melodic.

I have been speaking of the choice for truth as if lying were something we primarily do to others. Not so. Our even greater proclivity is for lying to ourselves. Of course the two types of dishonesty feed off each other in an ever-escalating orgy of deception. But while we can deceive some of the people some of the time, our capacity for self-deception is potentially unlimited as long as we are willing to pay the price of evil or insanity. And these are ultimately the costs. Self-deception is not a matter of being kind or gentle with oneself; on the contrary, it is as hateful as lying to others, and for the same reason: it adds to the darkness and confusion of the self, augmenting the Shadow layer by layer. Conversely, the choice to be honest with oneself is the choice for psychospiritual health and, therefore, the single most loving choice we can ever make for ourselves.

In the realm of personal belief, we are faced with many complex choices, and the certainties of science cannot readily be relied upon. If we choose to believe something is true, is it therefore true? If so, submitting to the truth would be nothing more than submitting to ourselves. Since God is synonymous with truth, in choosing to submit to God we are submitting to a truth higher than ourselves. In *People of the Lie,* I wrote that since we are endowed with the freedom to choose, we can submit to the wrong things. I also explained that there are only two states of being: submission to God and goodness, or the refusal to submit to anything beyond one's will, which automatically enslaves one to the forces of evil, to "the Father of Lies." And I quoted C. S. Lewis: "There is no neutral ground in the universe: every square inch, every split second is claimed by God and counterclaimed by Satan." Perhaps we may feel that we can stand exactly between God and the devil, uncommitted either to goodness or to evil. But "Not to choose is to choose." Fence-straddling eventually becomes intolerable and the choice of unsubmission is ultimately invalid.

CHOICES OF VOCATION

To most people, "vocation" simply means what one does for a living, one's occupation or career. The secular definition of "vocation" usually implies only income-producing activity. The religious definition, however, is more literal and yet far more complex. "Vocation" literally means calling. The religious meaning of "vocation," therefore, is what one is called to do, which may or may not coincide with one's occupation, with what one is actually doing.

In this sense vocation implies a relationship. For if someone is called, something must be doing the calling. I believe this something is God. God calls us human beings—whether skeptics or believers, whether Christian or not—to certain, often very specific activities. Furthermore, since God relates with us as individuals, this matter of calling is utterly individualized. What God calls me to do is not at all necessarily what God is calling you to do.

It is quite obvious that while one person may be called to be a homemaker, another may be called to be a lawyer, a scientist, or an advertising executive. There are different kinds of career callings; for many people, there are sequential callings. Midlife is often a time when there is a change in career. But what is less obvious are the spiritual and ethical issues relevant to one's vocation, cause, or product. As a scientist, am I called to work on weapons development? As a lawyer, am I called to defend someone I suspect is guilty? As a gynecologist, do I or do I not perform abortions?

Just as some discover that certain aspects of their vocation do not fit or feel right to them, others spend years—even a lifetime—fleeing their true vocation. A forty-year-old sergeant major in the Army once consulted me for a mild depression that he ascribed to his reassignment to Germany, upcoming in two weeks. He and his family were sick and tired of moving, he claimed. It was unusual for top-ranking enlisted men (or officers) to seek psychiatric consultation, especially for such a minor condition. Several other things were also extraordinary about this man. People do not get to be sergeants major without considerable intelligence and competence, but my patient exuded wit and gentility as well. Somehow I was not surprised to learn that painting was his hobby. He struck me as being artistic. After he told me he had been in the service for twenty-two years, I asked him, "Since you're so fed up with moving, why don't you retire?"

"I wouldn't know what to do with myself," he replied.

"You could paint as much as you wanted," I suggested.

"No, that's just a hobby," he said. "It's not something I could make a living at."

Having no idea of his talent, I was not in a position to rebut him on that score, but there were other ways to probe his resistance. "You're an obviously intelligent man with a fine track record," I countered. "You could get lots of good jobs."

"I haven't been to college," he said, "and I'm not cut out for selling insurance." At the suggestion that he consider going back to college and live on his retirement pay, he responded: "No, I'm too old. I wouldn't feel right around a bunch of kids."

I requested that he bring samples of his most recent paintings to our next appointment the following week. He brought two, an oil and a watercolor. Both were magnificent. They were modern, imaginative, even flamboyant, with an extraordinarily effective use of shape, shade, and color. When I inquired, he said that he did three or four paintings a year but never attempted to sell any of them, only gave them away to friends.

"Look," I said, "you've got real talent. I know it's a competitive field, but these are salable. Painting ought to be more than just a hobby for you."

"Talent's a subjective judgment," he demurred.

"So I'm the only one who's ever told you you have real talent?"

"No, but if you keep looking up in the sky, your feet are bound to stumble."

I then told him it seemed obvious that he had a problem with underachievement, probably rooted in fear of failure, or fear of success, or both. I offered to obtain for him a medical release from his assignment so that he could stay on post for us to work together exploring the roots of his problem. But he was adamant that it was his "duty" to proceed to Germany. I advised him how to get psychotherapy over there, but I doubt he took my advice. I suspect his resistance to his obvious vocation was so great that he would never follow the call no matter how clear or loud.

Given our free will, we have a choice to refuse to heed God's calling for us. The fact that we have a vocation doesn't necessarily mean that we will follow it. Conversely, the fact that we want to do something—or even have a talent for it—doesn't necessarily mean it is what God wants us to do.

Some people have a calling to marriage and family life; others have a calling to single or even monastic life. Whether one believes in fate or not, the embrace of a calling often comes only after much ambivalence. One woman initially experienced agonizing uncertainty when faced with the prospect of parenthood after she had already established her career and had several professional options with two college degrees in different fields. At the age of thirty-three she became pregnant—and also *open* to the prospect of motherhood—for the first time. "Before, I never could picture myself tied down to anyone—not one man and certainly not the lifelong commitment to a child," she told me. "I had vigorously rebelled against the idea of being responsible for the long-term well-being of anyone other than myself. I had become addicted to the 'freedom' of uncommitment, to living according to my own whims and desires. I didn't want to be dependent on anyone else and didn't want anyone dependent on me."

Through her openness and willingness to venture through uncertainty and doubt, she slowly emerged with a new sense of herself. "I found myself being pried into 'giving up' my totally independent lifestyle and began learning to like the idea of interdependence that made room for my mate and child," she said. "Then I couldn't imagine not having the child. I can't quite put my finger on this force that pushed me toward accepting this new image of myself as a mother and a committed partner. But somehow, when I finally stopped resisting it, I became transformed in a way that felt just right."

It is clear that while the fulfillment of a vocation does not guarantee happiness—as in the case of the tortured artist van Gogh—it does often set the stage for the peace of mind that may result from fulfillment. It is therefore frequently a pleasure to witness a human being doing what she or he was meant to do. We delight when we see a parent who truly loves taking care of children. There is such a sense of fit. Conversely, there is always a sense of dis-ease when we see people whose work and lifestyles do not fit their vocations. It seems such a shame, a waste. I believe God's unique vocation for each of us invariably calls us to personal success, but not necessarily in the world's stereotypical terms or means of measuring success. I have seen women who married into great wealth, for instance, who would be considered successful in the world's terms, whose jewels and position were the envy of multitudes, but who lived in despair because they were never called to marriage in the first place.

The Choice of Gratitude

A decade ago, I received two checks, one in payment by contract for a lecture I had given and the other an unasked-for, unanticipated donation for FCE. I generally support the expression "There's no such thing as a free lunch." But this was one of those moments of exception when I sat with an earned meal on one knee and a delicious, surprising gift on the other. For which do you suppose I was the more grateful?

It is easy to take a lot for granted—including good luck and unexpected gifts—in this life. Indeed, in this remarkably secular age, we are actually encouraged to think in terms of luck, as if good fortune has no more meaning than a roll of the dice. We imagine everything to be a matter of mere accident or chance, assuming that good luck and bad luck are equal, that they balance out and add up to zero or nothing. This attitude easily leads to the philosophy of despair called nihilism (derived from *nihil,* the Latin word for "nothing"). When it is brought to its logical conclusion, nihilism ultimately holds that there is nothing of any worth.

Yet there is another way to look at good luck and unexpected gifts. This theory posits a superhuman giver, God, who likes to give gifts to human creatures because He particularly loves us. Whether this God has anything to do with the downpours in our lives is uncertain, although in retrospect they often seem to have been blessings in disguise. As to those things that are recognizable gifts, some of us see a pattern of beneficence to them far greater and more constant than any pattern of misfortune. For this beneficent pattern of gift-giving we have a name: grace. If something is earned it is not a true gift. Grace, however, is unearned. It is free. It is gratis. The words grace, gratis, and gratitude flow into one another. If you perceive grace, you will naturally feel grateful.

A story told to me by a famous preacher involved a young Yankee who, on a business trip, had to drive through the South for the first time in his life. He had driven all night and was in a hurry. By the time he arrived in South Carolina, he was really hungry. Stopping at a roadside diner, he ordered a breakfast of scrambled eggs and sausage, and was taken by surprise when his order came back and there was a white blob of something on the plate.

"What's that?" he asked the waitress.

"Them's grits, suh," she replied in her strong southern accent.

"But I didn't order them," he said.

"You don't order grits," she responded. "They just come."

And that, said the preacher, is very much like grace. You don't order it. It just comes.

In my experience, the ability to appreciate pleasant surprises as gifts tends to be good for one's mental health. Those who perceive grace in the world are more likely to be grateful than those who don't. And grateful people are more likely to be happy than ungrateful ones. They are also more likely to make others happy. Feeling given to by the world, they feel predisposed to give back to the world.

Why do some people have such obviously grateful hearts while others have distinctly ungrateful ones? And why do still others fall in between, seeming relatively bland in both their gratitude and their resentment? I don't know. It would be simple to believe that children from nurturing homes will automatically grow up to be grateful adults, and that deprived homes regularly turn out malcontents. The problem is there's not much evidence to support this. Exceptions abound. I've known many who were raised in the midst of neglect, poverty, and even brutality who seemed to quite naturally live their adult lives praising the Lord, or at least praising life itself. Conversely, I've known a few from homes of love and comfort who seemed born ingrates. A grateful heart is a mysterious thing, and may even be genetic in origin.

So an "attitude of gratitude" may not entirely be a matter of choice. Indeed, it is my belief that a grateful heart is itself a gift. In other words, the capacity to appreciate gifts is a gift. It is also the greatest blessing a human being may possess other than a strong will. But that doesn't mean that a grateful heart cannot be nurtured by choice.

I once supervised a lay therapist in his work with a man in his forties, who had come to see him because of chronic depression. As depressions go, his was rather mild. Perhaps a more accurate description of the patient's condition was dyspepsia, an old-fashioned lay term for indigestion. It was as if the whole world gave him indigestion and made him want to burp and belch. Not much changed in his disposition for quite a while. Toward the end of the second year, however, the therapist I was supervising told me, "At the last session, my client came here very excited. He was exclaiming at the beauty of a sunset he'd seen while driving over the hills."

"Congratulations!" I responded.

"What do you mean?" he asked.

"Your patient's over the hump," I said. "He's getting better rapidly. It's the first time I've heard that this man took any delight in life. He's not so absorbed in negativity or so self-focused that he couldn't notice beauty around him and be grateful for it. This represents an extraordinary shift." I later learned that my prediction was on target. Within a few months, the patient was basically behaving like a new man, his therapist reported.

Indeed, how one responds to adversity and good or bad luck may be one of the truest measures of our ability to grow into gratefulness. We can look at some bad luck as a blessing in disguise. We can also maintain a sense of humility and not take good luck for granted. Do we complain about how bad the weather is most of the time or can we learn to appreciate the beauty and diversity of weather as a gift to us? If we are stuck in a traffic jam on a blustery winter day, do we sit and stew, even want to chew out the drivers ahead of us, or do we concentrate on the fact that we are blessed to have a car in the midst of a snowstorm? Are we inclined to complain about our jobs rather than work on ways to improve our skills?

When I was a child a friend of my father's gave me a number of Horatio Alger, Jr., books that were already out of print. I devoured them. The books' heroes were grateful for what they got. They didn't complain about adversity, but acted almost as if it were an opportunity instead of a curse to them. Reading those books in childhood was, I suspect, a profoundly positive influence in my young life. I worry about our society these days when such books are not only out of print but, by many, deemed corny.

THE CHOICE TO DIE GRACEFULLY

The final choice of our lives on this earth is whether or not we go out in style. For it's not a matter of whether to die but how. We have a lifetime to prepare. Unfortunately, the denial of aging in our culture goes hand-in-glove with the denial of death. For many, this denial circumvents the greatest learning of old age: how to accept limits. Our culture suggests that there are no limits—and furthermore, seems to suggest that there *shouldn't* be any. Of course, real life challenges this notion on every level. Yet no-limits thinking is at the heart of much of television advertising. One ad that particularly annoyed me showed a woman in her sixties (who, of course, looked fortyish) playing tennis. The message was that because of some medicine she took, her arthritis didn't keep her off the courts. The ad concluded with an invisible voice from the sidelines joyously exclaiming: "Live without limits!"

The reality is that we must live with limitations, even from the time we are young, quite exploratory, and generally vibrant. As we age, we face far greater limitations. We have by then made some choices—such as whether to be single or married, to work or to retire—that exclude other options. If someone becomes confined to a wheelchair, it would be foolish for him to believe that he can just hop on an airplane easily and go about business as usual.

It would be unnatural to welcome aging. A modicum of depression related to the losses inherent in growing old—or facing any change, for that matter—is natural. But just because it would be unnatural to invite aging does not mean we should deny the realities of aging and its painful process of stripping away. Aging eventually involves the stripping away of everything, including agility, sexual potency, physical beauty, and political power. Our options and choices become ever more limited and we are challenged to learn to live with these limitations.

Dying, of course, is the final stripping away. I've heard many people say that "if" they have got to go—as if they really had a choice—they would rather die suddenly. The reason that cancer and AIDS are so dreaded is that with such diseases one dies slowly. The gradual deterioration involves experiencing a total loss of control, and for most people this process is equated with a loss of dignity. The sense of indignity involved in stripping away is very real. But a distinction can be made between false dignity and true dignity, and there is a tremendous difference between the responses of the ego and those of the soul to the process of dying. Our egos often can't bear the loss of dignity from watching our bodies waste away. That's because dignity has everything to do with the ego and nothing to do with the soul. In confronting the choice to give up control, the ego vigorously rebels despite an inevitable losing battle. The soul, on the other hand, welcomes the stripping-away process. We can learn that as we give up control, we are also giving up false dignity, so that we may die gracefully with true dignity.

By dying gracefully I do not mean taking the route of euthanasia. Euthanasia basically involves trying to make something clean that is inherently messy. It is, in my opinion, an attempt to shortcut the existential and legitimate suffering of dying, thereby shortcutting the opportunity for learning and growth. Neither do I mean engaging in denial. In different forms of denial some people refuse to make out wills, choose not to talk about their feelings about death, or block it out altogether by making distant future plans even when they should know their time is limited. Denial may help ease the pain of being conscious of one's inevitable death, but it also keeps us stuck. It not only blocks meaningful communication, it also obstructs all learning toward life's close.

To die gracefully, I believe, is to make the choice to see dying as a learning opportunity and to welcome the stripping away as a cleansing so that the true dignity of the soul can shine through. In my novel *A Bed by the Window*, I describe some dying patients at a nursing home who seem to have haloes around them. This phenomenon is not restricted to fiction. Indeed, many people have noticed or heard about the "lightness" around those who have truly worked through the stage of depression and arrived at acceptance.

If we are willing to do so, we can become transformed—not by bitterness, but by humility—as we deal with the major losses that are an inevitable part of aging and the journey toward death. Perhaps the choice to die gracefully occurs when we finally learn and accept that all is according to how it should be. Whether one believes in an afterlife or not, to proceed gracefully into the arms of death is the ultimate acquiescence to an abiding conviction—even in the midst of paradoxical uncertainty—that every aspect of life contributes to the meaning of the whole. And, also paradoxically, the most important choice we make—the choice to die gracefully—is to choose to give up all choices and place our souls totally in the hands of the Real Power.

THE CHOICE OF EMPTINESS

Death is the ultimate emptiness. We are terrified of the void of death even if we believe we will come out the other side. Yet we don't *know* what the other side will be like.

There are many varieties of emptiness, but the most important (and the easiest to speak about without getting too mystical) is the "emptiness of not knowing." Despite living in a society that appears to push a "know-it-all" mentality and label incompetent those who don't always seem to be in the know, we still have a choice to not know without feeling incompetent or guilty about it. In fact, there are times in each of our lives when it is not only proper but healing to give up thinking we know all the answers.

The most healing experience of my adolescence was a gift by a man who related to me out of the emptiness of not knowing, and who served as a wonderfully positive role model to boot. In *A World Waiting to Be Born,* I described how, at the age of fifteen and in the middle of my junior year, I decided to leave Exeter. As I look back on that turning point in my life, I am amazed at the grace that gave me the courage to do it. After all, not only was I dropping out of a prestigious prep school against my parents' wishes, but I was walking away from a golden WASP track that had all been laid out for me. Hardly aware at that age just what I was doing, I was taking my first giant step out of my entire culture. That culture of the "establishment" was what one was supposed to aspire to, and I was throwing it away. And where was I to go? I was forging into the total unknown. I was so terrified that I thought I should seek the advice of some of Exeter's faculty before finalizing such a dreadful decision. But which of the faculty?

The first who came to mind was my adviser. He had barely spoken to me for two and a half years, but he was reputedly kind. A second obvious candidate was the crusty old dean of the school, known to be beloved by thousands of alumni. But I thought that three was a good number, and the third choice was more difficult. I finally hit upon Mr. Lynch, my math teacher and a somewhat younger man. I chose him not because we had any relationship or because he seemed to be a particularly warm sort of person—indeed, I found him a rather cold, mathematical kind of fish—but because he had a reputation as the faculty genius. He had been involved with some kind of high-level mathematics on the Manhattan Project, and I thought I should check out my decision with a "genius."

I went first to my kindly adviser, who let me talk for about two minutes and then gently broke in. "It's true that you're underachieving here at Exeter, Scotty," he said, "but not so seriously that you won't be able to graduate. It would be preferable for you to graduate from a school like Exeter with lesser grades than from a lesser school with better grades. It would also look bad on your record to switch horses in midstream. Besides, I'm sure your parents would be quite upset. So why don't you just go along and do the best you can?"

Next I went to the crusty old dean. He let me speak for thirty seconds. "Exeter is the best school in the world," he harrumphed. "Damn fool thing you're thinking of doing. Now you just pull yourself up by the bootstraps, young man!"

Feeling worse and worse, I went to see Mr. Lynch. He let me talk myself out. It took about five minutes. Then he said he didn't yet understand and asked if I would just talk some more—about Exeter, about my family, about God (he actually gave me permission to talk about God!), about anything that came into my head. So I rambled on for another ten minutes—fifteen minutes in all, which was pretty good for a depressed, inarticulate fifteen-year-old. When I was done, he inquired whether I would mind if he asked me some questions. Thriving on this adult attention, I replied, "Of course not," and he queried me about many different things for the next half-hour.

Finally, after forty-five minutes in all, this supposedly cold fish sat back in his chair with a pained expression on his face and said, "I'm sorry I can't help you. I don't have any advice to give you.

"You know," he continued, "it's impossible for one person to ever completely put himself in another person's shoes. But insofar as I can put myself in your shoes—and I'm glad I'm not there—I don't know what I would do if I were you. So, you see, I don't know how to advise you. I'm sorry that I've been unable to help."

It is just possible that that man saved my life. For when I entered Mr. Lynch's office that morning some forty-five years ago, I was close to suicidal. And when I left, I felt as if a thousand pounds had been taken off my back. Because if a *genius* didn't

know what to do, then it was all right for me not to know what
to do. And if I was considering a move that seemed so insane in
the world's terms, and a *genius* couldn't tell me that it was
clearly, obviously demented—well, then, maybe, just maybe, it
was something God was calling me to.

So it was that that man, who didn't have any answers or
quick formulas, who didn't know what I should do and chose to
practice emptiness—it was that man who provided the help I
needed. It was that man who listened to me, who gave me his
time, who tried to put himself in my shoes, who extended himself and sacrificed himself for me. It was that man who loved
me. And it was that man who healed me.

There are no simple or easy formulas. In handling all life
experiences, we must endure a degree of emptiness and the
agony of not knowing. As I wrote in *Further Along the Road Less
Traveled,* there are many things we often go through life blam-
ing others for. Since a big part of growing up is learning to forgive, each time we must reconsider and debate, "Should I
blame or should I forgive?" Or, "Am I being loving or am I being a doormat?" Or simply, "What is the thing to do?" It is a decision that must be made again in each situation and every
different time.

Although there is no certain formula, there is a guideline
to help in such decision making, which I first wrote about in
The Different Drum. It is to recognize that the unconscious is always one step ahead of the conscious mind. The problem is we
don't know whether it's ahead in the right direction or the
wrong direction. We don't always know if that still small voice
we hear is the voice of the Holy Spirit, or Satan, or maybe just
our glands. It is, therefore, impossible ever to know that what
we are doing is right at the time, since knowing is a function of
consciousness.

However, if your will is steadfastly to the good and if you
are willing to suffer fully when the good seems ambiguous
(which to me seems about 98.7 percent of the time), then your
unconscious will always be one step ahead of your conscious

mind in the right direction. In other words, you will do the right thing. But you won't have the luxury of knowing it at the time you are doing it. Indeed, you will do the right thing precisely because you've been willing to forgo that luxury. And if this guideline seems obscure, then you might want to remember that almost all the evil in this world is committed by people who are *absolutely* certain that they know what they are doing.

CHAPTER 5

Organizational Life Choices

※

WE MAY THINK THAT WE MAKE personal life choices as individuals, as if the individual existed more or less in isolation. But the reality is that we do not so exist. We human beings are social creatures, and virtually all our choices are made under the influence, and in the context of, the various organizations in which we participate. By organizations, I do not simply mean business organizations. Families are organizations, and many of the principles that hold true for families also hold true for businesses, and vice versa. On the largest scale, our whole society is an organization. On the smallest, every single social relationship we have is an organization. Anytime there is a relationship between two or more people, an organization of some sort is involved.

Consequently, the subject of organizational behavior encompasses virtually the entire field of human psychology, since virtually all human behavior occurs in the context of one or more organizations. Organizational behavior includes not only how individuals behave in temporary groups but also how groups—and even the organizations themselves—function. The field is enormous, but I would like to focus on organiza-

tional choices that seem to me most important, the decisions
we make and the actions we take that impinge upon other people—and how we treat others as well as ourselves—for good or
ill. If the decisions we make affect only ourselves, we can simply
do whatever we want to do, take responsibility for it, and deal
with the consequences of our actions. But when others are involved, this brings us very clearly into the realm of ethics and
the matter of civility.

CIVILITY

I have spent much of the past fifteen years in the attempt to resurrect two critical words from a meaningless death: community
and civility. When we speak of community in our current society, we usually mean any conglomeration of people. For instance, we will refer to Morristown, New Jersey, as a community.
But the fact of the matter is that Morristown, New Jersey, is
nothing but a geographical aggregate of people with a certain
tax base and a few social services in common, but precious little
else—if anything—that links them together as human beings.
Or we will refer to the Third Presbyterian Church of some town
as a community when, more often than not, the reality is that
the people sitting in the pews next to each other are unable to
talk to each other about the things that are most troubling and
important in their lives. I have come to refer to such aggregates
of people as pseudocommunities.

For me, community has to do with communication, and
real community should imply a sustained and high quality of
communication among its members. I first wrote about community in *The Different Drum: Community Making and Peace.* But
the major focus of my life these years has been not writing but
working with others in the establishment and development of
the Foundation for Community Encouragement (FCE). It is
the mission of this educational foundation to teach the principles of community, by which we mean healthy and authentic
communication within and between groups.

My work with FCE led me, at a time of social breakdown and increasing adversarialism, to an attempt to resurrect another word fallen into meaninglessness: "civility." All that is generally meant these days by "civility" is superficial politeness. But the fact is that people have been politely stabbing each other in the back and politely hurting each other for God knows how long. I was helped to arrive at a more meaningful definition of civility by an English gentleman of the last century, Oliver Hereford, who is famed for saying, "A gentleman is someone who never hurts another person's feelings unintentionally." What that means to me is that sometimes it may be necessary to hurt another person's feelings, but the key is intention, meaning awareness of what you are doing. Such awareness requires consciousness. So in my book on the subject, *A World Waiting to Be Born: Civility Rediscovered,* I defined "civility" not as mere superficial politeness, but as "consciously motivated organizational behavior that is ethical in submission to a higher power."

It can be assumed that anyone who has made the choice to be conscious wants to be a civil person. But there is a major problem here: in order to be civil, we must be conscious not only of our own motivations but also of the organization—or system—in which we are acting. Civility requires organizational as well as individual consciousness. Consequently, if we aspire to ever greater civility, we must increasingly think in terms of systems.

SYSTEMS

The most enjoyable part of my medical school education was the study of microscopic anatomy. All external appearances to the contrary, our bodies are mostly water. Consequently, when you look at thin slices of our organs under a microscope you cannot see much except pallid, indistinguishable filaments. But if you take these same slices, soak them for a while in selected dyes, and look again, suddenly you have entered a fairyland, a garden of delights compared to which Disneyland is downright insipid. No matter what our age, station, or even state of health, at this level we are all very beautiful on the inside.

Gradually, as I peered at one beautiful cell after another, microscopic slide after slide, month after month, something even more important dawned on me. Each and every cell was not only a system in itself, but also a minuscule part of a larger, even more complex system. The absorbing villi cells, the smooth muscle cells, and the connective tissue cells holding them together were all an integrated part of an organ—in this case, the small intestine. The small intestine, in turn, was a part of the digestive system. And the digestive system was integrated with other systems of the body. The fine filaments of the autonomic nerve cells that stimulated the digestive muscles to relax or contract and the glands to rest or secrete were minute parts of the nervous system, connecting all the way up through the spinal cord to other cells in the brain. Throughout each organ were the tiny cells of arteries or veins, all connected to the heart as part of the circulatory system. And in each artery or vein I could spy varieties of blood cells, originally manufactured in the bone marrow as little tiny parts of the hematopoietic system.

Actually, I had "known" for years that the human body—and the body of every other living thing, animal or plant—was a system. But prior to medical school, I had not been aware of the extraordinary complexity and beauty of such systems. It was at this point I was able to make another leap of consciousness to something, once again, I had long "known," but only dimly. Since each individual cell was a component of an organ, and each individual organ a component of a body system, and each such system a component of the body as a whole, was it not possible that my body was also part of a larger system still? In other words, might I—my individual self—be but a single cell of an organ of some gigantic organism? Of course. As a fledgling physician, I was connected, directly or indirectly, to countless other individual human cells. To my parents, who paid my tuition. To the older physicians who taught me. To the laboratory technicians who conducted the tests I ordered. To hospital administrators. To manufacturers who made the equipment I used. To the patients I used that equipment on. To growers in Mississippi and California who sold cotton to the North Carolina textile workers who made the clothes I wore. To ranchers in Kansas who grew the beef, and farmers in New Jersey who grew the lettuce I ate. To the truck drivers who transported all these things to me. To my landlord. To the barber who cut my hair. And on and on.

So it was (although I had not yet even heard the term) that I became a foursquare believer in "systems theory." The basic tenet of systems theory (which is actually not a theory but a fact) is that everything is a system. On a level more macroscopic than that of a cell or an organ or an organ system or an individual, all of us are component parts of the fabric of human society. We are just beginning to wake up to the fact that the whole of that society is connected to the waters, to the land, to the forests, and the atmosphere: the "ecosystem." Indeed, systems theorists often envision the entire planet as a single organism. Our earth is, of course, a part of the solar system. And as we begin to reach even farther into outer space, we will probably perceive a systemic nature to the galaxies and the universe itself.

Beyond the fact that everything that exists is part of a system, systems theory also holds that if you change one component of the system, all the other parts must also change. Only in the past few decades have we become somewhat aware of this fact in our society. We have come to realize that virtually everything we do has an effect upon our environment, and that these effects have the potential to either nurture us or destroy us.

As an example, virtually everyone who owns a car has had the experience of taking it to a shop for a minor repair only to have it conk out on the way back home. When this happens, you may curse the mechanic for having done some evil deed. But as a rule, no evil deed has been done at all. It is just that the presence of a brand-new part has caused a subtle change in the engine—the entire system—which requires an adjustment in the other parts, sometimes an adjustment those older parts are not able to make without themselves breaking down.

Human relationships are also a system: marriage, in particular. In our work as psychotherapists with couples, Lily coined the term "tenuousness," by which she meant that in a marriage each partner's definition of the other should be tenuous—namely, flexible rather than fixed. Again and again in our practice we saw that whenever one marital partner significantly changed or grew as a result of psychotherapy, the other partner would have to change or grow in response, or else the system—the marriage—would fall apart.

I do not mean to suggest that psychotherapy is the only variable in the equation. All manner of things can change the nature of a marriage. The nature of my marriage to Lily changed as soon as we had children. It changed again when the children were out of diapers. It changed once more when the children entered adolescence. And it changed again when they left home. Along the way, it had to change when our financial situation changed and we moved from being the recipients of philanthropy to roughly twenty years of breaking even to being significant contributors to charitable causes. It has certainly changed again as we moved from middle age into old age and my retirement.

So systems theory implies that we must be able to adjust—sometimes very quickly—or the system may break down. But to have the capacity to make such rapid changes, we must have an acute consciousness of the systems to which we belong. And there's the rub. We humans are conscious to varying degrees. And while almost everyone is conscious of himself as an entity and is aware of his more urgent needs and desires, we lack such clear awareness of our social motivations and of the Shadow from which those motivations may spring. Even with a relatively advanced degree of consciousness, most of us remain remarkably unconscious of the complex organizations and social systems to which we belong.

This lack of organizational and social consciousness is such a dramatic phenomenon that I have come to call it the hole in the mind. And while this hole is often gaping, sometimes it is more like a slice of Swiss cheese. For instance, a business executive is likely to have come to the awareness that his company is a complex system, but he may never once have stopped to think of his own family as a system. Others may be quite aware of their family as a system, but have little consciousness about the organization that employs them.

This hole in the mind—this unconsciousness concerning our organizations—is frequently fed by our narcissism. For instance, in a large manufacturing company, it is probable that most of the workers on the assembly line think of themselves as the core of the company and give little or no thought to the other employees and their roles. After all, they're the ones who actually make the product, are they not? The salespeople may also think of themselves as the core of the company. After all, they are the ones who sell the product, and if it didn't get sold there would be no company. But the marketing people are likely to think of themselves as the center of the company because the sales staff wouldn't be able to sell the product if they didn't market it well. Those in the financial division may think they are the center of the company, because they balance the books and keep the company solvent. And those in management may think of themselves as the most important, because they create the policies that guide the corporation, but they may have precious little empathy for the others in different roles who contribute to the whole.

The same is true of our society generally, and of the racism and classism that pervade it. The failure to be aware of others' contributions has led to a lack of civility, perhaps because we feel overwhelmed simply trying to become more conscious of ourselves and have no energy left over to develop our organizational and social consciousness. Nevertheless, there is no way that we can evolve into a more civil society until ever greater numbers of us are willing to make the choice not only to be personally conscious but also to think in terms of whole systems and expand our awareness in order to fill the hole in the mind.

ETHICS

I have a friend who was one of the first American pilots shot down and captured by the North Vietnamese. In the early days of his seven-year captivity, he and his fellow prisoners of war were systematically tortured. In an extraordinary book about his experiences, he makes it quite clear that his captors were engaging in fully conscious organizational behavior. They knew exactly what they were doing. They were conscious of their intent and the effect their beatings and even more brutal practices had on their victims. They knew that anyone will break under enough pain and that their torture would extract confessions—no matter how false—useful for propaganda purposes and serving their organizational mission. Yet, even those Americans who were horrified by the incivility of our prosecution of the Vietnam War would never consider torture to have been a civil response or in any way justified.

So civility is something more than organizational behavior that is merely "consciously motivated." It must be *ethical* as well. And all but the morally insane would agree that torture is inherently and grossly unethical. I use this example because it is so gross, not to sidestep the fact that a much more subtle incivility is the real, pervasive problem in our society. And it, too, is unethical. To be ethical is, at the very least, to be "humanistic," which by definition means having the attitude that people are precious and should be treated accordingly insofar as possible. We do not torture people if we think of them as precious.

Recently there has been much criticism of "secular humanism" by the religious right. I believe that many of these critics would be well advised to become more humanistic themselves. Nevertheless, I also believe they have a point. Secular humanism is like a house built on sand. When the going gets rough—when business is bad or strife is abroad—secular humanistic attitudes may easily be blown away. For example, the media have been recognized to be a particularly secular realm. And those who work in the media not only generally regard themselves as humanists but also think that their work to keep people informed is important in keeping society at least barely civil and humanistic. There is some truth in this. However, I know all too many instances of reporters easily and quickly throwing their humanism out the window in their eagerness to get a story.

The problem with secular humanism is that it says nothing about *why* human beings are precious, nor why they should be treated accordingly. Consequently, secular humanism, being unrooted in any kind of theology, is often a fair-weather phenomenon. That is why I define civil behavior not simply as "ethical," but specifically as "ethical in submission to a higher power." For if, as I have said, light, truth, and love are all synonyms of a sort for God, and if we are *truly* submitted to these things, our behavior will be godly even though we may not think of ourselves as religious.

As an example of such submission, let me return to the reporter who may throw his humanism out the window in order to get a story. Although that reporter may (not always) take pains not to lie (lest he be sued) and will, therefore, "stick to the facts," he is likely to retain complete license to decide upon which facts he will report and which he will not. In this sense, facts are like statistics. They can be used to say anything you want. In many situations, a reporter is completely free to draw a black picture, a white picture, or a gray picture. Unless he is a very conscientious individual, it is quite likely that his choice will be determined not by any deep submission to the truth so much as by what seems to make a good story. Even if the reporter is devoted to truth, there is a chain of command involved in the process of how a story gets interpreted. After the reporter has written it, his editors—who are not directly involved in the initial gathering of information—will add their own perspectives. They do so by means of the headline and by the length and placement of the story. From my point of view, the best stories are those that are gray, because the truth is generally complex. But it is my experience that many reporters would rather not submit themselves to such complexity, because it doesn't make for good, enticing headlines. Even they will admit to looking for a "slant" on a story, apparently forgetting that there is a difference between slanted stories and the truth.

In dealing with such ethical complexities, I have found the distinction between code ethics and situation ethics to be helpful, almost essential. Code ethics are derived from various ethical prescriptions that have been in use throughout history. The earliest known is the Code of Hammurabi. Far better known to us are the Ten Commandments. What such codes do is to pronounce certain acts to be bad, wrong, or impermissible under any circumstances. For instance, one of the Ten Commandments is "Thou shalt not kill." It isn't "Thou shalt not kill except in time of war," or "Thou shalt not kill except in self-defense"; it is "Thou shalt not kill," period. No ifs, ands, or buts.

The basic tenet of situation ethics, however, is that no ethical judgment can be made about an act without consideration of the circumstances in which it occurs. Unlike the Ten Commandments, situation ethics would allow for killing in such circumstances as wartime and self-defense.

Our society has evolved away from simplistic code ethics toward situational ethics. This is dramatically visible in our legal system. Go visit your lawyer and you are likely to see that her office is filled with bookshelves full of weighty tomes. What most of those heavy books contain are legal precedents of a situational nature. Such precedents will state, "Thou shalt not break a contract, except as in the case of *Jones v. Smith,* where such and such circumstances prevailed," or "Thou shalt not break a contract except in the kind of situation that occurred in *Brown v. Taylor.*"

To live by situational ethics, it is necessary for the individual to have the capacity to serve as an entire legal system within himself. To be healthy and whole, we must possess within our own minds a competent defense attorney, a competent prosecuting attorney, and a good judge. People with character disorders tend to have a very strong internal defense attorney, but a very weak conscience or internal prosecuting attorney. Those with neuroses tend to have a very strong prosecuting attorney but a weak defense attorney, who is unable to speak up for his client. Finally, there are those who have in their heads both a reasonably competent defense attorney and prosecuting attorney but then, for one reason or another, have great difficulty coming to decisions because they lack a good judge.

I heartily support the movement of society (and of individuals in their own personal decision making) toward situational ethics. As a psychiatrist, I am very familiar with the fact that rigid code ethics often have inhumane consequences. But there are two caveats to be considered. One is that the use of situation ethics means that there are no formulas, so healthy individuals have the responsibility to reconsider their behavior each and every time the situation changes ever so slightly. While it might be the right thing to blame someone in one situation, it might be the right thing to forgive him in a subtly different one. Without formulas, we never know at the time that what we are doing is right. We must have the capacity to operate out of the "emptiness of not knowing."

My other caveat is that I do not want to imply that code ethics are useless. Again, in recent years, the religious right has become more and more critical of situational ethics, and again they may have a small point—although I suspect that their proposals would be regressive. Consider, for instance, the concept of a just war. Given the current state of human evolution, in which it seems beyond us to get rid of war, I believe it was appropriate for the Catholic Church to use situational ethics in developing the concept of a just war. But I'm not sure we would even attempt to discriminate between just and unjust wars were it not for the existence of a persisting code ethic that states, "Thou shalt not kill."

INTERDEPENDENCE AND COLLABORATION

In *The Road Less Traveled,* I noted that we all have dependency needs and feelings, but that these do not constitute love and that to be driven by them is to fall into the terrible trap of dependency. It is a trap because it leaves the dependent individual continually feeling that he cannot be whole or happy without the almost constant attention of other people. Just one of the many problems such dependency can cause is pathological jealousy. Nothing that I said about dependency was wrong, but I should have balanced my castigation of it with a hymn in praise of interdependence.

At the time I wrote *The Road Less Traveled,* I was still operating to some degree under the ethic of good old American rugged individualism, which holds that we are all called to become independent, to stand on our own two feet, and to be captains of our own ship, if not necessarily masters of our own destiny. All that is fine; I believe that we are called to independence when possible. But the huge problem with the ethic of rugged individualism is that it neglects the other side of the coin: that we are also called to come to terms with our own sin, our inevitable imperfection and inadequacy, and our mutual interdependence. It is because the individualist ethic is only a half-truth that it encourages us to hide our weaknesses and failures and to feel ashamed of our limitations. It drives us to attempt to be superwomen and supermen, not only in the eyes of others but also in our own eyes. It pushes us, day in and day out, to look as if we "had it all together," and it leads to such phenomena as people sitting in the same pew but not able to talk to each other about their pain and yearning and disappointments, hiding behind their masks of composure so that they can look as if they are in total control of their lives.

In *The Different Drum,* written seven years later, I denounced this simplistic, one-sided, nonparadoxical, and therefore fallacious ethic and, in talking about community, began to champion interdependence. My most dramatic examples of the virtues of interdependence have come from my work in helping groups build community. But let me also sing its praises in the smallest of organizations: marriage, and my marriage to Lily, in particular. In our marriage, Lily's primary role has been that of homemaker and mine that of breadwinner. For some years we worried about the degree to which these roles were dictated by cultural, sexual stereotypes. Only gradually did we come to the peaceful realization that they were, in fact, not dictated by stereotypes but more by our own very different personalities.

From the beginning of our marriage I noted that Lily was mildly disorganized. Not infrequently she would become so engrossed in smelling the flowers that she would forget an appointment or neglect to write a promised letter. I, on the other hand, from the beginning, was what can be called goal-oriented—to put it mildly. I never had time to sniff a flower unless its bloom happened to coincide with my schedule, according to which every third Thursday afternoon from 2:00 to 2:30 was designated for flower-sniffing, barring rain.

Furthermore, I used to berate Lily for her inclination to speak in what I considered irrelevancies—details that got in the way of seeing the "big picture"—as well as her tendency to ignore civilization's most significant instrument, the clock. She was equally harsh about my maddening punctuality, my stodginess, and my insistence on speaking in paragraphs that began "First of all . . ." "Second . . ." "Third . . . ," and "In conclusion. . . ." Lily believed hers was the superior approach, and I upheld the excellence of mine. Lily bore the chief responsibility for raising our children. I do not mean to imply I had nothing whatsoever to do with them, but I cannot pretend that I was an ideally attentive parent. I was particularly inadequate when it came to playing with them. Have you ever tried to play well with children on schedule? Or when you get off schedule and all you can think about is the unfinished chapter you have to write? Lily, however, played with our children with an unending grace. She also contributed to my books. Indeed, as I wrote in the introduction to *The Road Less Traveled,* "she has been so giving that it is hardly possible to distinguish her wisdom . . . from my own." But she could not have organized her time well enough to write (and rewrite) sentences, paragraphs, and chapters week after week, month after month.

Slowly, therefore, Lily and I agreed to accept what once looked like vices as virtues, curses as blessings, liabilities as assets. Lily has the gift of flowing; I have the gift of organization. Over the years I have learned a bit about how to go with the flow and to be more patient and attentive in dealing with our children and others. Likewise, Lily realized that although she had made improvements, she would never be completely organized. But we have come to appreciate each other's very different styles as gifts and have slowly begun to incorporate the other's gift into ourselves. As a consequence, she and I are gradually becoming more whole as individuals. But this would not have been possible had we not first come to terms with our individual limitations and recognized the value of our interdependence.

The only problem with the word "interdependence" is that to some it may suggest "codependency." A fashionable word this past decade, "codependency" refers to a relationship in which the partners cater to—and thereby encourage—each other's weaknesses. Often it is properly decried. But I believe we need to be cautious about this, because a very real part of the learning of marriage is learning how to work around each other's limitations. When it is proper to work around such limitations, and when to criticize or to confront them, is a decision that can be made, again, only out of the agonizing "emptiness of not knowing."

While I do not wish to discard the word "interdependence," it may be helpful to think in terms of another word, "collaboration": laboring together. In our work with larger organizations, Lily and I have realized that such organizations often have a lot to learn about collaboration. But as we look at the organization of our marriage, we have concluded that we have actually done a pretty good job at laboring together. When collaboration is poor in an organization, the system can look quite ugly. But when the collaboration is good, not only is the organization efficient, but its system can be so beautiful to behold that it approaches a kind of mystical glory.

ACCOUNTABILITY AND STRUCTURE

Interdependence does not necessarily mean that the collaborating individuals have different roles. Usually, however, it does; and, as described, Lily and I have had very different roles in the thirty-seven-year-old organization of our marriage. And whenever there are different roles in an organization, two important factors immediately come into play: accountability and structure.

I am able to depend upon Lily for most of the homemaking because she not only does it but does it well. And she can depend upon me for the moneymaking for the same reason. We play these roles well because we consider ourselves responsible for doing so. In other words, we hold ourselves and each other accountable. On the negative side, accountability implies that someone is subject to being judged. On the positive side, it implies that the accountable person is trusted. Were Lily to significantly fail at her homemaking role—were she no longer accountable—I could no longer trust her to fulfill that role and would have to step in to take over. Such a takeover would be natural and simple if her loss of accountability was due to a temporary physical illness. For instance, when she had a breast abscess following the birth of our third child, it was the most natural thing in the world for me to take over the care of that infant and our two other young children. Had that not been a temporary condition, however, it would have meant a major restructuring of our marriage.

So differing roles and accountabilities imply structure. Within a small (but not necessarily at all simple) organization like marriage, roles and structure may be relatively informal. But the larger and more complex an organization becomes, the more it is essential that the accountability structure be formalized. Written job descriptions (or, as they are now sometimes called, responsibility profiles) are now required, and we have entered the realm of formal organizations.

Virtually every business school has a mandatory course en-

titled something like "Organizational Theory." And a standard
and enormously thick textbook with the same title will lay out
the full range of possible organizational structures for the business executive to choose from. While this range can be vast and
complicated, the subject is actually almost outrageously simple.
It has but one underlying principle, which is "contingency theory." Contingency theory (which, like systems theory, is not a
theory but a fact) simply states that there is no one best type of
organization. The best structure for a particular organization
or endeavor is *contingent upon* the purpose of the collective, collaborative endeavor, as well as other factors.

Among these other factors is the nature of the people involved. A think-tank organization is not going to draw the same
kind of people as a more traditional manufacturing company.
Marketing departments are not going to draw the same kind of
people as sales departments. Nowhere could this be more evident than in the organization of marriage. In accordance with
contingency theory, there is no one best organization of a marriage. Although Lily's and my marriage has been organized according to what seem to be stereotypical roles, that organization,
as I have suggested, is actually the product of our very different
personalities and callings and is not in any way something that
we hold forth as a correct model. Goodness cannot be stereo-
typed. I could offer you stereotypical formulas for bad marriages; I cannot offer an organizational formula for a good
marriage. Each situation is different because of the very different partners involved.

Whenever there is accountability structured into a system,
be it as small as a marriage or as huge as a corporation, there is
also an authority structure. This doesn't mean that authority
can't be shared. For instance, the money Lily and I save is split
equally between us. Any important decision about the children
and about major investments or expenses we have always made
conjointly. Nonetheless, as individuals, we each have limited authority within our own domains.

A corporation president on the board of directors of FCE
has taught us the term "the authority of knowledge." Lily can

fulfill her homemaking role without any day-to-day oversight from me precisely because she has such authority. For example, a couple of weeks ago, when I was about to do a few local errands, Lily asked me if I would pick up a bunch of parsley at the store. Although the only parsley there was severely wilted, I bought a bunch rather than make a forty-mile round trip to purchase some that was fresh. Nonetheless, I presented this wilted stuff to Lily with some chagrin. She immediately said, "Oh, that's no problem; you just soak it in water." Within a day, that parsley looked as fresh as when it was picked. Lily knows the tricks of her trade.

Our marriage is in no way hierarchical. Although there is a system of accountability, neither of us is the overall boss. But there is no way in larger systems, such as businesses, that you can have a structure of accountability without a chain of command. What that chain of command will look like can vary considerably from business to business, contingent upon the nature of the business, but somewhere the buck has to stop. Because they have had unpleasant experiences with hierarchical authority systems, many people tend to distrust all structure. They need to guard against this tendency. There can be highly dysfunctional structures, but structure is by no means all bad. Most of it is good. Indeed, over the years I have come to learn that not only children but adults very much need structure.

Employees often suffer grievously from a lack of structure. I first realized this when, at the age of thirty-one, I was assigned to be the director of psychiatry at the U.S. Army Medical Center on Okinawa. In this position I was to manage a department of approximately forty people. Until that time I had never managed anybody. Nor had I ever received anything faintly resembling management training. Yet from the moment I took over the department, I was perfectly clear in my own mind about what my management style would be. I was going to be just as different from every authoritarian boss who had ever been in charge of me as I could possibly be.

I had no idea how to define consensus, but I was going to strive for it. Certainly my model was a highly consultative one.

Not only did I never make an administrative decision without consulting everyone involved, I did my very best to see that, within the constraints of professional competence, the people under me made their own decisions whenever possible about the matters that affected their own lives. Because ours was a medical, "professional," department, I felt we could ignore the matter of rank. I discouraged them from addressing me as Major Peck. Soon everyone was calling me Scotty. I was Mr. Nice Guy. And it worked. The mood was euphoric. Everybody spoke glowingly about what a good leader I was and how relieved they were to be free of that stupid old lieutenant colonel, their previous commander. The work ran smoothly. The department morale was superb.

After just about six months, however, things began to go sour. The change was almost imperceptible at first. The euphoria was gone. The men stopped talking about what a great place it was to work. "All right," I told myself, "the honeymoon's over. What else could you expect? Now it's work as usual, but nothing's wrong." But by the nine-month mark things began to get worse. While the work went on, petty bickering started. I wondered whether there might be a problem, but I could see nothing to account for it. Certainly it had nothing to do with me, for hadn't I shown myself to be a born leader? By the year mark, however, it was clear there was a problem. The bickering had escalated and work was beginning to suffer. Little things were being left undone.

At this point fate seemed to come to my rescue. A major new outpatient medical complex was in the final stages of construction, and the hospital commander told me that the clinic, the largest part of our department, would move there. Our current offices were cramped, cold, and gloomy. The new ones would be modern and airy, with views over the Pacific and wall-to-wall carpeting. Surely the morale would improve at the prospect of such a pleasant move.

It didn't. It got worse. As moving day approached the entire staff grew ever more irritable. They began to squabble with each other about who would get which office in the new building. The packing of files fell way behind schedule. It was now finally obvious that it was my responsibility to do something. But what? I announced to the staff that we were going to meet over in the new conference room for the entirety of the next morning. And that we would continue to meet in that way every morning—even though it meant working in the evenings—until we got to the bottom of the problem.

The two four-hour meetings we had were the stormiest I have ever attended. Everyone took potshots at me and at each other. Everyone was angry. Everyone had something to complain about. Yet all the complaints were picky, superficial, and seemingly unreasonable. It was unrelieved chaos. But toward the end of the second morning, one of the young enlisted men said, "I feel I don't know where I stand." I asked him if he would elaborate. He couldn't. He became inarticulate and the group continued with its random conflict. But the young man's words reverberated through my mind. Earlier that morning someone else had said, "Everything's vague around here." And the day before, another young man had voiced the complaint: "It's like we're at sea." I told the group I needed time to think, that they should get back to work, and that we would not have any more of these meetings for the foreseeable future.

We returned to the old building and I sat in my office, staring at the ceiling, my lunch on the desk beside me, uneaten. Was it possible the department needed more structure than I had provided? What kind of structure? A clearer sense of rank? What did they want me to do—boss them around like a bunch of children? That was totally against my nature. But then most of them *were* rather young, after all. Could it be that they wanted me to be some kind of father figure? Yet if I started ordering them around like an autocrat, wouldn't they hate me? I wanted to be Mr. Nice Guy. But, come to think of it, it was not my job to be popular; it was my job to run the best possible department I could. Maybe they needed a stronger kind of leadership from me.

I called the noncommissioned officer in charge of the department and asked him to bring me the plans for the new building as soon as possible. When he returned, we unrolled the floor plan for the psychiatry outpatient clinic on my desk. I pointed to the larger corner office. "That will be mine," I announced. Then, pausing just long enough for him to note each assignment, I proceeded along the blueprint through the smaller offices: "We'll put Captain Ames here, you here, Sergeant Ryan there, Lieutenant Hobson here, Private Cooperman there, Captain Marshall here, Sergeant Mosely here, Private Enowitch there," and so on down the map. "Now please go inform each of them of the office I've assigned him to."

You could practically hear the howls of dismay all across the island. But by evening morale had begun to improve, and the next day I watched it escalate. By the end of the week, it was back to where it had been at its best. They still called me Scotty, and my overall style of leadership continued to be relatively— although no longer rigidly—nonauthoritarian. But morale stayed high for the remaining year of my duty.

You could think of this as a success story. I did eventually acknowledge that there was a problem and that it was my responsibility. I finally took the correct steps to diagnose it and was able to readjust my behavior to meet the needs of the organization. Indeed, it was a dramatic example of how a system can be successfully changed by a simple intervention. However, it can also be regarded as a story of failure. For the fact of the matter is that the department—the organization and the individuals within it—*suffered* for over six months on account of my poor leadership. It was indelibly clear that we had a significant morale problem at least six months before I took corrective action. Why did I take so long?

One reason was my self-esteem. I simply did not want to believe that there was anything wrong with me or that my leadership was anything other than perfect. Fueling that conceit, however, were my needs: my need to offer the department a simplistically compassionate, nonauthoritarian style of supervision, and my need to receive back the constant affection and gratitude of my subordinates. Until that final day I never even stopped to ask whether my needs matched those of the organization. It almost required a revelation for me to realize that it was not necessarily my job—my role in the organization—to be popular.

It also never occurred to me that there was anything other than one best way to run any organization. I had never heard of contingency theory back then. My group consciousness was so limited that I gave no thought to how remarkably young the members of the department were, and hence no thought to the possibility that the department might require a different style of leadership than an organization whose personnel were more mature. We had all suffered needlessly for months because of a lack of structure.

Although people often don't realize it, structures can be flexible. A significant part of the work at FCE is to teach organizations, both large and small, how to "operate in community." When operating in community, the group does not have a rigid authority structure; authority and leadership are shared, as they must be to maximize communication. But we could not do this work if it meant that organizations had to abandon their hierarchical authority structure altogether. We can do it only because it is possible for an organization to operate in a hierarchical mode most of the time, dealing with its day-to-day operations, but to switch to a community mode in response to certain issues and problems (such as those of diversity and morale) and whenever group decision making is required.

As I noted in *The Road Less Traveled,* one characteristic of individual mental health is what I call flexible response systems. These are also a characteristic of organizational health. An organization that has two modes of operating at its command and can use one or the other, contingent upon the circumstances, is obviously going to be healthier than an organization that can function only in a single way.

BOUNDARIES AND VULNERABILITY

Wherever a structure of accountability and differing roles has been established, there you will find boundaries. Such boundaries are a two-edged sword. On the one hand, they are essential. If personnel in the sales department felt totally free to march into the marketing department and tell it how to market the product, the result would be chaos. On the other hand, if the boundaries of these two different departments are so rigid that there can be no communication between them, immobilization and inefficient competitiveness will be the result. One reason FCE is brought into corporations to build community is in order to soften departmental boundaries that have become so rigid that they prevent important communication and functional interdependence.

The choices of a major business executive about how to deal with such boundary issues are choices relatively few have to exercise. But every human being has to deal with boundary issues within the organization of his or her marriage, nuclear family, extended family, network of friendship, and employment. Each of us as individuals must make choices day in and day out in defining our boundaries within the framework of any organization.

Perhaps the easiest of such choices involve the degree to which you are going to respect other people's boundaries. What makes these decisions easier is that you will eventually be punished, one way or another, for failing to perceive such boundaries and act accordingly. These boundaries will vary from individual to individual and culture to culture. Psychologists, for instance, have discerned that there is a specific distance at which most people in a given culture feel comfortable communicating with their fellows. In the United States, that distance is relatively large, and seldom do we talk with a new acquaintance unless our faces are a good three feet distant from each other. In India, on the other hand, the norm may be more like one foot. The relationship between this concept of actual physical space and boundaries is recognized in our current psychological lingo by the expression "to give each other space."

Such space, of course, is much more complex than mere footage. A dozen years ago, for example, Lily was riding the

Staten Island Ferry with her mother, who was in the early stages of senility at the time. While they were sitting on the ferry, her mother spied a gray hair in Lily's fine black crown, and without permission to do so, suddenly reached over and yanked that hair out. Lily naturally felt violated. This was not, of course, the same level of violation as rape or robbery or murder, but the episode makes the point that in lesser ways we violate other people's boundaries all the time and cause their resentment whenever we do so.

Nonetheless, boundaries must be violated at certain times. Perhaps the most agonizing decisions we ever have to make concern when to intervene in the affairs of our children, our friends, and, as we get older, our parents. How do you know when to intervene in the life of an adolescent or young adult child, and when to trust the way that she is flowing? Or when to confront a friend who seems to have taken the wrong path? Or when to step in to insist that elderly parents get the care they obviously need and just as obviously don't want? You don't. There is no formula. All such decisions must be made out of the "agony of not knowing." We are confronted, once again, with the paradoxes of life and the fact that we are almost at one and the same time called to respect the boundaries of others and, upon occasion, to interfere in their lives no matter how much they might hate us for it.

In my experience, however, a greater problem than that of learning an awareness of others' boundaries, and when and how to respect them, is the problem of choosing and setting our own boundaries. When I was still in the practice of psychotherapy, it seemed to me that at least half my patients had what I came to call drawbridge problems. Sooner or later I would say to them, "All of us live in a castle. Around the castle, there is a moat, and over the moat there is a drawbridge which we can lower open or raise shut, depending upon our will." The problem was that my patients' drawbridges did not work very well. Either they were laid open all the time, so that virtually anyone and everyone could amble into their personal space, prowl around, stay as long as they liked, and do whatever harm they would—or else their drawbridges were raised shut and stuck so that nobody and nothing could penetrate their isolated solitude. Neither case was benign.

These patients lacked freedom and the flexible response systems that are such a dramatic characteristic of mental health. For instance, in *The Road Less Traveled,* I discussed a woman who would sleep with every man she dated, which left her feeling so degraded that she would then cease dating altogether. It was a veritable revelation for her to learn that there are some men you don't want to let in through your front door, some you might want to let in through your front door and into your living room but not into your bedroom, and some you might want to let into your bedroom. She had never considered that there might be—might need to be—at least three different ways to respond to different men in any given situation. Nor had she perceived that she had the power to make such discriminating choices, to draw a line to establish and protect her boundaries.

It is our choice when to lower our drawbridges and when to raise them. But this choice leads us into yet another complexity. If we keep our drawbridges open, people or issues may come into our lives and hurt us, not so much physically as emotionally. The response of many to this dilemma is to keep their physical drawbridges somewhat open, but their emotional drawbridges firmly closed. It is as if an executive had an "open door" policy, but nobody who came in through that door ever affected him. One of our ongoing problems in life is to constantly choose the degree to which we are going to allow ourselves to be emotionally affected by issues and other people. This is the dilemma of vulnerability.

The word "vulnerability" means the ability to be wounded. In choosing how vulnerable we are going to be as human beings, it is essential that we make the distinction between wounding as in being hurt and wounding as in being damaged. To help make that distinction in my lectures, on occasion I used to ask if there was anyone in the audience who was willing to volunteer for an unknown but painful experiment. Fortunately, some brave soul always was. I would ask the volunteer to come up on stage and I would pinch his or her upper arm quite sharply. Then I would stand back and ask, "Did that hurt you?" The volunteer would reply vigorously that it did. Then I would ask, "Did it damage you?" The volunteer would usually—and sometimes reluctantly—acknowledge that while she or he had experienced pain, no permanent damage had been sustained as a result.

Under almost all circumstances, it would be plain stupid to walk into a situation where you are likely to be permanently damaged. But it might be very smart to open yourself up—within limits—to situations in which you would be likely to experience some emotional pain, such as in taking a risk to enter a relationship that has the potential to lead to commitment. Again it is necessary to distinguish between the path of smart selfishness and the path of stupid selfishness. Stupid selfishness, you will remember, is trying to avoid all emotional, existential suffering, whereas smart selfishness is distinguishing between suffering that is neurotic, unnecessary, and unproductive, and suffering that is inherent in life and productive of learning.

So it is necessary for our own emotional health and learning that we retain the capacity to choose to be open to being a vulnerable person. It is also necessary for meaningful communication and organizational behavior. As I wrote in *What Return Can I Make?*

> What happens when one person takes the risk to say to another: I'm confused, I'm not sure where I am going; I'm feeling lost and lonely; I'm tired and frightened. Will you help me? The effect of such vulnerability is almost invariably disarming. "I'm lonely and tired too," others are likely to say and open their arms to us.
>
> But what happens if we try to maintain a "macho" image of having it altogether, of being the top dog, when we gird ourselves about with our psychological

defenses? We become unapproachable, and our
neighbors guard themselves in their defenses, and our
human relationships become no more meaningful or
productive than two empty tanks bumping against
each other in the night.

I am not advising anyone to be totally vulnerable, nor to be
vulnerable at all times. Nonetheless, if you choose to be a healing presence in the world, it will be necessary to choose
throughout your life to retain the capacity to be wounded to at
least some degree. A justifiably famous book by Henri Nouwen
is entitled *The Wounded Healer*. The message of that book, as its
title suggests, is that if we are to be effective healers we must allow ourselves, within limits, to be continually wounded, and
that, indeed, it is only out of our woundedness that we can heal
or be healed.

But again, there must be limits. A man by the name of John
Kiley once introduced me to a Zen Buddhist–like expression:
"to weep with one eye." Weeping with one eye does not mean
that the suffering of vulnerability should be halfhearted but
only that one should generally not be damaged by it. The expression points to the distinction between empathy and sympathy. Empathy, the capacity to feel and to some degree take on
another person's pain, is always a virtue. Sympathy, on the other
hand, is more like symbiosis, or a total identification with the
other person. I am not saying that all sympathy is bad, but if you
wallow in another person's depression to such an extent that
you become depressed yourself, you have not only taken on an
unnecessary burden but made yourself unlikely to be able to
help that person.

This distinction is, of course, extremely important for psychotherapists. The single greatest talent a psychotherapist can
possess is the capacity to be simultaneously both involved and
detached. This is what is meant by weeping with one eye. It is
not, however, a talent to be developed just by psychotherapists;
it is a capacity that must be developed by anyone who desires to
be a healing presence in the world.

POWER

In *The Road Less Traveled,* I drew the distinction between spiritual and political power. Political power is essentially the capacity to force or influence others to do what you want them to do. It is a function of the structure of organizations. Political power does not actually reside within the person himself but rather in the position he holds in a hierarchy or in the money he happens to have to create organizations to do what he wants to be done. Political power is always "temporal." One may have it for a while, but eventually it will always be wrested away, if not by replacement or mandatory retirement, then by old age or, ultimately, death from either natural causes or assassination.

Spiritual power, on the other hand, has little to do with organization or structure. It resides not in position or in money but in the person's being. It is the capacity to influence others, often by example, simply by virtue of the kind of person that one is. Those who are politically powerful usually do not possess much in the way of spiritual power. Conversely, the spiritually powerful are as likely to be found among the poor and disenfranchised.

I do not mean to imply that there can be no overlap between political and spiritual power. Executives are subject to the very same temptations that Jesus confronted in the desert. Unlike Jesus, they are likely to flunk the test. They are reflections of Lord Acton's famous maxim: "Power tends to corrupt and absolute power corrupts absolutely." Although that is usually true, it has been my good fortune to know a number of extremely powerful executives who were not corrupt; rather, they were exceptionally self-reflective people with extraordinary insight and concern for others. And they suffered deeply in their work. By necessity they wept with one eye, but they maintained their capacity for vulnerability.

No experience in my life was more painful than when FCE was hit by the recession and, in 1991, after running heavily in the red for two years, had to downsize. As part of the management of that organization, I had to participate in the painful decision to lay off eight very competent people. Such pain is one of the reasons why most executives become hardened and lose their capacity for vulnerability. Yet only those few able to retain their capacity for vulnerability are the truly great leaders. Once again, as I wrote in *The Road Less Traveled*, "Perhaps the best measure of a person's greatness is his or her capacity to suffer."

It is easy to overestimate the political power of executives. In a high-ranking executive position, their hands are often tied. But not with respect to this overlap of political and spiritual power. The greatest power a top executive has is the ability to determine the spirit of the organization. If his spirit is mean in some way, that meanness will pervade the entire organization. This was impressed upon me when I worked in the federal government in Washington from 1970 to 1972, during the Nixon administration. The spirit of "dirty tricks" was virtually everywhere. On the other hand, in those perhaps rare instances when a top executive is a deeply honest person, you will probably find an unusually honest organization.

While political power is generally attainable by only a relative few, spiritual power can be attained by most. Although to a considerable extent it is a gift from God, beginning with the creation of the individual soul, people can choose to neglect or cultivate their souls. When you make the choice for consciousness, learning, and growth, then you have also chosen the path of spiritual power, which resides in your being and not in your position.

Throughout the centuries, theologians, in considering the dichotomy between being and doing, have invariably come down in favor of being. In other words, who you are—what kind of person you are—is much more important than what you actually do. That is hard to grasp in our action-oriented culture. I cannot tell you the number of times I went to Lily at the end of a day of my psychiatric practice and said to her, "I really did something phenomenal with Tom today. I made a brilliant intervention. It was a beautiful maneuver." The problem was that Tom would then come back for his next session and act as if nothing had happened. I would ask him after a while what he thought about our previous session. "What about it?" Tom would ask. I would then remind him of the brilliant thing I had done or said, and Tom would scratch his head, commenting, "I vaguely remember something about that."

On the other hand, Tom might come in for a session and exclaim, "God, Dr. Peck, what you said last week has totally revolutionized my life." Then it would be my turn to scratch my head and ask what I had said or done that was so important. Tom would answer, "Don't you remember at the end of our last session, just as I was leaving the office, you said such and such? Thank you. Thank you." I didn't remember whatever it was I had said that was so healing. It wasn't anything that I had done but rather something that had just "flowed" out of my being.

As a psychotherapist I used to be very interested in Jesus' "zap" cures (although the scientist in me would have liked some good follow-up studies). They are not the norm in the practice of psychiatry. Indeed, in my whole career, I have had only one zap cure, which occurred in the context of community. It was at a five-day community-building workshop for almost four hundred people at a beautiful retreat center in North Carolina. By the end of the third day, the group as a whole had reached "community," but there were still a few stragglers who weren't there yet and might never be. On the morning of the fourth day, I was carrying two cups of coffee from the dining room back to my own room for my solitary prayer time when I spied a woman sitting on the parapet with a towel clutched to her head, in the most obvious distress. I stopped, not because I wanted to become involved but simply because I was curious.

"My God, you look miserable," I said. "What's the matter?"

The lady clutched her towel even tighter and mumbled in agony, "I've got a migraine."

"I'm sorry," I responded. "I hope it gets better." And I proceeded on my way.

But as I moved off, I heard the woman say, "I'm so angry. I'm so damn angry!"

Again, I stopped, not to try to heal her but out of curiosity once more. "Why are you so angry?"

"I'm so angry at those damn charismatic phonies," she replied. "You know, the ones who during the singing raise their hands up in the air and wiggle them about. They're just trying to pretend to be pious."

"I think you're right that many of them are probably trying to look pious," I commented, "but I think probably some of them are just having fun."

The lady looked at me with suddenly wide eyes. "Oh, my God, I've never had fun," she blurted.

"Well, I hope someday you do," I remarked, and left with my coffee, intent upon my prayer time.

At the end of the day it was reported to me that this woman no longer had a migraine. She had been able to reach community and had spent the entire afternoon telling other members of her group, "Dr. Peck healed me. I've never had fun. Dr. Peck healed me." That was my one "zap" cure. I think it was no accident that it occurred at a time when I wasn't even trying to heal.

Indeed, the best psychotherapists eventually learn, if they hang in there long enough, to stop *trying* to heal their patients. What they can realistically set their sights on is building the best possible relationship—or community—with their patients; within that relationship, healing will naturally occur without their having to "do" anything. I believe that the power to heal, a spiritual power, comes from God. It is a gift. And I believe it is the intent of the Giver that it should be used in such a manner as to ultimately give it away. In other words, the best reason to have any kind of power—spiritual or temporal—is to use it so as to empower others.

CULTURE

Culture may be defined as the interlocking system of norms and values, implicit or explicit, within an organization. Every organization, even a marriage, has its own culture. We speak of family cultures. The subject of culture in business is much written about. Of course, every society has its own culture, and even those not accustomed to thinking in terms of systems are aware that American culture is different from French culture, which is different from Japanese culture, and so forth.

One of the most influential books of this century was Ruth Benedict's *Patterns of Culture,* in which she described at length three dramatically different "primitive" cultures. In one of the three, the gender roles we know were completely reversed. The men were accountable for the homemaking and child rearing, while the women were accountable for business and all the important political decisions. In contrast, another of the cultures Benedict studied was even more patriarchal than that of the United States back in the eighteenth or nineteenth century.

The message of this powerful book was that no culture is better than any other. And while a member of any one of them would have been confused in entering another, each of the three seemingly worked well. Benedict's book put forth the concept of cultural relativism, whose underlying principle is what is considered good in one culture may be considered bad in another. In other words, ethics are totally relative to culture. Somewhat like situational ethics, cultural relativism holds that judgments cannot be made about any culture except from within it.

The concept of cultural relativism has done much to broaden our minds—minds that very much needed broadening. For instance, I remember with great clarity that at the age of nineteen I, with a group of other Americans, got off a cruise ship that had docked in Naples. At eleven o'clock that evening, our group strolled along the streets on the edge of the beautiful Bay of Naples, and strolling with us were swarms of Neapolitans of every age. It was not the infants or the adults who caught my compatriots' eyes, but all the children between the ages of two and twelve who were running about. "Why, they ought to be in bed!" they exclaimed. "What kind of people are these Italians that they keep their children up at eleven at night? That's a terrible way to treat children."

What my compatriots failed to realize or take into account is that the siesta was an inviolate part of Italian culture—at least back then, more than forty years ago. Everyone, adults and chil-

dren alike, went to sleep between two and five in the afternoon.
Businesses were closed, then reopened around five or six in the
evening; and people normally didn't start eating dinner until
nine. The children were not "up past their bedtime" or being
mistreated in any way. Had my compatriots been more familiar
with the concept of cultural relativism, they might not have
demonstrated the arrogant judgmentalism that so many American tourists are guilty of even today.

Sometimes, however, it can be inappropriate to withhold
judgment. In 1969 Lily and I went to India for a sight-seeing vacation. Among Americans who visit India, there seem to be two
different types. One type returns raving about India's beauty.
The other comes home horrified by their experience. We belonged to the horrified type. We were horrified not only by the
poverty and the filth but also by the incredible inefficiency.
Throughout our eleven days we saw things routinely being
done poorly that could just as easily have been done well. For
the first time in our lives it occurred to us that while tolerance
is often a virtue, there could be such a thing as an excess of tolerance. India seemed to suffer from a vice of tolerance. We saw
people blandly tolerating what seemed to us intolerable inefficiency.

It was all a bit of a mystery to us until our next-to-last day
there, when we were having breakfast. A waiter spilled a pitcher
of cream on the dining room floor, but instead of cleaning it
up, he vanished. Other waiters, then headwaiters, then man-
agers came and looked at the puddle of cream and proceeded
to walk through it, spreading footprints of cream throughout
the dining room. We were seeing an example of the genesis of
India's filth. But why? And at that moment it finally dawned on
us: it was not the job of waiters or anybody present to clean up
puddles of cream. It was the low-caste sweeper's job, and he
didn't come on duty until afternoon. From that incident, as we
thought about it, we realized that virtually every inefficiency we
had seen was a result of the caste system, which, although supposedly outlawed, was still so deeply embedded in Indian culture as to govern the lives of every one of its citizens. Cultural

relativism would insist that there is nothing inherently wrong with the caste system. I disagree. In my estimation, it is a serious cultural flaw, not only because of its inherent incivility but also because of its extraordinary inefficiency and its degradation of an entire society.

America's culture is not without its flaws, although they are perhaps not of the same magnitude as the flaw of the caste system. I could point to dozens of major flaws in the culture of this nation, but to my mind the greatest problem for the United States at this point in time is not the flaws of its culture but the fact that its culture is breaking down. Since the beginning of the 1960s, all our major cultural norms have come into serious question. I believe that this has been proper. But it has left us in a position where many of our citizens are increasingly unsure about how to behave. We have demolished many of the old, rigid cultural norms and are still in the process of doing so. The big question now is whether we will be able to develop new and more workable norms. I do not know the answer to that question. The future of our society seems increasingly obscure.

Norms are generally established or reestablished, upheld or overturned, by those in power in organizations, whether they are families or businesses. Earlier, I made the point that one of the greatest powers business executives have is, through their spirit, to create the spirit of the organizations of which they are in charge. The other great power is an analogous one. It is to create the culture of the organization. It is not easy for a new top executive to change the culture of a company, but insofar as it can be changed, the change will begin at the top. No one has more responsibility for the culture of an organization than those in the highest positions of authority.

This responsibility is often abdicated, not only by business leaders but also by family leaders. In this time of cultural breakdown, more and more parents are unsure about how to behave as parents. It often seems that they now look to their children to establish the family culture, as if they are reluctant to exercise the authority that is necessary to establish clear family values and norms. Parents should not be despots, but neither should children have the responsibility of creating the family culture. If they are given that responsibility, they will become either very confused or tyrannical. The power to create the spirit of an organization is more than analogous to the power to create its culture. They are inseparable. Ultimately, it is in the culture of an organization that its spirit becomes embodied.

DYSFUNCTION VERSUS CIVILITY

It has become very fashionable these days to use the term "dysfunctional" for organizations, whether they are businesses or families. Indeed, it is so fashionable that, like "community" and "civility," the word is rapidly descending into meaninglessness. When I was still giving lectures, I used to ask my audiences on occasion: "Will anyone here who was not brought up in a dysfunctional family please raise your hand?" Not a hand would be raised. All organizations, whether families or businesses, are dysfunctional. But some are more dysfunctional than others.

A number of years ago I was asked to consult with a large department of a huge federal agency because it was so obviously dysfunctional. There were many problems in that department, but the biggest one was very easy to spot as soon as I looked at the department's hierarchical organizational chart. The head of the department (a man I will call Peter) was a senior civil servant. And when I saw that two of his deputies were political appointees, I was astonished. In my own years of government service, I had never heard of a political appointee who reported to a civil servant. Political appointees always held the top management positions. Peter and these two deputies all attempted to assure me that this was not so out of the ordinary, and that there was nothing wrong with the system. But many things were obviously wrong, and finally I found another experienced civil servant near the top who was willing to be honest with me. "Of course," he said. "Peter has been layered." Apparently the political appointees at the head of the agency so distrusted Peter that they had put two of their picks within his department to serve as spies and to undercut his authority whenever they saw fit.

I could discern no reason for Peter to be distrusted. Indeed, he was an unusually mature and competent man. What I discovered in this agency, rather, was an entire culture of distrust so severe that it could properly be termed a culture of paranoia. Since this culture had been generated at the top, by the highest-ranking political appointees—to whom I had no access—all my recommendations were disregarded, and the organization remained as dysfunctional after I departed as it had been when I came in.

"Dysfunctional" and "culture of paranoia" are abstract terms. Less abstract was the fact that a top-notch executive was rendered totally impotent and the time of two other executives was being utterly wasted in spying on him. This meant several hundred thousand taxpayer dollars down the drain. But more than that, the morale of the entire thousand-employee department was a shambles and its performance understandably poor as a result. The actual cost to the taxpayers, within that department alone, was in the millions. What it was for the entire agency, God only knows.

There are two morals to this story. If, as I have said, the most civil use of power is to give it away, then in this instance not only were those in the highest positions of power not giving it away, they were taking it away. The story's first moral is that such incivility is not cost-effective. To the contrary, it is viciously expensive and wasteful. The other moral is that it is extremely difficult to change a culture, no matter how uncivil and unproductive or dysfunctional it may be. We have seen that one tenet of systems theory is that whenever you change a part of the system, all the other parts have to change. Now we have arrived at another tenet: systems inherently resist change. They resist healing. The plain fact of the matter is that most organizations, despite the blatancy of their dysfunction and despite its cost-ineffectiveness, would rather remain dysfunctional than grow toward greater civility. Why is this so? Reflect on the complexity of the definition of civility, namely, that it is "consciously motivated organizational behavior that is ethical in submission to a higher power."

Civility does not come naturally. It takes consciousness and action to achieve. Incivility comes more naturally to us human beings, and because of laziness it is simply easier to be uncivil.

If that seems to be a pessimistic view, there is still room for optimism. It may be derived from my statement that all organizations are dysfunctional. What this means for you as heads of families and businesses is that you cannot do it perfectly. Things will never come out neat and tidy. But don't feel bad about ordinary failure. It is inherent in the complexity of the roles of parents and executives. Indeed, if you expect perfection, you may make things even worse. You are entitled to feel good about getting along as well as you can in this world. Despite the odds against doing things perfectly, you do the best you can. To be as civil as possible in these complex and demanding roles is the path of smart selfishness, even though it requires a great deal of psychospiritual exertion. Why bother, then, since incivility comes more easily than civility? The answer to that question, as I suggested in *A World Waiting to Be Born,* is that while incivility is easier, the creation of a relatively civil organization or culture is in the long run more cost-effective. It is also the route to creating something that is more healing and alive.

CHAPTER 6

Choices About Society

❉

WE HAVE MANY CHOICES TO MAKE as we play varying roles and face many tasks, responsibilities, and challenges in our families, work lives, and group affiliations. But our lives become even more complex when we look beyond our nuclear families and the particular organizations to which we belong or have contact with on a regular basis. Whether we are children, heads of families, students, or employees, we also belong to an even larger organization that we call society. We coexist as a collective of human beings stretching beyond the boundaries of different towns and cities, counties and states, regions and nations. We all are inevitably citizens of the world. And as members of this social order, we confront profound choices about what citizenship means.

A secular psychiatrist and old friend, who was one of the very first readers of *The Road Less Traveled,* wrote this to me about the book: "What I get from it is that there's no such thing as a free lunch." He was right in a certain respect. The support and nurturance we get from society do not come free. Some degree of responsibility beyond simply paying taxes accompanies the benefits of citizenship. But whether we're interested in being good citizens or not is another matter. If we have the energy and will to do so, we face the choice of how to be the best citizens we can be. We also have the option of copping out, of not caring, of avoiding all responsibility for the well-being of society. As is the case with any choice we make in life, which of these routes we take yields its own consequences.

If we more closely examine the complexities of citizenship and look at society realistically, inevitably we will be confronted by a number of paradoxes. Whenever you take into consideration the multiple dimensions of any situation, and if no pieces of reality are missing from the picture, you probably will be looking at a paradox. In other words, virtually all truth is paradoxical, and nowhere is this more evident than in the task of making our choices about society.

THE PARADOX OF GOOD AND EVIL

In one of his letters, the Apostle Paul wrote that this human society was ruled by "principalities and powers," his phrase for "the demonic." Whether we interpret the demonic as some external force or simply our human nature and "original sin," the notion that the devil is the ruler of this world has an enormous amount of truth to it. Given the prevalence of war, genocide, poverty, starvation, gross inequality in the distribution of wealth, racism and sexism, despair and hopelessness, drug abuse, white-collar crime in our institutions, violent crime on our streets, and child and spousal abuse in our homes, evil seems to be the order of the day.

It certainly looks that way most of the time—for the forces of evil are real and varied. Some religions claim that the factors perpetuating evil originate in human sin. Psychological explanations often point to the lack of individual and group consciousness. Many social commentators view the chaos in our culture, including a breakdown in family values and the emphasis on materialism and comfort at all costs, as the primary determinants of evil. The media are often blamed for their wicked influence. Let's look at each of these factors briefly to flesh out the paradoxical reality of good and evil that has a significant impact on our choices about society.

The word "Satan" originally meant adversary. In Christian

theology, Satan is also called the devil. We are being adversarial when we speak of "playing devil's advocate." Satan or the devil, mythologically, was originally a "good" angel who was cast out of heaven for disobedience and pride, and became the personification of evil and the adversary of man. A certain amount of adversarialism is good for our thinking and growth. Its flippant practice, however, may hide a hint of the sinister. Any adversarial position which is persistently contrary and opposed to human growth—and directly opposite to that which is godly—contains the harsh ingredients for the perpetuation of evil.

Among those ingredients may be human nature itself. I have little idea what role the devil plays in this world, but as I made quite clear in *People of the Lie*, given the dynamics of original sin, most people don't need the devil to recruit them to evil; they are quite capable of recruiting themselves. In *The Road Less Traveled*, I suggested that laziness might be the essence of what theologians call original sin. By laziness I do not so much mean physical lethargy as mental, emotional, or spiritual inertia. Original sin also includes our tendencies toward narcissism, fear, and pride. In combination, these human weaknesses not only contribute to evil but prevent people from acknowledging their Shadow. Out of touch with their own sins, those who lack the humility to see their weaknesses are the most capable of contributing to evil either knowingly or unknowingly. Wars tend to be started by individuals or groups lacking consciousness and devoid of integrity and wholeness. I wrote of this in *People of the Lie*. Using My Lai as a case study, I demonstrated how evil at an institutional and group level occurs when there is a fragmentation of consciousness—and conscience.

In *Further Along the Road Less Traveled* and *The Different Drum*, I wrote of the evil of compartmentalization. I described the time when I was working in Washington in 1970–72 and used to wander the halls of the Pentagon talking to people about the Vietnam War. They would say, "Well, Dr. Peck, we understand your concerns. Yes, we do. But you see, we're the ordnance branch here and we are only responsible for seeing to it that the napalm is manufactured and sent to Vietnam on time.

We really don't have anything to do with the war. The war is the responsibility of the policy branch. Go down the hall and talk to the people in policy."

So I would go down the hall and talk to the people in policy, and they would say, "Well, Dr. Peck, we understand your concerns. Yes, we do. But here in the policy branch, we simply execute policy, we don't really make policy. Policy is made at the White House." Thus, it appeared that the entire Pentagon had absolutely nothing to do with the Vietnam War.

This same kind of compartmentalization can happen in any large organization. It can happen in businesses and in other areas of government; it can happen in hospitals and universities; it can happen in churches. When any institution becomes large and compartmentalized, the conscience of that institution will often become so fragmented and diluted as to be virtually nonexistent, and the organization has the potential to become inherently evil.

The word "diabolic" is derived from the Greek *diaballein,* meaning to throw apart, fragment, or compartmentalize. Among the most diabolic aspects of the fragmentation of our collective consciousness are those things so common that they have become institutionalized. Where institutionalized evils such as racism, sexism, ageism, and homophobia exist, for example, we find the dual mechanisms of oppression and dehumanization. When certain segments of humanity are systemically regarded as disposable or irrelevant or are treated with derision, dire consequences for the integrity of the entire society are inevitable.

To do battle with institutionalized societal evils, we need remember that what we call good must be good for most people, most of the time, and not merely a matter of "Is it good for me?" This variant of the Golden Rule means that when we employ double standards condoning our own behavior but judging others harshly for the same breach or something lesser, we are in danger. For example, those who live in the nation's inner cities receive substantially longer prison terms than others for relatively minor crimes, like possession of small amounts of crack cocaine, according to statistics from the National Sentencing Project based in Washington, D.C. Suburban powder-cocaine users and middle- to upper-class users are rarely sentenced to prison for first offenses. They are more likely to get probation and be encouraged to receive treatment for their drug problems.

Often, the forces of evil are more subtle than blatant. Almost as horrific as evil itself is the denial of it, as in the case of those who go through life wearing rose-colored glasses. Indeed, the denial of evil can in some ways perpetuate evil itself. In *In Search of Stones,* I wrote about this tendency among a number of financially well-off people whose money insulates them in their world of opulence. They fail to actually see the poverty that exists so close to them, and thereby they avoid accepting any responsibility they may have for the problem. Many ride a train to work every day from their suburban havens to downtown New York City, never looking up from their newspapers as they pass the most impoverished sections of Harlem. The slums are rendered invisible and so, too, are those enmeshed in them.

On the other hand, there are those who take a cynical view of the world and seem to believe that evil lurks behind everything. Their vision is gloom-and-doom, even in the midst of innocence and beauty. They look for the worst in everything, never noticing that which is positive and life-affirming. When despair and cynicism are like demons to us, we risk perpetuating evil as well. Although we can't avoid our demons, we can choose not to welcome or to ally ourselves with them. To be healthy, we must personally do battle with them.

A despairing vision of society can become even more clouded by media influences. Through their focus on the drama of evil, the media perpetuate an unbalanced view of reality. When a credit card is stolen, it becomes a statistic, and the headlines bombard us with crime reports. But we rarely hear any statistics about credit cards left behind on counters and quietly returned (as is almost always the case). The media's general exclusion of good news leaves the public with the impression that evil truly rules the day. If "no news is good news," it would also appear that "good news is no news." We do not hear or read about the goodness that occurs routinely—on a daily basis—in the world.

It is easy to despair, to simply throw one's hands up and believe that, since the world is so evil, nothing and no one can make a difference. But if we are to look at our society realistically, we will recognize the powerful influences of both good and evil forces. The world is not all beautiful. Neither is it all bad. Thus, the most critical challenge we face is developing the ability to gain and maintain a balanced perspective. And from this perspective, there is cause for optimism, not despair.

A story told to me by my late father helps make the point. It is the story of an Oriental sage who, back in the 1950s, was interviewed by a reporter and asked whether he was an optimist or a pessimist.

"I'm an optimist, of course," the sage replied.

"But how can you be an optimist with all the problems in the world—overpopulation, cultural breakdown, war, crime, and corruption?" the reporter asked.

"Oh, I'm not an optimist about this century," the sage explained. "But I am profoundly optimistic about the next century."

Given the reality of the world today, my response would be along the same lines. I'm not an optimist about the twentieth century, but I am profoundly optimistic about the twenty-first century—if we can arrive there.

Keeping a balanced perspective will be essential. Just as it is necessary to develop one's consciousness in order to acknowledge the reality of evil and our own potential for sin and for contributing to evil, we also need to become increasingly conscious to identify and relish what is good and beautiful in this life. If we see the world as inherently evil, there is no reason to believe it can improve. But if we see that the forces for good in the world are, at the very least, on an equal footing with the forces for ill, there is great hope for the future.

In many ways, the world is changing for the better. As I wrote in *The Road Less Traveled,* over one hundred years ago child abuse was not only rampant in the United States but blandly overlooked. Back then, a parent could beat a child severely and commit no crime. Some two hundred years ago, many children, even those as young as seven, were forced to work in factories and mines practically all day. Some four hundred years ago, children weren't generally considered worthy of attention and respect as individuals with their own needs and rights in our society. But child protection efforts have improved tremendously in our century. We have established hotlines for reporting cases of child exploitation; investigations are routine and sometimes extensive in cases of suspected child abuse and neglect. Unless you can't see the forest for the trees, there's no denying that society has made vast improvements in protecting the interests and well-being of its youngest and most vulnerable citizens.

There is also profound proof of change for the better on a world level. Consider the issue of human rights. Governments are regularly monitored to determine how they treat their citizens, and some have suffered economic sanctions in response to major human rights violations, as was the case with the apartheid system in South Africa. In previous centuries, the notion of war crimes was nonexistent. Captured women and children were routinely raped and enslaved while the disembowelment of male prisoners of war was ritualistic behavior. Wars and war crimes persist, but recently we have begun to raise the issue of why humans so frequently go to great lengths to kill one another when a most decent peace would be quite feasible if we simply worked at it a little bit. We have established tribunals to try to punish those guilty of war crimes. We also now debate whether a war should be considered just or unjust and unnecessary. That we even raise these issues is an indication of how much positive change is emerging in this society and throughout the world.

It can be argued that one reason many view evil as more prevalent than ever is a result of the fact that our standards have improved. In any case, the evidence suggests that society is evolving for the better over the long haul. That would be im-

possible if society were wholly evil. The truth is that both good
and evil coexist as forces in this world; they always have and always will. I recognized that fact long ago. But I find it actually
easier to pinpoint with greater clarity why evil exists and
whence it comes than to ascertain the origins of goodness in
this world without reference to God. What St. Paul called "the
mystery of iniquity" is ultimately less mysterious than the mystery of human goodness.

While the prevailing Judeo-Christian view is that this is a
good world somehow contaminated by evil, as a mostly middle-
of-the-road Christian I prefer the view that this is a naturally evil
world somehow contaminated by goodness. We can look at children, for example, and rejoice in their innocence and spontaneity. But the fact is that we are all born liars, cheats, thieves,
and manipulators. So it's hardly remarkable that many of us
grow up to be adult liars, cheats, thieves, and manipulators.
What's harder to explain is why so many people grow up to be
good and honest. While capable of evil, in reality human beings
overall are often better than might be expected.

In my experience with the community-building workshops
sponsored by FCE, I've been immensely impressed by what I've
come to call "the routine heroism of human beings." It is also
common to discover how people in tragic circumstances such
as the Oklahoma City bombing, or in other crisis situations, rise
to the occasion. There is abundant evidence of how people can
be incredibly good when they are pulling together. Still, many
tend to take goodness for granted. There is a lesson for us all in
these words of wisdom, uttered by some anonymous soul: "A life
of all ease and comfort may not be as wonderful as we think it
would be. Only through sickness do we gain greater appreciation for good health. Through hunger we are taught to value
food. And knowing evil helps us to appreciate what is good."

If the coexistence of good and evil is paradoxical, we must
embrace that paradox so that we can learn to live our lives with
integrity. The crux of integrity is wholeness. And through wholeness as human beings we can practice the paradox of liberation
and celebration. Liberation theology proclaims that Christians

are called to play an active role in doing battle with the systemic sins and evils of society—called to take responsibility for liberating people from the burdens of poverty and oppression. Celebration theology has historically encouraged a focus on and celebration of the goodness and beauty found in the world.

In his book *Christian Wholeness,* Tom Langford probes the many paradoxes that Christians must embrace in order to be realistic and whole people, among which the paradox of celebration and liberation is but one. As Langford points out, people who focus exclusively on liberation become fanatic and glum, while those who focus only on celebration will be frothy, superficial, and glib. Once again, we are called to integration. Striving for wholeness makes it necessary for us to continually acknowledge and do battle with the forces of evil. At the same time, we must remain conscious of and deeply grateful for the forces of good.

In the battle between good and evil, we must be open to struggling throughout our lives. While there is reason to be pessimistic, there also is strong reason to believe that each of us can have some impact, however minuscule it may seem, on whether the world tilts toward change for good or ill. In a remark attributed to Edmund Burke, we have the basis for determining which of the two forces will ultimately win the day: "The only thing necessary for the triumph of evil is for good men [and women, I must add] to do nothing."

THE PARADOX OF HUMAN NATURE

The paradox of good and evil is essentially inherent in human nature. I have already spoken about "original sin." To balance out the paradox, I need to talk about what Matthew Fox has called "original blessing." It is, to put it quite simply, our capacity to change. If, as I have said, we are all born liars, cheats, thieves, and manipulators, to behave otherwise as adults would seem to be contrary to human nature. But we have the ability to alter human nature—if we choose to do so.

Whenever someone is bold enough to ask me, "Dr. Peck, what is human nature?" my first answer is likely to be "Human nature is to go to the bathroom in your pants."

That, after all, is the way each of us started out: doing what came naturally, letting go whenever we felt like it. But then what happened to us, when we were about two, is that our mothers (or fathers) began telling us, "You're a really nice kid and I like you a lot, but I'd sort of appreciate it if you'd clean up your act." Now, this request initially makes no sense whatsoever to the child. What makes sense is to let go when the urge hits, and the results always seem interesting. To the child, keeping a tight fanny and somehow getting to the toilet just in time to see this interesting stuff flushed away is totally unnatural.

But if there is a good relationship between the child and the parent, and if the parent is not too impatient or overcontrolling (and unfortunately, these favorable conditions are often not met, which is the major reason that we psychiatrists are so interested in toilet training), then something quite wonderful happens. The child says to himself: "You know, Mommy's a nice old gal, and she's been awfully good to me these last couple of years. I'd like to pay her back in some way, give her a present of some kind. But I'm just a puny, helpless little two-year-old. What present could I possibly be able to give her that she might want or need—except this one crazy thing?"

So what happens then is that as a gift of love to the mother, the child begins to do the profoundly unnatural: to hold that fanny tight and make it to the toilet on time. And by the time that same child is four or five, it has come to feel profoundly natural to go to the bathroom in the toilet. When, on the other hand, in a moment of stress or fatigue, he forgets and has an "accident," the child feels very unnatural about the whole messy business. What has occurred, in the space of two or three short years, is that out of love, the child has succeeded in changing his nature.

This capacity we have been given to change—this original blessing, the ability to transform ourselves—is so extraordinary that at other times when I am asked, "What is human nature?" I facetiously respond that there is no such thing. For what distinguishes us humans most from the other creatures is not our opposable thumb or our magnificent larynx or our huge cerebral cortex; it is our relative lack of instincts, those inherited, preformed patterns of behavior that, as far as we can ascertain, give the other creatures a much more fixed and predetermined nature than we have as humans. In other words, human beings are endowed with access to a much wider range of options—socially, psychologically, and physically—that give us flexibility in responding and handling a variety of circumstances and situations.

Much of my life I have been involved in peacemaking activities. Those who believe that a world of peace is an impossibility generally refer to themselves as realists. They have referred to me as an idealist—or, more frequently, as an empty-headed idealist or a fuzzy-headed idealist. And they have been right to a certain extent—not, I hope, about the empty- or fuzzy-headedness, but about the idealism. I would define an idealist as one who believes in the capacity for transformation of human nature. I am not, however, a romantic. I would define a romantic as one who not only believes in the capacity for transformation of human nature but also believes it ought to be easy. Romantics gravitate to simplistic formulas such as "Love conquers all." In my work as a psychiatrist it gradually became clear to me that many would not change and grow despite all the love in the world. Changing human nature isn't easy. But it is possible.

There are profound reasons why it isn't easy. What we call personality can best be defined as a *consistent* pattern of organization of psychic elements—a combination of thinking and behavior. "Consistent" is the key word in this definition. There is a consistency to the personality of individuals—and to the "personality" of cultures or nations as well—a consistency that has both a dark side and a light side, a good and a bad.

For instance, when I was still in practice and new patients came to see me, they would be likely to find me dressed in an open-collared shirt, a comfortable sweater, and perhaps even slippers. If they came back to see me a second time and found me in a tie and business suit, ready to leave for a speaking engagement, that would probably be all right. If they were to come back a third time, however, and found me in a long, flowing blue robe, wearing jewelry and blowing a joint, chances are they wouldn't come back to see me a fourth time. One of the reasons that many did keep returning for my services was that I was pretty much the same old Scotty every time they came. There was a consistency in my personality that allowed them to know where they stood. It gave them something to "hang their hats on." We need a certain amount of consistency—a degree of predictability—in our personalities so that we can function effectively in the world as trustworthy human beings.

The dark side of that consistency, however, is what we psychotherapists call resistance. The personality—whether that of an individual or a nation—inherently resists change. Change is threatening, even when it may be for the better. Most patients come to psychotherapy asking to change one way or another. But from the moment therapy begins, they start acting as if change were the last thing that they want to do, and they will often fight against it tooth and nail. Psychotherapy, designed to liberate, shines the light of truth upon our selves. The adage "The truth will set you free, but first it will make you damn mad" reflects the resistance of our human nature to change. It is clearly not easy for us to change. But it is possible—and that is our glory as human beings.

Our natural resistance to change—a result of our laziness, fear, or narcissism—is what is meant, I believe, by "original sin." At the very same time, the most distinguishing feature of our human nature—our "original blessing"—is our capacity to change if we so desire. Given free will, it is our individual choice whether to give in to our original sin, resist change, stagnate, and even deteriorate, or to work on our individual as well as societal transformation. It would be pointless to work for societal betterment if people could not change. Yet people are free not to change. This conflict between the inertia of not changing and the effort of changing was summed up by a very early Christian theologian, Origen, who said, "The Spirit stands for progress, and evil, by definition then, is that which refuses progress."

THE PARADOX OF ENTITLEMENT

I have already explored an aspect of "criminal thinking" known as the psychology of entitlement. Many people—whether they are rich or poor—tend to believe they are entitled to something for nothing, or to behave as if the world owes them rather than the other way around. Some feel entitled on the basis of a superiority complex, while for others the sense of entitlement arises from an inferiority complex. The latter seem to feel they have no responsibility for their own lot in life. The former believe they are due all their "success," even at the expense of others, whom they see as less deserving than they, often for irrelevant and insignificant reasons.

There are numerous reasons behind this seemingly pervasive attitude of entitlement. In *In Search of Stones,* I cite one such particularly American reason. It is the notion put forth by the Declaration of Independence: "We hold these truths to be self-evident, that all men are created equal, that they are endowed by their Creator with certain unalienable Rights, that among these are Life, Liberty and the pursuit of Happiness." I believe these words are, paradoxically, perhaps the most profound and the silliest words ever written. They constitute a magnificent and holy vision that accurately captures the essence of the human condition. At the same time, they are horribly misleading.

We are all equal in the sight of God. Beyond that, however, we are utterly unequal. We have different gifts and liabilities, different genes, different languages and cultures, different values and styles of thinking, different personal histories, different levels of competence, and on and on. Indeed, humanity might be properly labeled the unequal species. What most distinguishes us from all the other creatures is our extraordinary diversity and the variability of our behavior. Equal? In the moral sphere alone we range from the demonic to the gloriously angelic.

The false notion of our equality propels us into the pretense of pseudocommunity—the notion that everyone is the same—and when the pretense fails, as it must if we act with any intimacy or authenticity, it propels us to attempt to achieve equality by force: the force of gentle persuasion followed by less and less gentle persuasion. We totally misinterpret our task. Society's task is not to establish equality. It is to develop systems that deal humanely with our inequality—systems that, within reason, celebrate and encourage diversity.

The concept of human rights is central to the development of such systems; I wholeheartedly applaud the Bill of Rights appended to the U.S. Constitution and, generally, its interpretation by the courts. I am much more dubious, however, about the sweeping rights claimed by the Declaration of Independence: the rights to life, liberty, and the pursuit of happiness. As I approach serious old age, for instance, I am increasingly dubious about my right to life in certain respects. As an author and teacher, I must question my liberty to lie or even subtly distort. As a psychiatrist and theologian, knowing happiness to be either a side effect of some deeper pursuit or else the result of self-delusion, I'm not sure how worthy a pursuit happiness is. My still larger problem is with the aggregate of these rights. Add the rights of life, liberty, and the pursuit of happiness together and it sounds as if we have a right to peace—as if we are entitled to peace.

Again, this presents a paradox. One side of the paradox is that peace is a truly proper human aspiration. There is a difference between lethal and nonlethal conflict, however. We need the latter. If managed properly it actually tends to promote human dignity. Despite its supposed glories, war generally destroys our dignity. If we define peace as the absence of outright war, it is indeed noble to aspire to it, and we cannot aspire to something we feel we don't deserve. In this sense we should regard peace as a right. The other side of the paradox is that we have no right to deserve peace without working for it. All that I have ever said about community, and everything we know about peace, indicates that we have no reason whatsoever to expect it effortlessly, or to expect that once we have, through sacrifice, won peace, it will stay around for long without our having to lift a finger again.

Perhaps no pitfall is more dangerous than the assumption that we are entitled to peace. One way this notion of entitlement to peace works itself out is the assumption of vast numbers of Americans that all conflicts can be peacefully resolved. That is naive. Yet many others operate out of the opposite assumption, that no conflict can be resolved except through force—through violence or the threat of it. This assumption is cynical and self-fulfilling. The paradoxical reality at this point in human evolution is that some wars are unavoidable or "just," and some are unjust, unnecessary, and waged at horrifying cost out of sheer laziness and stupidity.

Although I've been speaking of peace between people, the same paradoxical principles hold true for achieving that much-yearned-for condition called inner peace. Although we have the right to desire it, we are no more entitled to inner peace than to outer peace. Yet many protest indignantly when life itself interrupts the happiness or serenity they have come to see as an entitlement. Moreover, in order to possess inner peace we are frequently required to first be willing to forsake it. Only those who can constantly lie to themselves without qualms have unqualified peace of mind. But if we do not want to be self-brain-damaged in this manner, we need to remember that there is something far more important than inner peace: integrity. Integrity requires, among other things, the willingness to endure discomfort for the sake of truth.

To remember this, it helps me to think about Jesus, who so often felt frustrated, angry, frightened, lonely, sad, and depressed—a man who clearly desired popularity but would not sell out for it and who taught us that life is something more than a popularity contest; a man who did not seem to have much "inner peace" as the world is accustomed to imagining it to be, yet who has been called the Prince of Peace. We must be

aware that there is a false kind of peace of mind that derives
from being out of touch with ourselves. True inner peace requires us to be intimate with every facet of ourselves—to be not
only invested in our rights but also concerned about our responsibilities.

THE PARADOX OF RESPONSIBILITY

As citizens, we are affected by a variety of issues at the local,
state, and national levels. Depending on the impact of these issues on our daily lives and the lives of others, different roles and
responsibilities may be required of us. Some attempt to meet
this challenge—to make a difference—by diligently voting in
every local and national election. Others choose the route of
participating in community organizations' efforts to help those
in need. Still others make financial contributions to support
causes of interest and concern to them. But many resist taking
any kind of responsibility. They find it easier instead to look to
others to be the messiahs to solve all the world's problems.
Rather than take any active role in gaining and maintaining certain rights, they feel no responsibility for making clear choices
about the quality of their citizenship. They may be able to claim
they are doing no harm to society, but the saying (attributed to
Eldridge Cleaver, during the 1960s) is true: "If you are not part
of the solution, then you are part of the problem."

The paradox is that we are responsible for everything and
at the same time we cannot be responsible for everything. The
answer to this—and to all paradoxes—is not to run with only
one side of the equation but to embrace both sides of the truth.
The writer William Faulkner, in a speech made when his daughter Jill graduated from high school, said: "Never be afraid to
raise your voice for honesty and truth and compassion against
injustice and lying and greed. If people all over the world, in
thousands of rooms like this one, would do this, it would change
the earth."

An unknown seamstress at a Montgomery, Alabama, department store in 1955, Rosa Parks helped change our nation when her refusal to yield her bus seat to a white man triggered a bus boycott that lasted 381 days. Her feet tired, and her dignity repeatedly tested, this forty-two-year-old black woman was arrested and subsequently fired from her job. Her simple action—and subsequent actions on the parts of many others—spurred a movement that led to tremendous legal reform in this country.

Not everyone can have the impact of a Rosa Parks, but we each can take a stand in the struggle against all kinds of evil in our world. Indeed, the battle against evil begins at home. We must deal with ourselves and our families first, and work to create healthier communication and interactions. "Think globally, act locally" is a good guideline.

Given geographical and other limitations that the average citizen faces, acting locally may be the only viable way to make a difference. But that does not mean our thinking must be restricted to that which is close to home. We always have the option to think globally on many issues. I can, if I choose to, be concerned only about the cost of medical care in the United States, simply because it affects me. But since I am a citizen of the world, I cannot close my eyes to events in the rest of the world. I have a responsibility to think about the civil wars and the genocide and other war crimes now rampant in Rwanda, Yugoslavia, and other parts of the world. Still, I have not taken the time to study these places as deeply as I studied the Vietnam War. With various demands already in my life, my plate is already too full. No one can study everything or take action and responsibility for everything without ultimately setting himself up for residence in a mental institution.

Yet it is not always enough to be concerned only with matters that directly affect ourselves. Beyond our own rights and standing up for our personhood, we need sometimes to be willing to take a stand on behalf of others, even when there seems no direct benefit to ourselves. Sometimes we must be willing to do so at our own risk. The responsibility for discerning when to go out on a limb is a choice that each individual must make, depending on what he or she is willing to give up or lose for the sake of standing for something.

There are times when we are truly in a bind about exactly where to draw lines of responsibility. In such cases, we need to do the best we can and then simply concede the rest to uncertainty. We will not always know for sure whether we could have done more—whether we should have spoken up when we heard a racial slur or intervened when we heard a neighbor verbally abusing his wife. In the face of complex and overwhelming social responsibilities, we must remember that if we become gripped by despair and burnout, we will be useless not only to ourselves but also to others.

I am reminded of an FCE Community Building Workshop during which a white male member of the group sent a note to a black woman who was speaking of the sense of agonizing responsibility she felt for promoting a positive image of her race. It was as if she had taken the weight of the entire world on her shoulders. The note read: "Do not feel totally, personally, irrevocably responsible for everything. That's my job." The kicker is that the note was signed "God." In other words, there are times in our lives—and in the world at large—when the most appropriate thing to do may be to temporarily, as the Alcoholics Anonymous saying goes, "let go and let God."

While we all can decide to do something to help our immediate families and communities, I cannot tell anybody specifically what it is he or she should do. Since we cannot be involved in everything, we must be selective about our level of action. For this we must discern our calling. And how God calls one person will not be the way He or She calls another. I don't consider any calling more noble than that of working with the poor. Yet it has become clear to me over many years that, much as I wanted to be noble, I do not seem to have a calling to do hands-on work with the poor.

Never was this made more clear to me than a decade ago when Lily and I were asked to do a week of volunteer work with the Church of the Savior in Washington, D.C., part of whose ministry was directed to the people in power in our federal government. During that week, we hoped that we might have the opportunity to meet briefly with Gordon Cosby, the dynamic founder of the church, whose primary ministry was to the inner-city poor of Washington. Our last day there began with a meeting at the World Bank at seven-thirty in the morning; there followed numerous appointments with various U.S. representatives and senators, a meeting with the organizers of prayer breakfasts, and many additional appointments with congress-people in the afternoon. By six o'clock that evening, we were utterly strung out and exhausted. Then we were informed that we could meet Cosby at one of the church's ghetto centers. Lily and I arrived for the meeting and were ushered downstairs to a basement room jammed with several hundred homeless people who were eating off tin trays while a rock band played on a tiny stage. The noise was deafening. Cosby hospitably suggested that we grab a tin tray of food and sit down beside him. I asked if we could talk someplace quiet, outside the dining hall. He obliged. When we finally met for a few minutes in a quiet room, it was a personal moment of crisis for me. "No one could admire the work that you are doing more than I, Gordon," I said, "precisely because I myself am not up to it. I don't seem to be called to it. I wish I had your calling, but I don't."

This doesn't mean I haven't been involved in other ways working on behalf of the poor and the homeless. The Foundation for Community Encouragement has done an enormous amount of work in areas of poverty. And I have for two decades spoken out against the states' decision to virtually shut down their mental hospitals and put the majority of their severely and chronically mentally ill patients out on the streets. Although this decision was dressed in sweet words about respecting the civil liberties of the mentally ill and the benefits of modern tranquilizers, plus a nice fantasy about "community mental health centers" that would take care of these people, I knew from the beginning that the motives were primarily economic and could see the problem of homelessness as an inevitable result of such crass economics.

But no matter how obnoxious I made myself (as in many of

my peacemaking activities), people generally did not listen. In this instance, as in others, it has often seemed to me that my energies have been wasted. But for years I have been consoled by an account of a patient of mine who attended a conference at which one of the Berrigan brothers (who have long been involved in radical civil disobedience on behalf of disarmament) was speaking. My patient said that at this conference someone asked Father Berrigan how he could continue over decades to do his work when it seemed to have no obvious results. He responded, "We don't even think about results. If we did, we would be dead by now. The results are not our concern. We just do what we think is right, what we feel we have to do, and leave the results up to God."

THE PARADOXES OF TIME AND MONEY

We must not only choose the level of our involvement and our responsibility as citizens but also consider the matter of timing. Deciding when to get involved is crucial, given that we can never do everything we may want to do in this life, and given the reality that our own resources—of time, energy, and money—are limited. I once met a woman of fifty-five whose children were grown and who was heavily involved in civil disobedience. She not only had the time and energy but also the tolerance for such activism; in fact, she regarded it as unproductive if she didn't go to jail at least once a month. But I doubt that God is likely to call a new mother, or a father whose income must support his family, to go to jail for civil disobedience.

As the saying goes, timing is everything. Many people already have their hands full making a living and raising their children. Others make a different choice. I have heard of a number of civil activists who were successful as society's movers and shakers but seemed to be failures as parents. Apparently they spent far more time on social causes than on their own children and homes. Yet some of these activists were obviously called to their work, and while they may have regretted not spending more time with their children, the world is very possibly better off for their sacrifices.

Many significant contributions are made to society through the giving of time, money, or other resources by strongly principled individuals who regard their citizenship as a responsibility. "Volunteerism" is the word we use to describe efforts at trying to do good in spheres beyond personal economic interests and family. As soon as a person stands up for something with no expectation of reward, his involvement in a cause is essentially voluntary. A philanthropist volunteers his money. A teacher may provide free after-school tutoring to children in a poor neighborhood. A student may assist at a homeless shelter. A homemaker may make weekly visits to spend quality time with lonely residents of a home for the elderly.

Doing volunteer work is a calling. It is as legitimate and as complex a choice as a career decision. I believe that most people should volunteer at some time or another, and that the process and outcome of doing so are always mutually beneficial to society and to the individual. Whether one does so in youth, middle age, or old age, volunteering presents an opportunity for learning and growing through service to others. The enthusiasm and energy of the young, and the availability, experience, and compassion of older people make them potentially very dedicated volunteers.

But the choice of volunteerism must be weighed by many factors, of which timing may be the most crucial. In the succinct words of Ecclesiastes:

> To every thing there is a season, and a time to every purpose under the heaven;
> A time to be born, and a time to die; a time to plant, and a time to pluck up that which is planted;
> A time to kill, and a time to heal; a time to break down, and a time to build up;
> A time to weep, and a time to laugh; a time to mourn, and a time to dance;
> A time to cast away stones, and a time to gather stones to-

gether; a time to embrace, and a time to refrain from
embracing;
A time to get, and a time to lose; a time to keep, and a
time to cast away;
A time to rend, and a time to sew; a time to keep silence,
and a time to speak;
A time to love, and a time to hate; a time of war, and a
time of peace.

Just as time is important, other resources also make a difference in one's ability to serve society. Many simplistically mis-
construe activism as a call to radical poverty, and thus reject it.
Working for the good of society need not be synonymous with a
total sacrifice of one's comfort. Some years ago I read the pro-
ceedings of a conference of community activists in Nova Scotia.
One of the speakers, who had spent many years on the front
lines of social action and volunteerism, said, "The greatest con-
tribution you can make to the poor is by not becoming one of
them." This statement may seem harsh, but out of my own experience it struck me, in part at least, as having the ring of
truth. FCE, for instance, has been able to do its peacemaking
and poverty work only because it is a financially solvent nonprofit organization.

While there's no virtue per se in abject poverty, there is the
real question of whether great wealth simply constitutes greed.
It depends, of course, on how that money is spent. There is
more than a grain of truth in the saying that money is the root
of all evil. But the flip side is equally compelling. Given that cap-
ital can also be used to do good, a man named Leonard Orr
once suggested that money can be viewed as "God in circula-
tion."

But when is enough money enough? Those intent on making money, or on keeping what they have already made, might
be inclined to answer, "Never." In my view, money is the means
to an end, not the end in itself. And if that end is to do good,
again there may never be enough money. In any case, the ques-

tion seldom arises unless there is "not enough" and decisions must be made concerning what to do about it.

It is often recognized that money is perhaps more likely to be enslaving than liberating. Money is a seductive mistress. In *In Search of Stones,* I wrote that I worry far more about money than I used to when we didn't have much of it. Some of this worry is appropriate. "A fool and his money are soon parted." But I have also worried about money more than necessary, and in inappropriate ways that could easily become an obsession. Counting up the numbers can certainly help relieve our anxieties about the future. But it can also lead to false pride and self-satisfaction, as if money were the measure of our worth.

I am perhaps more prone to this obsession than most. Born in May 1936, I am very much a Depression baby. Throughout our Park Avenue childhoods, my father would not only expound to my brother and me, "You boys have got to learn the value of a dollar," but also repeatedly proclaim, "We're going to the poorhouse." Part of me knew at the time that this was laughable. However, it sank in. As an adolescent, when I took my dates to dinner, I would sit in silent anguish if they ordered anything other than one of the least expensive entrees. I was able to get over that, but for many years after getting married and having children I worried we might end up going to the poorhouse. What if I had a stroke and couldn't work? What if we got sued? What if the bottom fell out of the stock market? What if inflation ran rampant? What if? What if?

In many minds, money and security are equivalents. But complete security is an illusion. Life is an inherently insecure business. At a very early age, I was granted a revelation that the only real security in life lies in relishing life's insecurity. I have preached this revelation ever since, yet to this day I continue to need to relearn it. Money is a kind of security, and there can never be enough—at least, not when we are chasing after the illusion of total security.

I know perfectly well that those very wealthy people who never give away anything have been damned to chase after that empty illusion. I know because a part of them is in me. I may not have fallen prey as completely as they to the idolatry of money, but the fact remains that nothing continues to interfere more with my prayer life than concerns about my income, investments, and book sales. Some spiritual writers have diagnosed the human race as suffering from a "psychology of scarcity"; they urge us to a "psychology of abundance"—a sense that there will always be enough and that God will plentifully provide. I believe in this teaching. It's just that as a Depression baby I'm hard pressed to follow it, try as I might.

What truly constitutes wealth? In worldly terms, it is the possession of money and valuable things. But if we were to measure wealth in other ways, besides mere dollars, many who are poor in possessions are spiritually rich, and many who own much are spiritually impoverished. From a psychospiritual perspective, the truly wealthy are those who have an ongoing relationship with God and have learned that by giving of themselves they also receive much.

Whether we are blessed with gifts of the spirit or worldly wealth or both, demands accompany those blessings. We have heard it said that from the one to whom much is given (in the way of talent, money, or other resources) much is expected. Thus, one of the greatest dilemmas for those who have accumulated any measure of wealth is the decision whether—and to what extent—they should share that wealth to benefit others. When should those with money start giving it away? There's no clear formula, of course. But what is clear to me is that, as with power, the real purpose of having money is to share it with others. Too much money, like too much power, poses a danger for society as well as for the individual who keeps it for himself instead of giving it away.

A Personal Case Study

Lily and I did truly extensive volunteer work in our late middle years, from roughly the end of 1984 to the end of 1995. Our ability to devote so much of our time and other resources came on the heels of the commercial success of *The Road Less Traveled*. And in 1984, the second year we earned significantly more than we needed, we began looking at where we could volunteer our time or contribute money to an important cause. The cause that captured our interest above all others was peace, and Lily and I began to talk about starting a foundation of some sort. For a few months we toyed with the notion of establishing something that would bring together the five hundred or so different peace organizations. But the more we considered it, the more likely it seemed that whatever we might set up would just become the 501st peace group.

Gradually, we came to realize that community making was more fundamental than peace—that, in fact, community making must precede peace. So in December 1984, in conjunction with nine others, we established the Foundation for Community Encouragement. FCE is a tax-exempt, nonprofit, public-education foundation whose mission is to teach the principles of community—that is, the principles of healthy communication within and between groups. The statement of its founding vision reads:

> There is a yearning in the heart for peace. Because of the wounds—the rejections—we have received in past relationships, we are frightened by the risks. In our fear, we discount the dream of authentic community as merely visionary. But there are rules by which people can come back together, by which the old wounds are healed. It is the mission of the Foundation for Community Encouragement to teach these rules—to make hope real again—to make the vision actually manifest in a world which has almost forgotten the glory of what it means to be human.

In *The Different Drum* (subtitled *Community Making and Peace* to signify the progression), I expounded on the value of community making as the crucial precursor to peace. Community building helps remove barriers to communication, such as the smugness many people start out with because of their job titles, income, degrees, and religious, cultural, and racial identities. When these barriers come down through the learning of emptiness, we experience a temporary state of consciousness in which the mind is utterly open and receptive and therefore totally alert. It is through this process that we also allow room for healing—and even miracles of a sort—to occur. Community building helps cut through people's sophistication to get to the heart of their innocence. It encourages people to profoundly examine their motives, feelings, judgments, and reactions, and hence it expands the consciousness of self and ultimately consciousness of others.

For those eleven years, Lily and I volunteered roughly a third of our income and a third of our time to working with FCE. We each spent about twenty hours a week working on behalf of the organization. Being part of FCE was very much like having children. We never dreamed of how much work it would be. We also never dreamed of how much we would gain and learn from it.

As I wrote in *In Search of Stones,* when we started FCE we were a bunch of do-gooders who didn't know anything about how to do good by running a nonprofit organization. Had you asked me back then what strategic planning was, I might have told you it was probably something they did over at the Pentagon. In particular, we had no idea how to run a business, which a nonprofit organization, every bit as much as a profit-making one, must be if it is to be successful. Again, we were operating in the dark. I had to learn. We had to learn. We had to learn not only about strategic planning but all about marketing, conference coordinating, management of volunteers, upsizing and downsizing, fund-raising and development, computer systems and mailing lists, mission and vision statements, accounting procedures, and so on. We also had to learn even more important things, such as how bigger isn't necessarily better, how to coordinate, and how to clarify roles and power issues.

Most of what we learned in those dozen years came as a result of working with many others in the management of FCE, and it has often been painful learning. At one point or another, we have made almost every managerial mistake in the book. I have already mentioned how far and away the most agonizing financial decision we have ever had to make was not in regard to our personal finances but in regard to this charitable organization. FCE was hit devastatingly hard by the 1990–92 recession, and survived only because, over the course of six months, we reduced its annual budget from $750,000 to $250,000 through "downsizing"—that euphemism for laying off competent employees.

As a WASP who grew up with certain instructions for how to conduct one's life with at least a modicum of dignity, the hardest thing I had to do for FCE was raise funds. I had been taught never to beg. After three years of doing so, I expressed my agony and frustration in a 1987 poem entitled "A Beggar's Life (Confessions of a Fund-raiser)":

I beg
Prowling the streets,
Stalking for targets.
Do I ever even see
The faces anymore?
Or just the clothes?

By the clothes I judge them.
That one looks poor. He looks disheveled. She
Looks ordinary. That one looks inconsequential.
Ah, but this one!
This one looks wealthy.
This one looks substantial.
This one looks influential.
I move in for the kill, and
Am brushed aside.

Am I not like them all,
Looking for a better life?
The problem, you see, is that I am not

A good beggar.
I prowl endlessly, yet at night
Sink into flophouse dreams,
Not even knowing if I will be able
To make next week's rent.

I wonder:
Would I not do better, were I to look at
Their faces?

I have colleagues
In this profession. Most
Tell me I am right to not look
At the faces. They have the same
Categories of clothes
As I, yet some seem more successful, and
I wonder why?

Do they look
At the faces? A few say
Yes,
From the faces you can see the guilt
And prey upon it.

I cannot play
That trick. It is not
That I am moral. It is that I might
Also see their need, and then how would I know
Who is who,
Who the beggar, and whether I,
With such limited resources,
Am not the one called to give?

Limited resources,
That's the problem. Can't spread yourself
Too thin, they say, and that's the truth.
I can't go down all the streets
At all hours and, certainly,

I can't look into
All the faces.

But I don't do well.
Some days, I also wonder
If I would not do better just standing still.
I have a friend, a blind man,
Who does real well.
He just sits there,
Not having to move,
With his scarred eyes all rolled up,
And they give and give.

But they wouldn't give to me,
Would they,
Just for being there?

And I don't have the courage
To gouge out my eyes
Even though I wouldn't have to worry
About making all those choices
And looking at the faces
Anymore.

So I keep moving along,
Trying to look at just the clothes,
Hustling as best I can,
But I don't do well.
It's a beggar's life.

That was the downside. I couldn't have done it without the
upside. For one thing, I knew that begging was honored in
many religions and that the humiliation of it all could be
looked upon as a spiritual discipline. Certainly I believe it was
fortunate for me that at the very time I could begin to sit back
and rely upon my portfolio of stocks and bonds, God happened
to put me in a position where I had to rely on the providence of
others. And then there was the matter of making new and good

friends. It is hard not to love someone who gives you money for a cause you believe to be worthy. And strangely, large donations often seemed to come when we most needed but least expected them, as if they were manifestations of grace.

It can be either very easy or very difficult to give away money. Julius Rosenwald, the entrepreneurial genius behind Sears, Roebuck and founder of the Julius Rosenwald Fund, once declared: "It is almost always easier to make a million dollars honestly than to dispose of it wisely." A number of FCE's small donors and a few of its large ones simply said, "Here's my check. It seems as if you're doing good work and we'd like to help you out, but that's as far as we want to get involved." We were very grateful to them. But others who donated large sums of money sometimes felt it was incumbent upon them to see that it was managed well. That meant a further investment of their time, and so made it more difficult to give away money than to make it. Even so, it may also have been more emotionally rewarding—as it was for Lily and me.

Many have given FCE hundreds of thousands of dollars, but just as important, many have also given it their time. Currently FCE has only four full-time employees. Yet its influence is greater than ever because a hundred people have volunteered the time. Volunteering is hard work. Because they are not paid, many who volunteer assume that they can just show up whenever they want to, but true volunteerism demands much more. Those who depend on volunteers to help their organizations succeed often find that the central problem is getting a commitment from them. Over the years, our organization has been blessed with an army of fully committed volunteers.

In hindsight, it seems to me that FCE has survived and is currently flourishing thanks to the hard work of these committed volunteers and because of its integrity as an organization. While we made every possible mistake, we did so with integrity, and somehow that seemed to save the mistakes from being total disasters. To act with integrity also meant that we had to integrate good business principles with our principles of community. That was not cheaply achieved. It required that we learn still more about management and the nature of organizational culture and consensual decision making—and learn more deeply about community itself. One of our informal mottos became "FCE goes deeper." So we ventured ever further into the depths of what community is all about within the framework of our own organization, discovering for ourselves both the profound limitations and equally profound virtues of community in the workplace.

It was good that we did so. When we started FCE, the market for community building was that part of the general public interested in a temporary, individual experience of personal growth. Gradually, however, as more people had the experience of community, the primary market became organizations that sought greater effectiveness and creativity. We were able to meet this growing demand with integrity only because we knew something about the complexities of integrating community principles with business operations—and that was largely a result of having practiced on ourselves.

More than anything else, what I've learned through FCE is a vastly increased awareness of how different people are—and how we need those differences. In *A World Waiting to Be Born,* I wrote that years before FCE one of my first teachers in this realm was a decade younger than I. Peter was a young enlisted man, a "psych tech" who served under me in Okinawa. When I arrived at my new assignment, I found there were not nearly enough trained psychotherapists to meet the demand; yet a dozen of these twenty-year-old techs were sitting around with little or nothing to do. So I told them to start doing psychotherapy and I would provide them with on-the-job training. It was quickly apparent that half were not up to the job, and I set them to other tasks. But six had a natural talent for the role. One was Peter. For two years he served with distinction as a therapist. Then his enlistment was up and it was time for him to return home to the United States. As we were saying good-bye, I asked him about his plans and was aghast when he told me he intended to start a milk distribution business. "But you're a fine psychotherapist," I exclaimed. "I could help you get into a good master's program. The G.I. Bill would pay for it."

"No, thanks, my plans are set," Peter firmly replied. But I persisted, outlining all the advantages of a career as a practicing psychotherapist. Finally, with an understandable edge to his voice, Peter silenced me by saying, "Look, Scotty, can't you get it into your head that not everyone is like you, that not everyone with the opportunity *wants* to be a psychotherapist?"

As well as illustrating my own narcissism, the story demonstrates that people who have a talent for something don't therefore necessarily have a vocation for it. Secular vocational counselors know the best occupations for people are those in which their aptitude and interest coincide. But God is generous to many and bestows on them multiple gifts—interests as well as talents. The pattern of such gifts, however, is always unique to the individual. Each of us is created differently. I have gifts that you do not have. You have gifts that I do not have. And this is why we need each other.

Our common narcissistic failure to appreciate the separateness, the differentness, of others bedevils business life every bit as much as it does our family and personal lives. Let me give you an example of the same sick dynamic—the failure to appreciate diversity among us—at work in an even larger setting, creating a hateful and destructive schism within an entire profession. I was tentatively asked some time ago to consult about a conflict between the two governing bodies of one of America's medical specialties. The "American College" primarily represented the practitioners in the field, while the "American Academy" primarily represented its researchers. The members of both groups were highly intelligent, extremely well-educated, and supposedly civilized physicians. Yet for over a decade the relationship between these "sister" organizations had gradually been degenerating into extreme incivility.

I quickly learned that the practice of this specialty, on the frontiers of medicine, was much more an art than a science. Those who belonged to the College were treating patients on the front lines and had to operate mostly by guesswork and intuition. It was no accident, therefore, that they were men and women not only accustomed to ambiguity but actually excited by it. On the other hand, like all scientific research, medical research requires extreme precision and clarity. By virtue of the ground-breaking nature of the specialty, it required exactness even more stringently than other fields. Consequently, the members of the Academy were women and men who hated vagueness and regarded ambiguity as their enemy.

After just two phone calls, I was able to ascertain that the major source of conflict between the two organizations was the difference in the personalities of their members. This extended even to their communication styles, which, beyond any matter of substance, seemed almost designed to antagonize each other. Failing even to acknowledge their different predominant personality types—much less appreciate the need for them—each body had come to assume that the other's hostility was malicious in intent. Unfortunately, both made the decision not to pursue reconciliation. Once hooked on conflict, many organizations, like individuals, would rather fight than switch.

Had these separate organizational bodies been willing to proceed with the consultation, they would have discovered that we now possess a distinct educational "technology" to heal such unnecessary organizational conflicts. This, which we call community-building technology, is a system of group learning techniques that cut through people's everyday narcissism, allowing them not only to see one another's differences but also to accept them. It is not painless learning, but it is effective. Through it people actually experience their mutual interdependence on one another's gifts. They learn in their hearts what the Apostle Paul meant by "mystical body" when he said:

> Now there are diversities of gifts, but the same Spirit. . . .
> For to one is given by the Spirit the word of wisdom; to
> another the word of knowledge by the same Spirit; to
> another faith by the same Spirit; to another the gifts of
> healing by the same Spirit; to another the working of

miracles; to another prophecy; to another discerning
of spirits; to another divers kinds of tongues; to another the interpretation of tongues. . . . As the body is
one, and hath many members, and all the members of
that one body, being many, are one body . . . the body
is not one member, but many.

If the foot shall say, Because I am not the hand, I
am not of the body; is it therefore not of the body?
And if the ear shall say, Because I am not the eye, I am
not of the body; is it therefore not of the body? If the
whole body were an eye, where were the hearing? If
the whole were hearing, where were the smelling? But
now hath God set the members of every one of them
in the body, as it hath pleased him. And if they were all
one member, where were the body? . . . And the eye
cannot say unto the hand, I have no need of thee: nor
again the head to the feet, I have no need of you. . . .
But God hath tempered the body together, having
given more abundant honor to that part which lacked:
That there should be no schism in the body; but that
the members should have the same care one for another. And whether one member suffer, all the members suffer with it; or one member be honored, all the
members rejoice with it.

Is it an accident, do you suppose, that we humans are created in such variety and called in so many divergent ways? How
else could there be a society? We, the collective race, the body
of humanity, need our practicing physicians and researchers,
our executive and legislative branches, our marketers and salespeople, our farmers and steelworkers, priests and plumbers, au-
thors and publishers, athletes and entertainers, prophets and
bureaucrats. Yes, occasionally the threads may become a bit un-
raveled, but what a wonderfully variegated fabric we are!

That is the lesson we learned through our work at FCE. But
for all that Lily and I have given, we have received even more in
return. We have gained friends among a global community and

amassed a great deal of new knowledge about ourselves and others. Without FCE—as without our children—I would be a very stupid man.

Now that Lily and I are entering old age, we have largely retired from FCE and other activities that were once part of our routine. But the learning continues—including that of learning how to retire gracefully. Actually, from the start our intent was to work toward helping FCE become independent of us. We were keenly aware of and concerned about what tends to happen when individuals build organizations and later leave them. There are countless examples of successful "evangelists" who started organizations only to have a stroke or commit an indiscretion, with the result that their churches or theme parks collapsed. Our goal was to avoid that at FCE. So we have handed over the reins, encouraging others to be independent of us, giving up our power to empower others who are indeed quite capable of carrying on FCE's mission.

My father didn't retire until forced to do so by advanced age—he was in his eighties—so it has seemed strange to break from the tradition of my upbringing that one must die in the saddle. But I've learned that there is nothing wrong with doing things differently. In fact, a founding FCE board member, Janice Barfield, was a major role model for me in this way. She said God was telling her to retire, and she did so with grace after serving eight years. Through her leadership she gave me permission to follow her footsteps after eleven. The decision to retire is a personal choice and we each must follow our own path.

I believe that I have been given the green light from God to refrain from taking on any major responsibility beyond my ongoing writing projects. Since I've been a responsibility-aholic all my life, this was not a simple step to take. I had to learn to say no and encourage others to assume the responsibilities that I no longer felt able to accept. Play has taken on a far more important role in my life. But it feels right to me—and even seems all right with God—that I should actually enjoy retirement.

In a life together full of blessings, Lily and I feel the adventure of retirement is another blessing. We have not stopped learning. I still continue to write; family and friends remain central in our lives; and we intend to make contributions to those social causes that have always been important to us. We now play golf a good deal of the time and enjoy it not only for relaxation but also as a new and strange learning experience. We are traveling abroad ever more frequently—another learning experience.

Not long ago I said to Lily, "These really are our golden years."

"Hell," she retorted, "they're our platinum years!"

PART III

The Other Side
of Complexity

CHAPTER 7

The "Science" of God

❋

IN THE END, ALL THINGS POINT to God. . . .

I said earlier that the organization of this book evolved from a single sentence, a quote attributed to Justice Oliver Wendell Holmes, Jr.: "I don't give a fig for the simplicity this side of complexity, but I would die for the simplicity on the other side."

To journey to the other side of complexity, we are challenged to make a radical shift in thought. We are invited to move way beyond any simplistic understanding in order to consider what strict scientists might call the God Theory. Walking this other side is to embark on a path into the invisible realm. We cannot discover the radical truths of God through a rigid stance of static certainty. A cautious yet commanding sense of "knowing with humility" is required.

Like life, the other side of complexity is not always linear, nor static. It is, much like life, ultimately a process. This process involves mystery at its core, but it also encompasses a journey of change, of healing, and of the acquisition of wisdom. On this journey into the other side we may experience a sense of epiphany—those flashes of insight where many things that seemed quite complex begin to make more sense when viewed from a spiritual perspective. To do so, we can no longer simplistically interpret life through the limited lens of materialism.

Like all transitions in life, the transitions we make toward understanding the other side of complexity are likely to be difficult, even chaotic. We will encounter paradox, and in learning to understand paradox, we will experience psychic pain. In particular, it is the pain of loss of old ideas and the sense of certainty they provided. Just when we get comfortable with all that we think we know, something will come along to rattle us out of complacency. Thus, it is imperative that we be open-minded and courageous on this journey. We must gather all our resources—emotional, intellectual, and spiritual—to endure the sense of loss involved in letting go of the barriers to our ability to think paradoxically, to think with integrity.

One paradox is that the simplicity on the other side does not always look simple. God, for instance, often seems like an extraordinarily complex being. As a Christian, I have frequently found it useful to divide God into the traditional three parts: Father, Son, and Holy Spirit. At the very same time I embrace paradox and know in the deepest sense that God is One. But when I say that in the end, all things point to God, what things do I mean—and what proof can be offered, if any? Let's explore "the God Theory" and the scientific—though mostly indirect—evidence that seems to point nowhere else but to God.

SCIENCE AND GOD

Where does science fit into the scheme of things surrounding God? Scientific geniuses, including Carl Jung and Albert Einstein, have been among those who left the world a legacy through their works, which advanced the search for meaning in life and understanding of the universe. And both made personal proclamations that their scientific inquiries had led them to conclude that God is indeed real. But despite the assured observations of divinity from some of science's brightest minds, we still can't cite any specific scientific proof to support the existence of God.

Any proclamation about the existence of God elicits at least a bit of skepticism—and properly so—precisely because it can't be proven by traditional scientific measures. In fact, in this

Age of Reason, science itself has become a sort of god. The problem, however, is that God cannot be measured or captured. To measure something is to experience it in a certain dimension, a dimension in which we can make observations of great accuracy. The use of measurement has enabled science to make enormous strides in understanding the material universe. But by virtue of its success, measurement has become a kind of scientific idol. The result is an attitude on the part of many scientists of not mere skepticism but outright rejection of anything that cannot be measured. It is as if they were to say, "What we cannot measure, we cannot know; there is no point in worrying about what we cannot know; therefore, what cannot be measured is unimportant and unworthy of our observation." Because of this attitude many scientists exclude from their serious consideration all matters that are—or seem to be—intangible. Including, of course, the matter of God.

But if we cannot capture or measure God, neither can we fully measure and "capture" light, gravity, or subatomic particles, despite their obvious existence. Indeed, in exploring such phenomena as the nature of light, gravity, electromagnetism, and quantum mechanics, physical science has matured over the past century to the point where it has increasingly recognized that at a certain level reality is utterly paradoxical. As I quoted J. Robert Oppenheimer in *The Road Less Traveled:*

> To what appear to be the simplest questions, we will tend to give either no answer or an answer which will at first sight be reminiscent more of a strange catechism than of the straightforward affirmatives of physical science. If we ask, for instance, whether the position of the electron remains the same, we must say "no"; if we ask whether the electron's position changes with time, we must say "no"; if we ask whether the electron is at rest, we must say "no"; if we ask whether it is in motion, we must say "no." The Buddha has given such answers when interrogated as to the conditions of

man's self after his death; but they are not the familiar answers for the tradition of seventeenth and eighteenth century science.

But there are enough hints about human spiritual behavior to constitute a science of sorts, and a wealth of happenings that cannot be explained without resorting to "the God Theory." In fact, many things in science that we think of as great truths are mainly theories in the minds of most scientists. The "Big Bang theory" of the origin of the universe, for instance, is just that: a theory. So all things point to God only to some people. And given the fact that God cannot be measured, many simply do not believe in Her existence. Materialists and those who are highly secular require proof in the form of visible evidence. Basically, materialists live by a central belief that reality is only that which the five senses can detect. In other words, their motto is likely to be "What you see is what you get."

Secularism is a more complex phenomenon. Perhaps it can most simply be defined by comparing it with its opposite. This is what the theologian Michael Novak did so clearly when he distinguished between what he called the sacred consciousness and the secular consciousness. The individual with a secular consciousness essentially thinks that he is the center of the universe. Such people tend to be quite intelligent. They know full well that they are but one of six billion human beings scratching out an existence on the surface of a medium-sized planet that is a small fragment of a tiny solar system within a galaxy among countless galaxies, and that each of those other human beings also thinks that he is the center of the universe. Consequently, intelligent though they may be, people with a secular consciousness are prone to feel a bit lost within this hugeness and, despite their "centrality," to often experience a sense of meaninglessness and insignificance.

The person with a sacred consciousness, on the other hand, does not think of himself as the center of the universe. For him the center resides elsewhere, specifically in God—in the Sacred. Yet despite this lack of centrality, he is actually less likely to feel himself insignificant or meaningless than the secularist is, because he sees himself existing in relationship with that Sacred Other, and it is from this relationship that he derives his meaning and significance.

Sometimes people fall in between, with one foot planted in sacred consciousness and the other in secular consciousness. Moreover, there are different types of secularism and religiosity. So part of the "science" of God is not only to consider that which is unexplainable to materialists, but also to come to terms with the fact that people are different in their relationship to God. To do so it's necessary to briefly explain the difference between spirituality and religion.

SPIRITUALITY AND RELIGION

When I was still lecturing, I commonly found my audiences confused over these terms. For that reason, I have gradually come to restrict my definition of religion to that which involves an organized body of beliefs with a specific creed and membership boundaries. Spirituality is much broader, and for my definition of spirituality, I refer to the words that William James used to define religion. In his classic work *The Varieties of Religious Experience,* James described it as "the attempt to be in harmony with an unseen order of things." For me, that covers everyone's spirituality or lack thereof. As a self-designated Christian, however, I personally not only believe that there is a "Higher Power" behind the visible order of things, but also that It is not neutral—that It actively wants us to be in harmony with It.

Obviously, many people are religious but not spiritual, and vice versa. One of the most secular persons I've ever met was a Catholic nun with whom I worked for a year. She had been in a convent for twenty-five years and had no desire to be anything but a nun. Despite the fact that she did everything nuns do—making confession and service to the community, for example—she gave virtually no thought to God in her daily life.

There are also many who are spiritual but not religious. And there are those who are a combination of both, as I am. I am specifically Christian yet quite ecumenical. I grew up in a primarily secular environment; my spiritual development was enabled by all the world's great religions, and it wasn't until I was forty-three that I was baptized, nondenominationally, as a Christian. With minor exceptions, I believe wholeheartedly in Christian doctrine. On the other hand, I also make use of the teachings of other great religions. *What Return Can I Make? Dimensions of the Christian Experience (Gifts for the Journey)* is the only specifically Christian book I've ever written; all the rest have been more spiritual than religious.

I believe that the differences between those who are actively religious or spiritual and those who are not are generally not so much random as developmental. People, like myself, change in their lives regarding the nature of their spirituality, and I've come to see that there is a profound tendency for these changes to follow a sequence, or stages.

STAGES OF SPIRITUAL GROWTH

My theory on the stages of spiritual growth was first suggested in *The Road Less Traveled,* but I wasn't as clear about it back then as I am now. The person best known for writing on this subject is Professor James Fowler of the Candler School of Theology of Emory University and the author of, among other works, *Stages of Faith.* On the basis of Fowler's work and my own experience as a psychiatrist, I realized there were more or less distinct stages of spiritual development. Fowler offers six such stages, which I condensed into four and wrote about in much greater depth in *A Different Drum* and to a lesser extent in *Further Along the Road Less Traveled.* What follows is a very brief description:

• Stage I, which I label Chaotic, Antisocial. In this most primitive stage, people may appear religious or secular but, either way, their "belief system" is profoundly superficial. They are essentially unprincipled. Stage I may be thought of as a stage of Lawlessness.

• Stage II, which I label Formal, Institutional. This is the stage of the Letter of the Law, in which religious "fundamentalists" (meaning most religious people) are to be found.

• Stage III, which I label Skeptic, Individual. Here is where the majority of secularists are found. People in this stage are usually scientific-minded, rational, moral, and humane. Their outlook is predominantly materialistic. They tend to be not only skeptical of the spiritual but uninterested in anything that cannot be proven.

• Stage IV, which I label Mystical, Communal. In this most mature stage of religious development, which may be thought of as that of the Spirit of the Law, women and men are rational but do not make a fetish of rationalism. They have begun to doubt their own doubts. They feel deeply connected to "an unseen order of things," although they cannot fully define it. They are comfortable with the mystery of the sacred.

I must caution that these stages should not be viewed simplistically. Superficially, many people might appear to be in a more advanced stage than they truly are. A considerable number of "New Agers" and scientists, for instance, are basically "fundamentalists," while some "evangelicals" are Stage IV mystics. Furthermore, not only are there gradations within each stage, but also people who are in transition from one stage to the next. And while some are developing, others, for various reasons, are deeply stuck or fixated in a particular stage. Nevertheless, the stages are essentially developmental, which means, for one thing, that the secularists of Stage III are actually more spiritually developed than the majority of religious people. Many in Stage II are highly critical of the "secular humanists" in Stage III but would be well advised to become more humanist themselves.

There are some who worry that categorizing people in

stages of spiritual growth may have a fragmenting effect—that the designation of different kinds of believers may be destructive to community in general and the "community of the faithful" in particular. While I understand the concern about hierarchies and their potential for elitism, I do not feel the worry is justified. The supposed "community" of the faithful has been noted in history for excluding, punishing, and frequently even murdering the doubter, the skeptic, and others who did not fit the mold. And my own repeated personal experience with the knowledge that we are at different stages of spiritual development facilitates rather than hampers the formation and maintenance of true communities. Still, it is good for us to bear in mind that the relatively undeveloped are quite capable of community and advanced growth, and that the most developed of us still retain vestiges of the earlier stages. As Edward Sanford Martin described it in his poem, "My Name Is Legion,"

> Within my earthly temple there's a crowd;
> There's one of us that's humble, one that's proud,
> There's one that's broken-hearted for his sins,
> There's one that unrepentant sits and grins;
> There's one that loves his neighbor as himself,
> And one that cares for naught but fame and pelf.
> From much corroding care I should be free
> If I could once determine which is me.

In this common journey of spiritual growth, it may help us all to remember the basic meaning of the word "Israel." The Old Testament, quite early in the drama, tells us of Jacob. He was clearly a Stage I chap—a liar, thief, and manipulator who has cheated his brother out of his inheritance. As this part of the story or myth opens, Jacob is in trouble—as is typical of Stage I people. On the lam from his brother, wandering through the desert, one evening he leaves his family to sleep alone. In the middle of the night, however, he is accosted by a strongly built stranger. They do battle with each other in the darkness. The desperate struggle lasts hour after hour, as they wrestle together. But finally, just as the first glimmer of dawn comes to the horizon, Jacob feels himself beginning to get the upper hand. Exulting, he throws all his resources into vanquishing this stranger who has assaulted him for no apparent reason.

Something extraordinary then happens. The stranger reaches out and lightly touches Jacob's thigh, and it is instantly, effortlessly pulled out of joint and broken. Crippled, Jacob then clings to the stranger, not to continue an obviously lost battle—he is an utterly defeated, broken man—but because he knows now that he is in the presence of divinity. So in that first faint light of dawn, he pleads with his adversary not to leave before giving him a blessing. The stranger agrees, and not only blesses Jacob but tells him, "Henceforth you will be called Israel, meaning he who has struggled with God." And Jacob limps off into the future.

There are today three meanings to the word "Israel." One refers to a rather small area of the earth's surface on the eastern coast of the Mediterranean, currently a nation-state with a brief, already tortured history. A second refers to the Jewish people, dispersed the world over, with a long and tortured history. But the most basic meaning refers to the people who have struggled with God. As such it includes all the Stage I people, who have just begun the struggle, who do not yet know by whom they've been assaulted, who are still in the midst of total darkness before seeing their first dawn, before even receiving their first breaking and their first blessing. Israel also includes those people once broken and once blessed, the Stage II fundamentalist Hindus and Muslims and Jews and Christians and Buddhists throughout the world. Included, too, are those twice broken and twice blessed: the atheists and the agnostics and skeptics, whether in Russia or England or Argentina or in this country, who question and thereby continue the great struggle. And finally it includes the thrice broken and thrice blessed mystics from all the cultures of the earth, who have even come to seek future breakings for the blessings they now know will follow. Israel includes the entirety of our struggling infant humanity. It is the whole potential community on the planet. We are all Israel.

PSYCHOSPIRITUAL AND HISTORICAL BAGGAGE

We are often prevented from seeing this aspect of our common humanity, in part because of the psychospiritual baggage we usually carry, unaware of how it shapes our worldview when it comes to religion and the spiritual issues that have an impact on our lives and on our perceptions of God's role in them. This psychospiritual baggage is often unconstructive and unnecessary. Some is the result of religious excesses, such as the Inquisition. The original relationship between religion and science was one of integration. And this integration had a name—philosophy. Early philosophers like Plato and Aristotle and Thomas Aquinas were men of scientific bent. They thought in terms of evidence and questioned premises, but they also were totally convinced that God was the essential reality.

In the sixteenth century, however, the relationship between science and religion began to go sour; and hit bottom in 1633 when Galileo was summoned before the Inquisition. The results of that event were decidedly unpleasant. They were unpleasant for Galileo, who was forced to recant his belief in Copernican theory—that the planets revolve around the sun—and was placed under house arrest for the remainder of his life. However, in short order things got even more unpleasant for the Church, which to this day has itself been recanting.

In response to this vast stress, there emerged toward the end of the seventeenth and the beginning of the eighteenth century an unwritten social contract that divided up the territory between government, science, and religion. Not consciously developed, it was an almost spontaneous response to the needs of the day, and it has done more than anything else to determine the nature of our science and our religion ever since.

In the early 1700s, Isaac Newton was president of the Royal Society of London for Improving Natural Knowledge. According to the unwritten contract, then already in place, natural knowledge was distinguished from supernatural knowledge. "Natural knowledge" had become the province of science, "supernatural knowledge" was now the province of religion, and according to the rules of the contract, never the twain should meet. One effect of that separation was the emasculation of philosophy. Since natural knowledge became the domain of scientists and supernatural knowledge that of the theologians, the poor philosophers were left only with what fell through the cracks, which was not much.

In some ways, this unwritten social contract might be looked upon as one of the great intellectual happenings of humankind. All manner of good came from it: the Inquisition faded away, religious folk stopped burning witches; the coffers of the Church remained full for several centuries; slavery was abolished; democracy was established without anarchy; and, perhaps because it did restrict itself to natural phenomena, science thrived, giving birth to a technological revolution beyond anybody's wildest expectations, even to the point of paving the way for the development of a planetary culture.

The problem is that this unwritten social contract no longer works. Indeed, at this point in time, it is becoming downright diabolic. As I have already noted, the word "diabolic" comes from the Greek *diaballein*, which means to throw apart or to separate, to compartmentalize. It is the opposite of "symbolic," which comes from the word *symballein*, meaning to throw together, to unify. This unwritten social contract is tearing us apart.

Thanks to the secularization of education, we can't even teach values in our public schools, for example. Although public schools teach science, there seems to be a view that religion shouldn't be touched. Nobody has sued—except a few fundamentalists who objected to evolutionary theory—over the teaching of science, but the subjects of religion and spirituality are considered so controversial that no one dares design a reasonable and basic curriculum. There's absolutely no valid reason not to teach religion; it can be done in much the objective manner in which science is taught, with a focus on all religions and their key concepts. Since values are ultimately related to basic religious ideas, the approach to teaching values can be along the same lines, with no partiality to any particular ideas but a general overview with specific concepts and theories.

In reality, we currently teach our children materialism by not teaching spirituality and, by implication, we are sending a message that values are simply not important. Those who object to values being taught fail to see that we already have interjected a basic nihilistic value into school curriculums. Nihilism suggests that there's no unseen order to things, that anything goes and there is no particular meaning in life's experiences. To teach values is to suggest that things do matter. But whose values and which values should be taught? That is the dilemma, and its resolution is not to teach any one set; it is to present students with a complete overview and then dare to let them decide for themselves.

Let me point out the effect of the unwritten contract not just throughout American culture but specifically upon my own field of psychiatry. Psychiatry, defining itself as scientific, has totally neglected the spiritual. I doubt that it is possible for a psychiatrist to complete his or her residency training without significant exposure to stage theory: Freud's stages of psychosexual development, Piaget's stages of cognitive development, and Erikson's stages of maturation and their predictable crises. Yet, to my knowledge, in their training psychiatrists receive absolutely no exposure to the stages of spiritual development. The primary reason for this fact is that training programs for psychiatrists have simply not regarded it as their responsibility to know or teach anything about spirituality.

We carry not only this collective historical baggage but also the baggage of our own personal experiences of how we were treated by the church when we raised doubts or experienced periods of alienation from human fellowship as well as alienation from God. The Inquisition is gone but current religious excesses still lead to the fixation of many in Stage III secularism. Dogmatism and bigotry among fundamentalists of all faiths leave no room for doubt and uncertainty. Many are deeply angry for being rejected by their church because they've had doubts. Often, their first response to anything spiritual after years of suffering from such rejection is "Oh, no, not that stuff again." To move on rather than remain stuck, they may need to learn to forgive their faith for its Stage II rigidity and intolerance.

Then there is the purely psychological baggage that causes many to become stuck in their spiritual growth. When I was still in practice, I served as a consultant to a convent that required its postulants to receive a psychiatric evaluation before entering the novitiate. One evaluation I did was of a forty-five-year-old woman who had been described by her novice director and religious instructor as a "wonderful postulant." The only red flag was that the other postulants weren't particularly friendly toward her. There was nothing specific they didn't like; they just didn't respond warmly to her.

When I met her, what immediately struck me was that she carried herself more like a giggly eight-year-old girl than a forty-five-year-old woman. As she talked about her spiritual life, there was nothing spontaneous. She came across as a good little girl who knew all the right things to say and who took great pride in reeling off her catechism.

I was compelled to probe beyond her religious life. When I asked about her childhood, she replied that it was "wonderfully happy." Since our younger years are so frequently painful, I immediately pricked up my ears, asking for more information about this wonderful childhood. She told me about an incident involving herself, then eight, and her sister, who was nine years old at the time. One day while they were in the bathtub, her sister playfully warned her, "Watch out! Oogle's coming," a reference to the girls' mutually made-up play pal, a friendly ghost. The eight-year-old instinctively dove under the water. Her mother, she then recalled, beat her.

"Beat you?" I queried. "Why?"

"Because I got my hair wet, of course."

As her recollections of other important events in her life surfaced during our session together, it became obvious that the woman's description of a "wonderfully happy" childhood was only one version of the story—a simplistic and comforting one perhaps. I learned that when she was twelve years old, her mother became incapacitated with multiple sclerosis and died seven years later. By now it was clear to me that the woman's giggly, childish manner was the result of her having become fixated at a preadolescent emotional stage.

In many ways, the personalities of children in their latency stage parallel Stage II spirituality. Indeed, we call the years between five and twelve the latency period precisely because children this age are "latent"—meaning not much trouble. Although mischievous at times, they naturally tend to believe everything Mommy and Daddy say. With adolescence, however, all hell breaks loose as they naturally tend to question everything. But how can you rebel against a mother who beats you merely for getting your hair wet, who becomes crippled just when your adolescence has begun, and then dies around the time when this normal period of adolescent rebellion should ideally be almost complete? This forty-five-year-old woman's failure to experience adolescent rebellion was also reflected in her spirituality. The origins of the childlike quality she had in general and of her deference to anything involving Church authority were easy to pinpoint.

I have previously written that there are parallels between the stages of spiritual development and the psychosexual developmental stages with which psychiatrists are generally familiar— Stage I corresponding in some ways to the first five years of life, Stage II to the latency period, Stage III to adolescence and early adulthood, and Stage IV to the last half of life in healthy human development. Like the psychosocial developmental stages, the stages of spiritual development are sequential. They cannot be skipped over. And just as there are fixations of psychosexual development, so people may become spiritually fixated in one of these stages, sometimes for some of the same reasons.

I need also note again that the "diagnosis" of a person's spirituality should not be made on superficial appearances or simplistic assumptions. Just because a man is a scientist, he may look as if he is in Stage III when actually he has a primarily Stage II spirituality. Another may mouth mystical sayings in Stage IV language but actually be a Stage I con artist. And a small minority may not fit very well into any developmental stage. Those we call borderline personalities, for instance, tend to have one foot in Stage I, the other foot in Stage II, one hand in Stage III, and the other hand in Stage IV. It is no accident that they are labeled borderline, since they tend to be all over the place.

The greatest problem encountered in all the stages is that, except for Stage IV people (who envision themselves as pilgrims on an ongoing journey), many think they have arrived. A Stage II fundamentalist is likely to think he has got it all figured out with God captured in his back pocket, while a diehard secularist thinks she is so sophisticated that "I've got no place else to go beyond here."

Some people need to grow out of religion, like the woman named Kathy whose story I told in *The Road Less Traveled*. She was a primitive, Stage II Catholic who displayed more of an attachment to the form of her religion than to its spirit. And there are some people who need to grow more into religion, as was the case with the extremely secular Theodore, whose story I also told in the same book, and who represented another example of the baggage that can cripple the spiritual growth process without psychotherapy for healing.

INTEGRATION AND INTEGRITY

Looking back over the course of human history, we can discern both the strengths and the limitations inherent in the Age of Faith. But only recently are we beginning to see the limitations of the Age of Reason, which is where we now find ourselves as a society. Were we still embedded in the Age of Faith, I suspect it would be blind faith that I, as a member of the "Enlighten-ment," would be attacking. Today, however, while I am a great advocate of reason, I am very much against unimaginative and narrow-minded reason. When we think we should know *the* rea-son for everything and that there is only one reason—when the concept of overdetermination is foreign to our minds—we are cursed by either/or thinking. Such limited thinking has led us to believe that education should be either secular or religious, that riots are caused either by a breakdown in family values or by oppressive racism, that one must be either a Democrat or a Republican, a conservative or a liberal.

The truth is there is room for both faith and reason. And only when we are able to integrate the attributes of faith and reason into our lives can we come closer to what constitutes integrity. I don't know who originally coined the term, but a few theologians—including me—are increasingly exalting the "Holy Conjunction." The Holy Conjunction is the word "and." Instead of an either/or style of mentation, we are pushing for both/and thinking. We are not trying to get rid of reason but promote "reason plus." Reason *and* mystery. Reason *and* emo-tion. Reason *and* intuition. Reason *and* revelation. Reason *and* wisdom. Reason *and* love.

So we are envisioning a world where a business can make a profit and be ethical. Where a government can promote politi-cal order and social justice. Where medicine can be practiced with technological proficiency and compassion. Where children can be taught science and religion. Our vision is one of integra-tion. By integration we do not mean squashing two or more things together into a colorless, unisex blob. When we talk of in-tegrating science and faith, we are not speaking of returning to an age of primitive faith, where science is discounted, any more than we are arguing for the status quo where a limited science is idolized while faith is relegated to an hour on Sunday. The Holy Conjunction is the conjunction of integrity.

I have often wondered what might lie beyond the Age of Reason. I don't know. But I hope it will be the Age of Integration. In that age science and religion will work hand in hand, and both will be more sophisticated as a result. Before we can arrive at the Age of Integration, however, we ourselves must become more sophisticated in our thinking. Specifically, we must come to learn how to think paradoxically because we will encounter paradox whenever reason becomes integrated by the Holy Conjunction.

Several years ago, I had the opportunity to offer a set of ten recommendations to the state commissioners of education who had gathered to wrestle with the complex issue of the teaching of values in public schools. One of my recommendations was that Zen Buddhism should be taught in the fifth grade. I was not speaking tongue in cheek. Zen is the ideal training ground for paradox. Without my twenty years of meandering around with Zen Buddhism, I don't think there is any way I could have been prepared to swallow the literally God-awful paradoxes that lie at the core of Christian doctrine. It is around the age of ten that children are first able to deal with paradox, and it is a critical moment for imprinting which should not be lost. I doubt, however, that the commissioners took this recommendation seriously.

It is not going to be easy for people to learn how to think paradoxically in this Age of Reason. Indeed, "paradox" is often translated from its Greek root as "contrary to reason." But paradox is not actually unreasonable. It seems that way because we tend to think in words—and particularly in nouns. Nouns are categories, and language compartmentalizes. "Cat" is the category for certain furry land animals with whiskers. "Fish" is the category for water creatures with scales. Consequently, a creature that falls into the cat category cannot fall into the fish category—unless it is a "catfish," but then we know that a catfish really belongs in the fish compartment. "Life" and "death" are opposite compartments. Even verbs are categorical. "To find" is the opposite of "to lose." What, then, are we to do with someone who teaches us the paradox, "Whosoever will save his life shall lose it; and whosoever shall lose his life will find it"?

GRACE AND SERENDIPITY

However hard we may try, the reality is that we humans can never will miracles into being. This fact, this lack of control, is one of the reasons the secular generally turn a blind eye to the miraculous in life. They fail to see the grace—and hence the proof—of God and God's love.

In my primary identity as a scientist, I want and like proof. Being as much a logical sort as a mystical one, I expect statistical proof whenever possible to convince me of things. But throughout my twenties and thirties and as I continued to mature, I've become more and more impressed by the frequency of statistically highly improbable events. In their very improbability, I gradually began to see the fingerprints of God. On the basis of such events in my own life and in the lives of patients (many recounted in *The Road Less Traveled* and subsequent books), I know that grace is real. There is a pattern to these highly improbable events: almost all seemed to have a beneficial outcome. I had stumbled upon a synonym for grace: serendipity.

Webster's dictionary defines serendipity as "the gift of finding valuable or agreeable things not sought for." This definition has several intriguing features. One is that serendipity is termed a gift, which implies that some people possess it while others don't, that some people are lucky and others are not. It is a major thesis of mine that grace, manifested in part by "valuable or agreeable things not sought for," is available to everyone. But while some take advantage of it, others do not.

One of the reasons for the human tendency to resist grace is that we are not fully aware of its presence. We don't find valuable things not sought for because we fail to appreciate the value of the gift when it is given to us. In other words, serendipitous events occur to all of us, but frequently we fail to recognize their serendipitous nature; we consider such events unremarkable, and consequently we fail to take full advantage of them.

The indications of grace and/or serendipity as I have described them seem to have the following characteristics:

• They serve to nurture—support, protect, and enhance—human life and spiritual growth.

• The mechanism of their action is either incompletely understandable (as in the case of dreams) or totally obscure (as in the case of paranormal phenomena) according to the principles of natural law as interpreted by current scientific thinking.

• Their occurrence is frequent, routine, commonplace, and essentially universal among humanity.

• Although they are potentially influenced by human consciousness, their origin is outside the conscious will and beyond the process of conscious decision making.

In other words, I have come to believe that their commonality indicates that these phenomena are part of or manifestations of a single phenomenon: a powerful force that originates outside of human consciousness and nurtures the spiritual growth of human beings. We who are properly skeptical and scientific-minded may be inclined to dismiss this force since we can't touch it and have no decent way to measure it. Yet it exists. It is real.

Our understanding of that is limited, again, by our difficulty in dealing with paradox. We want to identify things rationally. The paradox of grace is that, on the one hand, it is earned. I've already mentioned a number of reasons why our becoming blessed by grace is a matter of choice. On the other hand, try as we might to obtain grace, it may yet elude us. In other words, we do not come to grace; grace comes to us. The paradox that we both choose grace and are chosen by grace is the essence of the phenomenon of serendipity, which was defined as "the gift of finding valuable or agreeable things not sought for." Buddha found enlightenment only when he stopped seeking it—when he let it come to him. But who can doubt that enlightenment came to him precisely because he had devoted at least sixteen years of his life to seeking it, sixteen years in preparation? He had both to seek it and not seek it.

I've often been asked if I have had any experiences of grace since I wrote *The Road Less Traveled* twenty years ago. Indeed, they just go on and on. And while hardly the most recent example, there is one that is particularly memorable. Approximately eight years ago, I was on my way to a speaking engagement in Minneapolis. Flying time was then very precious to me, because that was when I got to do the majority of my writing. So I always carried a yellow legal pad with me. Because I am shy, I usually do not like to talk to the person next to me, particularly if he is intoxicated. So even when I am not writing, I make it look as if I am to protect my privacy.

On this particular morning, when I got on the plane in Hartford, my seatmate, who was quite sober, was a man in his early forties. I gave him my usual nonverbal messages that I didn't want to talk to him, and was delighted to see him give me equally strong nonverbal messages that he didn't want to talk to me either. So we sat there in silence together, I with my yellow pad and he reading a novel, for an hour-long flight to Buffalo. Then we silently got off the airplane together and silently shared the same waiting room in Buffalo for an hour-long layover. Then we silently got back on the airplane together. It was not until forty-five minutes east of Buffalo and west of Minneapolis that the first words passed between us when, out of a literally as well as figuratively clear blue sky, this man looked up from the novel he was reading and said, "I hate to bother you, but you don't happen, by any chance, to know the meaning of the word 'serendipity,' do you?"

I responded that as far as I knew I was the only person who had written a substantial portion of a book on the subject, and that it was perhaps serendipity that at the precise moment he wanted to know the meaning of the word, he happened to be sitting in outer space next to an authority on the subject. (Think of the improbability of that occurrence! Also keep in mind that I have defined grace in terms of occurrences that are not only statistically highly improbable but also have beneficial outcomes.)

When that sort of thing happens, sometimes even I have to put away my yellow pad, and the two of us began to talk. He asked me what the book that had something to do with serendipity was about. I told him that it was a kind of integration of psychology and religion. "Well, I don't know about religion anymore," my seatmate said, and told me that he was an Iowa boy, born and bred—born into the Methodist Church and sustained by it for decades. Perhaps because I looked like the kind of person he could talk to, and certainly a person he would never have to see again, he went on to tell me, "I'm not sure that I buy this virgin birth bit anymore. To be perfectly honest, I even have some questions about the resurrection. So I'm feeling kind of bad about it, because it looks like I'm going to have to leave the church."

In response, I began to talk about the healthiness of skepticism and doubt. I told him that in *The Road Less Traveled* I had written, "The path to holiness lies through questioning everything." And I explained how such questioning was necessary for someone to move from a hand-me-down religion to a fully mature, personal one. When we parted at the Minneapolis airport, my seatmate said, "I don't have the foggiest idea what all of this means, but maybe I don't have to leave the church after all."

REVELATION

I believe that the radical healing influence of grace is manifested to us not only through such wildly improbable circumstances but also through revelation. Whenever something happens that is beyond coincidence, the chances are great that the hand of God is at work. But does God actually ever directly speak to us or reveal Himself to us? The answer is yes.

The most common way is through Her "still, small voice." You may recall my story about a friend of mine—a woman in her thirties—who went running one morning just as she was preparing to leave home to go to work. She hadn't planned to run, but could not shake that still, small voice urging her to do so. As a result of following the guidance of that voice and the healing of the experience, when she recounted it to me a few days later she exclaimed with exhilaration, "To think that the

Creator of the whole universe would take time out to go running with me!"

My clearest, recent encounter with God's still, small voice occurred in early fall 1995, after I had completed the first draft of my novel *In Heaven as on Earth* and it had been accepted for publication. The moment for rewriting was upon me, and I had a problem. In the first draft, I had used myself as the main character and I was certain this needed to be changed in the second draft. For the rewriting I needed to step outside myself and otherwise improve the development of the character. Yet I've never been very good at stepping outside myself. Moreover, the nature of the plot demanded that the main character be a man very much like me—specifically, someone who was an intellectual with psychiatric training and an amateur theologian to boot. It was a problem, indeed, and I had not the faintest idea how to solve it.

It was at this point one afternoon, when I was working on something else and my problem was on the back burner, that I heard a still, small voice say, "Read the Book of Daniel." I shook my head slightly. I knew that the Book of Daniel was in the Old Testament. And like almost every schoolchild, I knew that Daniel was a prophet who for some reason had been thrown into the lions' den and had managed by God's grace to survive. Beyond that I knew nothing. I had never read the Book of Daniel. I had never had any intention to, and I had absolutely no idea why this voice should be telling me to read it. I shook my head and returned to dictating letters.

The next afternoon, while searching for some papers in my wife's office, the voice came back. "Read the Book of Daniel," it repeated. This time I did not shake my head. Somewhat experienced with the Holy Spirit's capacity for persistence, I recognized that God might be nudging me toward something, although God only knew what or why. Still, I was in no hurry.

At noon the following day, while I was taking my daily walk, the voice came back, even more insistent: "Scotty, *when* are you going to read the Book of Daniel?" it asked. So, as soon as I returned, having nothing more clearly pressing to do, I pulled out one of our Bibles and read the Book of Daniel. I learned many things. But the most useful thing for me at that moment was the realization that there were dramatic parallels between Daniel and myself. Although far the more courageous, faithful, and noble, he, too, was clearly an intellectual. As an interpreter of dreams he became something of a psychiatrist, and later, as a prophet, something of a theologian. So it was that my own life had evolved, and it quickly dawned on me that I had the solution to my problem: henceforth the central character of my novel would be a Daniel, not Scotty. And both the similarities and the differences between us allowed me to step outside myself in a myriad of little ways to make that character believable.

This example of God's nurturance of me is all the more remarkable given that I am not only a poor scholar in general but a particularly poor student of the Bible. As far as the New Testament is concerned, I've never been able to get through Revelation and I've had hard sledding with the Letters. As for the Old Testament, I've simply not read much of it. And as with the Book of Daniel, I've not much cared to. What is to be made of this sort of phenomenon? Many who have written about creativity without mentioning God have offered examples of how the solution to a difficult problem can suddenly come to someone when she is not actively thinking about it. But in these examples, the solution is immediately recognized and welcomed. It is not experienced as coming from outside oneself. Yet here I received not a solution to my problem but the gift of a path to the solution. The gift made no sense to me; I was unaware that it had any relation to my problem. It was a path I would not ordinarily have followed. I did not welcome it. Indeed, my first reaction was to reject the gift because it seemed so alien to my ego.

As problems go, mine was not huge. Am I suggesting that God would go out of Her way to help me with such a relatively small problem? Yes, that is exactly what I am suggesting. Why God should care about me so much, I do not really know. But millions have reported experiences such as I've described. And for me, these sorts of experiences of grace and revelation are evidence not only of the existence of God but also of the fact that She nurtures us on an ongoing basis.

To experience Her "still, small voice" is a strange phenomenon. It is not in the least a great, booming, masculine voice from heaven. As the Bible puts it, the voice is indeed "still" and "small"—so still and small it is hardly a voice at all. It seems to originate inside of us and for many may be indistinguishable from a thought. Only it is not their own thought.

No wonder many feel so confused about discerning revelations. The closeness between this "voice" and an ordinary thought calls for a word of caution. One would be ill-advised to go around ascribing all or most of one's thoughts to be the word of God. That can quickly lead to insanity. But there are some guidelines for discernment. First, it's important to take time (unless you are in an emergency situation) to "reality-test" whether what you hear might be the voice of the Holy Spirit or merely your own thought. And you will have that time. Indeed, if you disregard the voice at first, it will almost always repeat itself, as did the urging to read Daniel. Second, this voice of the Holy Spirit (or Comforter, as Jesus called it) is always constructive, never destructive. It may call upon you to do something different, and that may feel slightly risky, but it won't be a major risk. If you hear a voice telling you to kill yourself, to cheat or steal, or to blow all your life savings on a yacht, get yourself to a psychiatrist.

On the other hand, the voice will usually seem just a little bit "crazy." This is what distinguishes it from your own thought. There is a faintly alien quality to it, as if it came from elsewhere (which it does). This is inevitable. The Holy Spirit doesn't need to speak to us to tell us something we already know or to push us in ways we don't need to be pushed. It comes to us with something new and unexpected—to open us up and therefore, by definition, to gently break through our existing boundaries and barriers. Consequently, one's usual reaction upon first hearing the voice of the Holy Spirit is to shake one's head.

One of the other ways God speaks to us—attempts to nurture us—is through some of our dreams, particularly those that Carl Jung labeled "big dreams." When I was in practice, some of my patients, aware of the fact that dreams could contain answers to their problems, avidly sought these answers by deliberately, mechanically, and with considerable effort recording each and every one of their dreams in complete detail. But there wasn't enough time in therapy to analyze most dreams; besides, I found that such voluminous dream material could prevent work in more fruitful areas of analysis. Such patients had to be taught to stop searching after their dreams and to let their dreams come to them, to let their unconscious choose which dreams should enter consciousness. This teaching itself was quite difficult, demanding that the patient give up a certain amount of control and assume a more passive relationship to his or her own mind. But once a patient learned to make no conscious effort to clutch at dreams, the remembered dream material could not only decrease in quantity but also dramatically increase in quality. The result then could be an opportunity for the patient's dreams—these gifts from the unconscious now no longer sought for—to elegantly facilitate the healing process.

I also had patients who entered psychotherapy with absolutely no awareness or understanding of the immense value that dreams could have to them. Consequently, they would discard from consciousness all dream material as worthless and unimportant. These patients had to be taught to remember their dreams and then how to appreciate and perceive the treasure within them. To utilize dreams effectively, we must work to be aware of their value and to take advantage of them when they come to us. And we must work sometimes at not seeking them or expecting them. We must let them be true gifts. That is what Jung meant by a "big dream." It is one that almost shrieks to us, "Remember me!"

Why are so many immune to the evidence—that still, small voice and our dreams, among other things—of grace and revelation? I believe there are two primary reasons. One is that people are threatened by change. Most with either a fundamentalist or secular mind-set are simply not likely to be open to the evidence that could call their mind-set into question. The other is that there is something particularly frightening about seriously acknowledging God for the first time. With the dethronement of one's ego involved in favor of putting God in the lead of our lives, there is a distinct loss of control (as there was in coming to terms with my own recounted "big dream" of God doing the driving).

For many secularists, the rejection of any evidence of God is not simply a neutral or passive sort of phenomenon. It is common these days to speak, for example, of addicts and others who reject massive evidence of their problem as being "in denial." Such denial is a fiercely active psychological process. In this respect, I believe we can think of some secularists as being addicted to their secularism. Or fundamentalists to their simplism. No amount of challenging evidence is going to change their minds. It isn't simply that they don't have the same access to God as everyone else has; it is that they have chosen to avoid and deny it.

THE EGO AND THE SOUL

In many ways, the acceptance of any evidence of God involves a battle between the ego and the soul. Earlier I defined the soul as "a God-created, God-nurtured, unique, developable, immortal human spirit." Each of these modifiers is crucial. Of particular importance is that the soul is "God-nurtured," by which I mean that not only did God create us at the moment of our conception but that God, through grace, continues to nurture us throughout our lives. I believe there would be no purpose in Her doing so unless She wanted something from us: the development of our souls. But how are souls different from egos?

I have previously described the ego as the governing part of our personality. Ego development—the maturation of this governor—is very much related to the development of our consciousness. When people speak of someone's "ego," what is usually referred to is someone's self-image, self-perception, and will. This encompasses not only some personality characteristics (often our more negative and defensive ones) but also what we think about and value in life. Like the soul, our ego can grow, change, and develop, but that doesn't mean it will.

One of the biggest differences between the soul and the ego is that the ego is closer to the surface of who we are or believe ourselves to be, whereas the soul goes deeper, to the core of our being—so deep that we may not be aware of it. This was the case when I made the decision to quit Exeter, the prep school I had attended for two and a half years. I recounted some of the details of this story in a previous chapter, as I often have elsewhere, because it marked the beginning of my encounter with my soul.

Everyone has a sense of their own "I," a sense of I-dentity. This "I" is sometimes referred to as the ego, sometimes the self. My ego wanted to please my parents, to tough it out and follow in my brother's footsteps in graduating from Exeter. I had wanted to go to Exeter. I wanted myself to succeed there. I most definitely didn't want to be a quitter. But if I didn't want to quit, then *who* was doing it? Gradually I found myself unable or unwilling to do what I thought I wanted to, even though it wasn't clear to me why at the time. Obviously, something was going on inside of me that was different from what my WASP upbringing had trained me to want.

Most psychiatrists would simply say that my ego was conflicted. Some would say more specifically that my ego was in conflict with my true self, implying that the self is somehow larger and deeper than the ego. The latter explanation I can live with, but it seems to me to beg the question. What is this "true self"? Why doesn't it get defined? Could it be the soul, and if so, why isn't it identified as such? And what might be the definition of the soul?

Secular psychiatrists would say that the true self—the whole self—is a conglomerate of psychic components: the id, ego, and superego; the conscious and the unconscious; the genetically determined temperament and our accumulated experiential

learning. No wonder I might have been in conflict, having so
many different parts! These parts are real, and can indeed be in
conflict. Moreover, effective psychotherapy can be accomplished using this "conglomerate" model. The problem was
that I didn't feel like a walking conglomerate at Exeter. And
strangely, the older I grew and the more I recognized the reality of these different parts of me, the less I felt like a conglomerate. I felt something deeper yet was going on, something very
important that somehow made me larger than myself. I had
come to recognize that I had a soul.

It's important to bear in mind that souls and egos, being
different phenomena, naturally operate on different levels. Although I believe the distinction between the soul and the ego is
both valid and important, this doesn't mean there is no interaction between the two. I strongly believe that a conversion—
change and growth—in the soul will dramatically change certain
ways in which the ego functions, and will do so for the better.
Similarly, I also believe that ego learning will encourage soul
development. But exactly how the soul and ego interact remains mysterious.

Most secularists acknowledge the uniqueness of persons
but see no need to make any "mystical" distinction between the
soul and the ego. "Since everyone has a unique genetic com-
plement as well as their own unique set of life experiences,"
they are likely to say, "naturally everybody's ego is different." To
the contrary, there seems to me to be a relative sameness among
egos, while human souls are unique. Yet while I can tell you a lot
about the ego, I can tell you very little about the soul. Although
egos can be described in general, almost banal terms, the
uniqueness of each individual's soul cannot be adequately captured in words. The soul is one's true spirit and, like God, it is a
spirit too slippery to capture.

The uniqueness of the soul shows itself most whenever
someone seriously elects a path of psychospiritual growth for
the remainder of his or her lifetime. It is as if psychopathology
of the ego is like mud, and the more it gets cleared away, the
more the soul underneath will shine forth in glory, in a distinct

pattern of glorious color that can be found nowhere else on earth. And while I am certain that God creates a human soul differently each and every time, this doesn't mean there are no unanswerable questions. Nonetheless, however mysterious, the process of soul creation is individualized. The uniqueness of individual persons is undeniable (except at peril to your own soul) and cannot be explained by mere psychology or biology.

The secular tendency to deny the soul is also a denial of the heart. There is a self-fulfilling quality in secularism; the thinking goes: "Since God doesn't exist, I will discount any evidence that hints at God." It is hardly surprising, then, that those individuals who are cut off from a sense of their own soul are also quick to dismiss the human heart. When there's a lack of integration of one's feelings and thinking—a distrust of feelings—the result is often the denial of one's own heart.

The case of Theodore in *The Road Less Traveled* was an example. In the course of his treatment, I asked him to listen to Neil Diamond's soundtrack for "Jonathan Livingston Seagull." It is a profoundly spiritual work of music, and I had hoped it would nudge Theodore a bit in the direction of spiritual growth. But he couldn't stand it. He called the music "disgustingly sentimental," words which, I believe, revealed his rejection of his own heart at the time.

I recognize that not everyone will have the same experience or strong reaction to songs I find soul-stirring. But at the very least, if someone is in touch with his own heart, he will make some room for sentimentality, will have a soft spot for the things that matter most to him. For those who are spiritually oriented, the body, mind, and heart are viewed as integral parts of their whole being. They are not ashamed to be "softhearted"; on the contrary, they worry most during those times when circumstances seem to demand that they be coldhearted.

I have written that this divorce between the head and heart, between intellect and emotion, is a common spiritual condition among sophisticated twentieth-century men and women. I have found many people, for example, to be Christians in their hearts while they are simultaneously intellectual atheists; sometimes it is the other way around. It is truly a pity. The former people—many of whom are generous, gentle, honest, and dedicated to their fellow human beings—are often filled with despair, finding little meaning in existence and at the same time denying the joyful or soothing voices of their heart, labeling the heart's messages sentimental, unrealistic, or childish. Lacking faith in their innermost selves, they are hurting unnecessarily.

The deepest healing occurs not in the mind, but in the heart or soul. And if the heart is "hardened," no words can penetrate it. Conversely, when one has undergone what the pithy Old Testament Jews called a circumcision of the heart, the reality of God's healing presence in our lives—and the rest of the world—becomes less difficult to acknowledge.

KENOSIS

When I wrote in *The Road Less Traveled* that the purpose of growth was for us to become more conscious and, in turn, evolve, I suggested that this evolutionary path in human life points directly to God. God wants us to learn and develop in this life and, I believe, actually nurtures us in doing so. But when I went on to suggest that God ultimately wants us to evolve toward becoming God—like God—that statement caused a great deal of theological indigestion. It seemed to be a potentially Satanic notion. After all, did not Satan think he could be like God or as good as God?

I could have prevented much of this indigestion had I gone on to write about the great paradox involved. The paradox is that we ourselves cannot become like God except by bumping ourselves off, except through the humility of emptiness. There is an important word in theology for this endeavor: kenosis, which is the process of the self emptying itself of self. It is the essence of the message of the great spiritual masters, like Buddha and Christ, throughout human history. We need to pare away our egos. The paradox that "Whosoever will lose his life for My sake shall find it" can be paraphrased as "Whoever is willing to lose his ego will find his soul."

The image used in Christianity for the goal of the kenotic process is that of the empty vessel. We need to retain enough of our ego—the governing part of our personality—to be a functioning container. Otherwise, we would have no identity at all. Beyond that, however, the whole point of spiritual growth is to get rid of our ego sufficiently to become empty enough to be filled with God's Spirit, with our true soul. That this is possible was expressed by St. Paul when he said, "I live now not with my own life but the life of Christ Jesus living in me."

So we have returned once again to this crucial matter of emptiness. It will be remembered that I spoke of it as the key to the unlearning and relearning that we must go through all our lives if we are to grow and to become as healed and fully human as possible. It will also be remembered that I spoke of how much this unlearning feels like dying. In years past, monks and nuns routinely engaged in a practice called mortification. The word is derived from the Latin *mortis,* "death," and means "the discipline of daily dying." While they may have overdone it with self-flagellation and the wearing of hair shirts, nonetheless they were onto something. Through mortification, they were attempting to practice kenosis.

I have also referred to the fact that not only individuals but also groups need to go through this kenotic process of self-emptying in order to become and stay healthy. I noted that the crucial stage of the community-building process we have labeled "emptiness." Now it is time to describe all the stages of growth that routinely occur when groups deliberately attempt to form themselves into communities.

Pseudocommunity

In order to avoid the pain of unlearning and change, when groups assemble to form community, they first attempt to pretend that they already are a community. The basic pretense is that all the members are the same, a pretense that is sustained by the practice of an unwritten set of rules that everyone knows: good manners. In this stage, the members are exquisitely polite to each other in order to avoid any disagreement in their desire to deny their individual differences. But the reality is that people, with their unique souls as well as egos, are all different, which is why we call this pretense of sameness pseudocommunity.

Chaos

Once individual differences are allowed (or, as in the community-building process, encouraged) to surface, the group goes about the business of trying to obliterate those differences. The primary method used is "healing," "fixing," or "converting." But people do not like to be easily healed or fixed, so in a short time the victims turn around and start trying to heal the self-appointed healers and to convert the self-appointed converters. It is glorious chaos. It is also noisy, argumentative, and unproductive. No one is listening to anyone else.

Emptiness

There are only three ways out of chaos. One is to revert to an even more profound pseudocommunity. Another is to organize away chaos by creating committees and subcommittees; but such organization is never in and of itself "community." The third way, we tell groups, is "into and through emptiness." If a sufficient number of the members of the group hear us, what then begins to happen is a very painful, gradual process of the members emptying themselves of the barriers to communication. The most common barriers include expectations, preconceptions, prejudices, rigidity of ideology or theology, and the needs to heal, convert, fix, or solve. As the group enters this stage of emptiness—the most critical stage of its learning—it looks very much like an organism that has totally lost its way. Indeed, the feeling is like dying. This is the time of kenosis. But if the group can hang in there together—as, amazingly, occurs almost all the time with proper leadership—this work of kenosis or dying will succeed, and from it renewal will emerge.

Community

When a group's death has been completed and it is open and empty, it enters community. In this final stage a soft quietness descends. It is a kind of peace, often preceded and followed by an abundance of individual expressions of personal experiences and emotions, tears of sadness and tears of joy. This is when an extraordinary amount of healing and converting begins to occur—now that no one is deliberately trying to convert or heal. From this point, true community is born.

Not every group that becomes a community follows this paradigm exactly. Communities that temporarily form in response to crisis, for example, may skip over one or more stages for the time being. And although I have spoken glowingly of the virtues of community when barriers to communication are finally transcended, this does not by any means suggest that it is now all easy. Once community is achieved, depending on a group's goals and tasks, maintaining it will become an ongoing challenge. But the experience of having grown from emptiness leaves a lasting imprint. And the most common emotional response to the spirit of true community is joy and love.

PRAYER AND FAITH

Everyone prays. The most diehard secularists pray in moments of agony or ecstasy, even if they are not aware of it. Instinctively, they will cry out during orgasm: "Oh, God!" or "Oh, Christ!" Similarly, when they are lying in bed racked with the flu, every bone aching, they are likely to moan, "Oh, God." Or their thoughts turn to God in moments of terror, a phenomenon that has led to the famous saying "There are no atheists in the foxholes." One of the differences between secularists and those of religious or spiritual persuasion is that we (the latter) occasionally think about God during the 99.5 percent of the time when we're not in agony or ecstasy.

But what is prayer? Time and again I must point out to people that there are many things in life, such as consciousness, community, love, and soul—all of which have something to do with God—that are too large to submit to any single, adequate definition. People have been praying for millennia, and one would think that theologians would have arrived at a fully adequate definition of prayer, but they have not.

Most people think of prayer as simply "speaking to God." This definition is not all that bad as long as we realize that there are innumerable ways of speaking to God. Hence, such prayer can be divided into many types: group prayer and individual prayer; formal and informal prayer; prayers of praise and adoration and gratitude; prayers of repentance and forgiveness; petitionary prayers for others or for oneself, and so on. I would also classify meditation as prayer, and again there are many kinds of meditation. While not all kinds would be defined as self-emptying, I believe the best forms of meditation are those when we deliberately quiet and empty ourselves in order to be able to listen to God or for God. This doesn't mean that God will answer. Spiritual experiences are actually unlikely to happen to one when praying, but many of us have a sense that an active prayer life increases the chances of having—and identifying—spiritual experiences at other times.

Then there is the matter of thinking and its relationship to prayer. Thinking well can and does merge into prayer. Although not wholly adequate, my favorite definition of prayer—one that doesn't even mention God—is that of Matthew Fox. As I mentioned much earlier, Fox defines prayer as "a radical response to the mysteries of life." Most of my time at prayer, I am not so much talking to God or listening to God as I am just thinking, but doing so with God in mind. Before I can respond radically to the mysteries of life, I first have to think about them deeply, as well as think about the mysteries of my own life and the whole range of potential options of response to them. "God, I wonder how this looks to You . . . through Your eyes?" I am pondering. This type of prayer is often referred to as contemplative prayer. And usually it is wordless. One of the reasons I like Fox's definition so much is its implication that prayer ultimately needs to be translated into action, but I myself find I cannot act well except out of contemplation.

There is great virtue in routine prayer. Although I am a Christian, I believe all the other great religions have some kernel of truth that Christianity may lack, and hence some ways of doing it better. The little bit of Islamic theology I have read seems to contain the word "remember" with unusual frequency. I think it is no accident that the Muslims build towers in their towns and cry out to the faithful five times a day to remind them to pray—and, by praying, to remember God. The ordinary Muslim believer does as a matter of daily routine what only highly contemplative Christian monks and nuns do.

Although there is great virtue in both public and formal prayer, my general preference is for private, personal prayer. Rightly or wrongly, I suspect that the more personal our prayers are, the more God likes them. But prayer is a two-way street. For our prayers to be personal (except in moments of agony or ecstasy), we need to have at least some smidgen of belief that there is a Person at the other end who is going to hear and possibly respond. This brings us to the matter of faith and its relationship to prayer. Why a "Person" at the other end? When I was in college, my favorite quotation was a remark of Voltaire's: "God created man in His own image, and then man went and returned the compliment." Voltaire was referring to our tendency to anthropomorphize God as a man or a woman with bodily features. It seemed to me that God must be infinitely more different than we can possibly imagine Him or Her to be. And so She or He is. Nonetheless, in the days since college, I have also come to realize that the very deepest means we have to even begin to comprehend the nature of God is to project onto Him or Her the very best of our own human nature. In other words, God is, among other things and above all things, *humane*.

There are other things I have learned since college. Back

then I used to think that faith preceded prayer, and that only those with a great deal of faith would pray a great deal. Some years ago, however, I ran across an ancient Christian motto—so ancient that it was in Latin: "Lex orandi, lex credendi," which translated means "The rule of prayer precedes the rule of faith." In other words, I had things reversed. The deeper truth is that if one prays a lot, then, and only then, will one be likely to grow in faith.

Why grow in faith? Once again, in my youth, I had it backward. I used to think that if I understood the world better, I might have more faith in God. But then I ran across a saying of one of the saints: "Do not seek understanding that you might have faith; seek faith that you might understand."

It was with my gradually increasing knowledge of such pieces of "science" that I was able to be of some help to a wonderful, initially secular woman, Annie, who came to see me because of her excessive worrying. We identified that at least one major root of her problem was her lack of faith in God, and ever so slowly I was able to teach her to pray. After some years of infrequent appointments, she came to see me one day and announced, "Dr. Peck, I am so poor at this business. I still don't know how to pray. Much of the time my only prayer—it comes from someplace in the Bible, I think—is 'I believe, Lord; help my unbelief.' It's so pathetic."

"Annie," I responded, "that happens to be one of the most sophisticated prayers ever spoken."

While this woman's growth in faith (as is typical of the transition from Stage III to Stage IV) was very gradual, occasionally the evolution of faith may be very rapid, as if one's eyes had suddenly been opened. Indeed, the experience can be frightening. My lecture audiences used to be made up primarily of people who were making the transition from Stage III to Stage IV or were already deeply in Stage IV. I would often ask them, "For how many of you here has the journey ever been moving so rapidly that you wondered whether or not you were going crazy?" Most raised their hands in understanding. I would go on to note: "That's one reason for good spiritual directors; they can tell you whether you're going crazy or not." Occasionally, sudden "explosions" of faith may indeed be the result of a mental illness. As often as not, however, what people need at such times is sophisticated reassurance (which a great many secular psychiatrists or psychotherapists are not able to provide).

I have been speaking of the gaining of faith. What about its opposite—the loss of faith? It is a very real phenomenon, occurring routinely in those who are in the process of growing out of Stage II into Stage III. It, too, can be scary, which is the reason for a small, recently founded organization, Fundamentalists Anonymous, a self-help group for people dealing with the immense anxieties that may be associated with relinquishing a very clear-cut, rigid, doctrinaire sort of faith. Loss of faith may also be particularly painful for those who have a formal or professional religious identity. Many a clergyman has entered the ministry while in Stage II, only to evolve into Stage III and find himself in the position of getting up in the pulpit every Sunday and talking about a God in Whom he is no longer sure he even believes. He, too, needs sophisticated reassurance that can only be given by someone who understands the stages of what Fowler calls "faith development."

We also need to glance briefly at a phenomenon that could be called the testing of faith, which may happen to any religious person at a time of crisis. Usually the crisis is survived and the faith survives with it. But there is another type of testing that is actually more predictable and most likely to happen to highly developed spiritual people who have long been in Stage IV. For this phenomenon, St. John of the Cross in the sixteenth century coined the phrase "the dark night of the soul."

The dark night of the soul is a point where God seems to be totally absent, and often for a prolonged period of time. To the person in it, the still, small voice she has come to distinguish as God's seems to have faded or stopped altogether. Dreams that once provided revelations seem to have dried up. It is not a matter of crisis or even affliction; it is just a deep sense that God, who was once present and active in her life, has gone on vacation and seems totally inaccessible, perhaps forever.

Might God deliberately make Herself inaccessible? It is conceivable, when we think of how appropriate it is that a mature faith needs to be tested. In *What Return Can I Make? (Gifts for the Journey)*, I used the analogy of a young child, perhaps two years old, who will have no trouble believing in Mommy's presence and care when she is right there in the room with him. But when he can't see her, he will panic and begin to think that she no longer exists. As his faith in her is so tested over several years, however, he will slowly come to learn that she has other concerns to tend to. Gradually he will realize that Mommy is probably just down the hall making his bed, that she has not truly vanished or abandoned him, that she is still actively loving and caring for him—only in a different manner than that which he had originally counted on.

Certainly, by the time they have reached the dark night of the soul, most of the faithful remain faithful. They continue to pray and praise the seemingly absent God, as Job did by and large. Their motto might be that of Jesus on the cross, when he cried out, "My God, my God, why have You forsaken me?" But it was still God Whom Jesus was calling to, praying to. It may also help them to know that more than a few designated saints who were not martyrs—who died in bed—spent their last days, months, or years in the dark night before they moved on.

PROCESS THEOLOGY

Many of us, secularists and spiritual people alike, question the existence of God most when we look at our world and ask why there is so much pain and suffering and downright evil. In other words, why aren't things perfect? It is simply not enough to answer: "God's ways are mysterious." No answer can be offered with certainty. What I can do, however, is offer some relatively modern, speculative additions to the more ancient, traditional, and, I believe, inadequate "God theory."

Traditional, primitive God theory posits a God who is omnipotent. But such a simplistic vision of God fails to account for evil or to take into account both a good deal of the Bible and common sense. While in the beginning God may have created everything (and even this is subject to question), by the third chapter of Genesis, the very first book of the Bible, there are already problems. God expels Adam and Eve from the perfect Garden of Eden and tells them that henceforth they shall have to suffer. Why? Is God sadistic?

The answer, I believe, is that God has to operate within constraints, even if they are constraints that He Himself created. When it is said that "God created us in his own image," what is meant by that more than anything else, I believe, is that God gave us free will. You cannot give someone free will and at the same time hold a machine gun to his back. Free will means that we are free, and such freedom means that we are free to choose for either good or evil. The moment when God granted us free will was the moment when human evil—as well as human goodness—was let loose in the world. Having once granted us free will, God is no longer omnipotent. He has constrained Himself, and no matter how much it might hurt Him, in most respects He simply has to let us be.

Genesis 3 suggests that this constraining decision to let us be is also associated with the existence of death (and, by implication, disease and aging). How we have agonized over these "curses"! Yet, as long as we bear in mind that the death of the body does not necessarily mean the death of the soul, I am not sure that aging and illness and death are curses at all. I curse them myself from time to time, but in my more rational moments, I see them as being an integral part of the natural order of things, an order that God Herself established. I don't mean to imply that God is totally helpless. What I do mean to imply is that God is not so omnipotent that She doesn't have to operate within the constraints of this natural order of illness, aging, death, and physical decay. And within the more terrible constraints of allowing human evil, even on such a mass scale as the Holocaust.

The notion that God is not simplistically omnipotent but must operate within certain constraints is not the only modern addendum to the primitive God Theory. An equally important addendum has come over the course of the past fifty years to be called process theology, which challenges the traditional notion of a God who is a static, unchanging being. It suggests that, like all living beings, God is "in process": living, suffering, and growing right alongside of us, albeit just a step or two ahead of us. While the origin of process theology is attributed to Alfred North Whitehead within this century, it was actually one well embedded in Mormon theology over a century ago. The Mormons have long had a saying: "As man is, God was. As God is, man will become."

In my novel *In Heaven as on Earth,* I proposed a sort of addendum to process theology, suggesting that creation (including the creation of souls, human and otherwise) might be an ongoing experiment. Insofar as God is a creator, why shouldn't She be an experimenter every bit as much as human scientists—albeit a bit more imaginative, sophisticated, and artistic? We scientists are generally comfortable with the fact that many, if not most, of our experiments "fail." That is, they are trials. There is always room for improvement. Might we not look upon a highly imperfect—even evil—soul as a "failed experiment"? We also know that we have as much to learn from failed experiments as from successful ones. They are what send us back to the drawing board; perhaps they do so for God, too. It makes sense once we stop thinking of God as omniscient, omnipotent, and unchanging—when we begin to think of Her as being in process and start to seriously consider the essence of process theology.

In *A World Waiting to Be Born,* I have written about how I first stumbled onto the concept of process theology. The moment was fifteen years ago; I was sitting in my office with a thirty-five-year-old patient. She was a very attractive person, perhaps only as much as eight pounds over the standard weight for women of her age and height. The preceding evening, at a joyful restaurant party, she was so relaxed she had ordered and eaten an ice cream sundae for dessert. Now she was lamenting,

"How could I have been so stupid? After only six days I broke my diet! Now I have to start all over again. I hate myself for being so undisciplined. An ice cream sundae, for Christ's sake! Butterscotch sauce. Thick, gooey. I mean, I couldn't have chosen anything that had more calories. One of these days I'll . . ."

As she went on and on in that vein, I found myself drifting off slightly, musing over how utterly typical she was of a large category of women who are physically appealing, yet who spend endless ergs of energy obsessing about their weight, even the most minor deviations in it. What was going on with them? In the midst of this wondering, I suddenly interrupted her, blurting out, "What makes you think that God doesn't have to diet?"

She looked at me as if I had gone crazy. "Why did you say that?" she asked.

I scratched my head, replying, "I don't know." But I had to think about why I had said it, and as I did, I realized that I was onto something. My patient was laboring under the fantasy that if she went on enough diets or discovered just the right diet or received enough psychotherapy, she would achieve a state in which she could either eat all she wanted without gaining an ounce, or else, whenever she did gain that ounce, could instantly and effortlessly lose it. A strange fantasy, come to think of it. "Maybe God puts on five pounds," I explained to her, "and then He has to take them off. Only He doesn't make a big deal out of it, which is perhaps why He's God."

The delusion my patient labored under was a static notion of perfection. It is a very common but destructive notion that perfection is an unchanging state. It is so common because it is so purely logical. If something is perfect and it changes, it can only become different from what it was. And if it becomes different from what it was, then logic holds that it has become imperfect. But if something is truly perfect, it cannot, by definition, become imperfect. Hence perfection must be unchanging. And so we think, "God is as God was and always will be."

But that's not the way I think anymore. It's also hardly what the Bible suggests. And increasingly it's not what theologians are beginning to think. Thank God! If there is anything that characterizes life, it is change. What most distinguishes the animate from the inanimate is "irritability." Something that's animate moves when you poke it. It doesn't just sit there. It's alive. It goes this way and that way. It grows, it dies, it decays, it is reborn. It changes. All life is in process. And since I choose to have a living God, I believe that my God is also in process, learning and growing and perhaps even laughing and dancing.

This new concept of process theology is so critically important not only because it adds a large piece to the puzzle of imperfection—even evil—in the world, but also because it implies that it is good for people to be in a state of change. The same holds true for our organizations and society, for all life itself. The healthier we are, the more we will be "in process." The more vibrant, the more lively we are, the more we will be changing. And the closer to perfection we are, the more rapidly we will be changing. And as we change, we can expect ourselves, the organizations to which we belong, and even our society to be in flux and in turmoil. We will know, not only in our heads but in our hearts, that if we let God into ourselves, we will be welcoming even more flux and turmoil. An individual who has developed a conscious relationship with God will probably be engaged in developing that relationship—often with anguish and struggle—for the rest of his or her ever-changing life.

We will know when we see ourselves or our organizations as comfortable, complacent, or particularly stable entities that we are undoubtedly in a state—or at least a phase—of decay. And if we see ourselves or our organizations suffering, struggling, searching this way and that for new solutions, constantly revising and reviving, our tendency will not only be to give ourselves or them the benefit of the doubt but to suspect that we may have stumbled upon a particularly Godly phenomenon.

Returning to the question of why things aren't perfect, it is for the same reasons that even Utopia will not be stable or static. It will be evolving. Utopia should not be thought of as a condition that we reach, because no sooner will we reach it than we will move on. It will not be a condition without suffering, without the stress and strain that necessarily accompany change or development.

Contrary to popular notions, Utopia does not mean all will be sweetness and light. Rather, it will be a society moving with maximal vitality toward maximal vitality. In other words, as long as there is a role for God to play and room for grace, Utopia may not be impossible to achieve after all. But it will be impossible to achieve if we hold on to our traditional vision of perfection, defined as static by our limited human understanding. Utopia will always be in the future, because it is not a state arrived at but a state of becoming. Indeed, we might think on our more optimistic days of Utopia as having already started, albeit barely.

GLORY

In the end all things point to God.

All things. I could go on and on, but I feel as if I'm in the same position as St. John when he wrote of Jesus at the conclusion of his Gospel:

> And there are also many other things which Jesus did, the which, if they should be written every one, I suppose that even the world itself could not contain the books that should be written. A-men.

I, too, could talk about all manner of other things unexplainable without resorting to God. About special people. About Jesus, who was so extraordinary that no one could have dreamed him up. But Jesus is a red flag for some who have been abused by the abusers of Jesus. So take another inexplicable human, Abraham Lincoln, and see if you can categorize him without resorting to divinity.

Or I could talk of mystical experiences, of sudden changes of perception, when without drugs or disease, we occasionally flit in and out of what seems another universe. I could speak of demons and angels. I could rhapsodize about God and nature—the God of the mountains and rivers, the God of sunrises and sunsets, of forests and storms. Or of music and melodies that are timeless. Or of romance and sex, where God deliberately gave us a taste of Himself—and of Her power, more subtle than dynamite, yet potentially as dangerous. Or of what transpires when a group reaches community or an exorcism has been successfully completed—when God seems to have entered an otherwise ordinary room and all that the people present can do is cry tears of gratitude and joy.

God is too immense to be limited to any chapter or book or even bible. Yet there is one word for our human experience whenever we happen—seemingly by accident—to tap into, to participate consciously in, that immensity. It is the experience of glory.

And how we yearn for it! Blindly, usually falsely, and more often than not destructively, we seek after glory as nothing else. Fleeting "happiness," even sexual ecstasy, can't compare. Despite all the pitfalls of this pursuit, it happens to be one of the many indirect "proofs" for the existence of God. As C. S. Lewis pointed out in his great sermon, "The Weight of Glory," God in His gentleness would never have created us with an appetite for something unreal or utterly unobtainable. We hunger only because there is food. We thirst because there is drink. We would not scream with sexual desire if there were no possibility of sexual fulfillment. So it is with glory. We yearn for it as we do for nothing else precisely because there is a God urging us on to union with Her.

But make no mistake: real glory is an attribute only of God. Since glory is the most potent object of all our desires, our desire for it is the one most subject to perversion. There is a name for this perversion: idolatry—the worship of false idols or cheap substitutes for God. As one name for the devil suggests, the varieties of idolatry are "Legion": money, sex, novelty, political power, security, possessions, and on and on. All are false gods. True glory is ours only insofar as we submit ourselves to the true God. But who . . . what . . . where . . . is the true God?

COCREATION

In *Denial of the Soul* I pointed out, with many qualifications, that suicide, including euthanasia, is usually an action not of courage but of the most questionable hubris. The reason for this seemingly harsh assessment is that we are not our own creators, and hence we do not have the moral right to be our own destroyers.

Humankind does not have the power to make the sun rise or set. We can predict and respond to the weather, but we do not determine what it will be day to day. I do not know how to create an iris or a rose; I can only steward one. So it is with myself. Presumably even more complicated than a flower, I could not possibly have even imagined myself into existence. But to a considerable extent I can choose to decently nurture or not nurture myself. In other words, while I cannot be my own creator, I can play a role as cocreator.

The concept of "cocreatorship" and the responsibility it entails have become quite popular in theology in recent years. But I have not read of this responsibility being extended to its ultimate. The fact is that we humans are free to choose our own vision of God, and no choice we make can be as potent in our personal lives or our role as agents of society. So we come to a crescendo of paradox. On the one hand, God is unquestionably our creator. On the other, in choosing the kind of God we believe in, we are, in a sense, creating God, not only for ourselves but also for others who will see God reflected in our beliefs, our actions, and in our very spirit.

But bear in mind that we cannot *know* God in the traditional scientific sense. A Hasidic story passed on to me by Erich Fromm makes the point. It is the story of a good Jewish man—let us call him Mordecai—who prayed one day, "O God, let me know Your true name, even as angels do." The Lord heard his prayer and granted it, allowing Mordecai to know His true name. Whereupon Mordecai crept under the bed and yelped in sheer animal terror, "O God, let me forget Your true name." And the Lord God heard that prayer and granted it also. Something of the same point was made by the Apostle Paul when he said, "It is a terrifying thing to fall into the hands of the living God." Yet . . .

In the end all things point to God. . . .

Let me turn now from the more or less abstract and prosaic science of God to poetry, and conclude this summation of my thinking in a very different tone by personally addressing the nameless and unknowable One.

CHAPTER 8

The "Poetry" of God

❉

Dear God,
Darling Lord:

Do You remember that reporter?
The one who pretended to be religious.
And then when I had talked for days about You,
Concluded by commenting,
"It's clear to me, Scotty,
That you could never really communicate
With your parents.
You must have been a very lonely child.
I wonder if
That doesn't have a lot to do
With your belief in God?"

Of course, I knew
At that point, we had lost it.

"Do you mean
Is God
My imaginary companion?"
I responded rhetorically.

"Actually, I don't think
I was a particularly lonely child,"
I went on.
"All children are lonely.
My parents were attentive
And I could talk to them about things small.
I had at least a modicum of friends
—more than most—
And more still as I got older.

"But is God my imaginary companion?
Oh, yes. Indeed, yes.
Yet, as I've been trying to tell you,
That's just one of a thousand
Reasons I believe."

Naturally, it had no effect.

But the fact is,
You have been beside me
In this imagination
For longer than I can remember,
And it's been a great trip together,
Hasn't it, Lord?

Now I'm old
I cannot be sure
Whether we're near the end
Or still merely preparing
To blast off.

But of this I'm sure:
There is not one moment I can declare
You to have been absent from me.
Note my words.
You created me to be precise with words.
I was not saying
I've always felt Your presence
Or been aware of You.
Frankly, most of the time
I haven't even bothered to think of You.

You've been so good to me.

Oh, there were a few bad years early on.
The year in the fourth grade in a new school
And two years later
When I was ten and couldn't understand
Why all my classmates suddenly
Turned on me again.
How could I have understood,
Unaware You had created me a leader who,
Without intent,
Threatened the top dog?
(It was thirty more years before
I realized what had transpired—
Before I even realized I was
A leader.)
But those
Were less than two years
Out of twelve. The rest
Were magical.

What can I say?
There was an icehouse
Behind our summer home.
And an orchard where the neighbor's sheep
Grazed, and in September
The white clouds grazed the sky,
And I knew my parents loved me.

And I knew
You were behind it all,
Like the icehouse . . . deep, deep,
Ancient, cool in the summer, and, above all,
Providing.
It is a paradox.
At one and the same time
I was grateful and I took You
for granted. Like the icehouse,
You were just there.

At thirteen I went to boarding school.
It was a place without love. Everything
Was wrong.
They said it was right.
Thirty months it took me
To think for myself. I walked out,
Not yet an adult exactly,
But a man who knew his soul
Belonged to You and, never again,
To fashion.

Yes, those were tough years.
The toughest. They were also when
I can first remember talking about You.
Vaguely I recall arguing Your existence
With my adolescent friends.
Or was it Your nonexistence?
It doesn't matter. What matters
Is that I was thinking about You.

Fifteen was the last bad year.
There have been bad moments since
—maybe even a few of tragedy—
But no bad years.
Some years it has even seemed as if
You had placed me on a kind of
Grand vacation.

I cannot imagine
Anything
I could ever have done
To deserve
Such kindness.

Was it at five . . .
Or ten or fifteen that
I first decided to speak
The truth
When I could have gotten away
With a lie?
I can't recall.
Certainly by college, honesty
Had become my habit
(Some have said my compulsion).
I do not mean I never withhold
A piece of truth now and then;
Only that it is painful for me
To love in such a way.

But I try not to withhold
Even a smidgen
From myself,
And if there is a secret
To all my good fortune, I suppose
That is it.
But it is not my doing.

It was You who planted in me the seed—
This burning thirst for the Real.
Besides,
Since You know the reality
Of my heart, to what end
Should I seek to deceive
Except to isolate myself from You?
And that is the very last thing
I could ever desire.

Do You remember
That book I was asked to praise,
The one with the title *Intuition?*
It never mentioned You.
That might have been pardonable,
Save that it drew no distinction
Between intuition and revelation.
I did not feel I could bless such a book
That left You out.
But was I being fair?
Perhaps its author was right and I was wrong.
Perhaps You did not exist.
So I sat down to think about it.
First, I thought about how much of my own work
Was predicated on You. I had a large stake
In You. Could I relinquish that?
If it were the reality,
Could I disavow You?
Yes.
Then I was utterly free
To contemplate Your nonexistence.

I began with the usual:
Famine and flood, drought and destruction;
Poverty, greed, war and torture;
Hate, lying, and manipulation;
Disease, mental and physical,
And all things unfair.
But it was of no use.
There was no evil I could blame on You,
That required You for its explanation.
Weep, yes, but
Blame You, no.

Then there was human goodness.
As have others, I could speculate
On how altruism may have been bred into us
For its survival value. Oh, yes,
I knew about sociobiology and other
Modern notions.
And while I could choose
To see Your hand in these matters,
I could also choose
Not to.

The same with beauty.
Trees and flowers, valleys and mountains,
Streams, rivers, lakes, oceans
And all manner of water and weather
Shriek to me
Of Your creation.
Yet, if need be, I could close my ears.
There is nothing that compels me
To find Your presence in sunrise or sunset,
Starlight or moonlight or all things
Green.
Wondrous, ever so wondrous,
But I cannot insist upon Your design.
It is not beyond me to imagine
A wondrous accident.

No, these big things I can deal with.
It is the little things,
This business of revelation,
I cannot handle:
The occasional dream,
More elegant by far than
My capacity for construction;
The quiet voice one might think
Is that of my waking brain
Save that when it rarely speaks
It teaches me with wisdom
Beyond any brain;
And those coincidences
Which might be merely amusing
If they could be understood as such.

I cannot explain these "little" things
Except to know that in them
You have revealed Yourself. . . .
And I cannot explain why
Except that You love me. . . .
And that I cannot explain
Except that You love us all.

None of this has been in my control.
Never have You operated by my schedule.
Yes, my Dearest,
I talk of You as if
You were my imaginary companion,
But only as if.
If You really were imaginary,
Then You would obey my imagination,
Leaping in form and time
In accordance with my desire.
But that's not the way it works,
Is it? And it is I who must strive
To be obedient.

No, my Companion,
You keep me strange company,
Coming to me
Whenever, however, and
In whatever form
You desire,
Utterly unpredictable.

The Hindus, I am told,
Have a concept they call
"The God of the Void."
If they are referring
To Your silence when I want Your voice,
To Your apparent absence
When I want Your presence,
To Your unpredictability,
To Your namelessness,
To the fact that You are far more ephemeral
Than my imagination,
Then I think I know
What they mean.

But You are not a void.
Although You are more likely
To come to me when I am empty—
To us when we are empty—
You Yourself are not emptiness
Without form.
Like us—
More than us—
You are capable of emptying Yourself,
Of setting Yourself aside
For the sake of love.
But You are not a void.
Rather I should call You
A God of Fullness.

I am not ready
To know Your true name
Nor yet to see You
Face to face.
But mysterious though You may be,
You are no cipher,
And there are things I can tell the world,
With gladness, about exactly
Who You are.

Most important,
You are a Person.

Why do we have such trouble with this,
Wishing to neuter You
Into some abstract "force"?
I know. I did it myself. I wanted
To be sophisticated. I wanted to be sure
People knew You weren't
My imaginary companion,
Some mere heavenly projection of myself
As the proverbial wise old man
With a long white beard.
How many years was it
Before I could finally speak my heart,
To publicly acknowledge
Your Personhood?

I am so slow.

You don't have a long white beard.
You do not even have a body,
As we are accustomed to think
Of bodies.
But You have a personality,
A personality definite beyond our own,
A personality vibrant beyond our imagination.
And how could this be
Were You not a Person?

So it is of Your personality I speak,
Your uncapturable Spirit,
And my language will be that of emotion—
Not of genes or beards or protoplasm,
Although I sometimes suppose You are
The ultimate protoplasm.

The obvious
Is that You are a
Loving God.
Trying to be scientific
In my published work, I have
Shied away from the emotion of love
And all its capacity for self-deception.
"The proof of the pudding is in the eating,"
As my grandfather would have said, or
"Handsome is as handsome does."
And I have insisted upon so-called
Operational definitions of love.
Which has been all to the good,
Save that it may have obscured the fact
We cannot be loving unless we want to be,
And that behind the wanting lies
An emotion—
The most unsimple and demanding
Emotion there is.

Real love demands
That we suffer—that I allow
My beloved to break my heart, piece by piece,
Yet still carry on,
Continuing to love with a heart
That is ever larger as the result.

On the eve of his execution
For plotting, out of love, to murder
Hitler, the Christian martyr Dietrich Bonhoeffer
Wrote: "Only a suffering God will do."
You, dear God, have not called me to quite
Such agonizing complexity. Nonetheless,
You have permitted me a taste of it
When I have been called to intervene
In the lives of others. Thinking
Of how You have intervened in my own life
With unfailing goodness of judgment,
I sense the awesome energy
Required, and I know You have brooded
Over me with a devotion
I can barely understand.
I can only assume
You suffer so over us all,
And I am not sure I became an adult
Until I began
To feel sorrow for You.

But You—
Needless to say—
Are a paradoxical God,
And what amazes me even more
Than Your continual suffering is Your
Persistent gaiety. You are a
Playful God,
And one of the things I know about You
Is Your sense of humor—
If for no other reason than it is clear
You love to confound me.
As soon as I think
I have obtained a handle on Your creation,
You instantly come along to ask,
"But what about this, Scotty?"
This defilement of my certainty
Is so routine
I have been forced to conclude
You must take a certain
Delight in it.

In the face
Of all the sorrows of the world
I am sometimes tempted to despair.
And this is what I find most strange
About You: I can feel Your suffering,
But never have I sensed in You
One second of despair. Unlike me,
Your delight in Your creation seems constant.
You are, to me, an amazingly cheerful God,
And I pray that some day I shall learn
Your secret.

You are also
A sexy God.
Now I sense You male, now female,
But never neuter.
Indeed, sex is one of Your tricks,
Infinitely confounding, yet
Among other things, the most glorious
Play we humans are allowed—
So glorious I cannot explain the pleasure
Save to posit it as a gift
Deliberately offered to give us
A taste for You
And Your playfulness.
I used to speak of this
In a lecture. It was the one
Where the audience was most likely
To weep with passion
Except for those
Who walked out, simply
Unable to bear
Your intimacy.

Yet You are a God
Of restraint.
Having given us, in Your image,
Free will, You never dictate,
Never threaten or punish.
I do not know the boundaries
Of your power, but sometimes I wonder
If You can only create,
Having long ago forever forsaken
The capacity to destroy
Anything.

You give us our "space,"
Forcing nothing,
And not once have I ever been
Violated by You. You are the
Gentlest of Beings.

You love variety.
In variety You delight.
I sit in a meadow
On a summer afternoon,
And from a single spot I can observe
A hundred different plants,
A dozen species of winged insects,
And had I the vision,
Within the soil,
I could watch colonies of bacteria
And whole societies of viruses
Intermingling.

But what impresses me most
Is the variety of humans,
Each with unique limitations,
Each with unique gifts.
From them You have given me
So many friends, all different,
And my entire life has been spent
In a web of exchange.
Often I have not exchanged well.
Forgive me, Lord,
For all those I have failed.

I thank You for my friends
And, most specially,
For my best friend.
Thirty-seven years ago,
When Lily and I were wed,
I did not know who she was.
Nor she me.
Nor much about ourselves.
Nor anything about marriage at all.
The learning was often to be painful,
Although without it
There would have been nothing.
Somehow we made it through,
And it would be wrong not to give ourselves
Any credit. But tell me this:
Utterly innocent back then,
How did I know
In my blind ignorance
That Lily—more different
Than I could imagine—
Was right for me?
I cannot explain it
Unless You were invisibly at my side,
Guiding me while I, like Jacob,
Was unaware. And I,
Like Jacob, must also now exclaim:
"Surely God was in this place, and I,
I did not know it."

In the end,
All things point to You.

We are old now—
Early old we have lived so hard—
And it is a time of waiting,
Tending to our aching bodies
As best we can for whatever little You
Have left in store for us
Here.

Like the old,
We look back,
Facing failures and enjoying
The successes of our past.
We can account for the failures. The successes
Seem the more mysterious. Again
We take some credit, but again
We know You have helped us
In all we have achieved.

This looking back is part of detaching. Mostly
We are looking forward.
Much as I have enjoyed this world
I have forever felt one part
Alien, as if I did not quite
Belong here. A decade ago,
After a five-day meeting that he led,
Jim—a most extraordinary man—commented,
"Scotty, I have no idea
What planet we're from
But it seems to have been
The same one."
A year later, almost to the day,
Walking across a street in France,
Jim was hit by a car from behind.
It killed him instantly. My reaction
Was one part grief and two parts
Envy.

Around that time I read a work of
Science fiction. Its story was that
Of aliens who, in the guise of humans,
Colonized earth. At one point
A few of their number were given
The opportunity to return
To their original planet. I threw
The book down on my bedclothes,
Sobbing to You,
"Lord, I want to go home.
Please take me home."

Now,
A decade later,
I do not feel so frantic
As it becomes ever more clear
It won't be so long before
I get my wish.

I'm coming home, Lord!

I have no desire
To disparage this world.
The older I am the more I can see
How precious it is to You.
You have set it before us
For a purpose. You have laid it out
Like a jigsaw puzzle to which
The box has been lost. But the pieces
Are so colorful we children cannot help
But pick them up and start to play.
Painstakingly, we put one piece together
With another.

The puzzle is huge.
Eventually it dawns on us
We will never begin to have enough time
To complete it. This may be
A moment for despair, tempting us
To discard You, You are so much larger than us.
Yet, if we are alert, there are other
Lessons to be learned. In fact,
The puzzle is so huge it is amazing
We can put one piece together with another
At all. It seems almost
Pure luck, save that it happens so frequently
We sense our hands and eyes have been guided
By an instinct we cannot explain. Who
Has not had the experience? Then
Those few pieces put together
Offer us tiny glimpses of the whole
And it looks beautiful . . . designedly enticing. Finally,
We find in those few attached fragments occasional
Cryptic messages. Once I interdigitated
Pieces that fit into a strange sign.
It was in French and read:
"Aimez-vous les Uns les Autres."

Do with this what you will.
I myself have chosen, by Your grace,
To see it as something more
Than a childish game. And some soon day
I imagine I may even see
The picture on the box, or,
Led deeper into Your mystery,
Be handed a jigsaw or else,
As a trembling apprentice,
Even a paintbrush.

In the meantime
Thank you for letting me know
That it is You
Who are the name of the game.

Acknowledgments

⁂

As was the case with my previous books, there is no way I can thank the hundreds who have supported me in writing this one. And, as usual, I must thank those same key people who keep hanging in with me year after year, book after book: Gail Puterbaugh, Susan Poitras, Valerie Duffy; my agent, Jonathan Dolger; my "senior" editors, Fred Hills and Burton Beals; and the one who has hung in longer than anyone, my ever-growing wife of thirty-seven years, Lily.

But this is not my usual book, and there is one person I have to single out for my very special appreciation. Because so much of its subject matter has been so close to me for so long, I have needed a very special kind of editorial assistance to help me see the woods for the trees. The right person for this job had to be someone of particular sophistication in the diverse areas of psychology, theology, and editing. Indeed, I had to wait the better part of a year for serendipity to bring this "just right" person to my door. That person was Fannie LeFlore. It was a pleasure to work with someone with such tact, humor, humanity, and fierce intelligence. Thank you, Fannie. I couldn't have done it without you.

Notes

ABBREVIATIONS

MSP	=	M. Scott Peck
TRLT	=	*The Road Less Traveled: A New Psychology of Love, Traditional Values and Spiritual Growth* (New York: Simon & Schuster, 1978)
POL	=	*People of the Lie: The Hope for Healing Human Evil* (New York: Simon & Schuster, 1983)
FARLT	=	*Further Along the Road Less Traveled: The Unending Journey Toward Spiritual Growth* (New York: Simon & Schuster, 1993)
DD	=	*The Different Drum: Community Making and Peace* (New York: Simon & Schuster, 1987)
WWTBB	=	*A World Waiting to Be Born: Civility Rediscovered* (New York: Bantam Books, 1993)
TFS	=	*The Friendly Snowflake: A Fable of Faith, Love and Family* (Atlanta: Turner Publishing, 1992)
BBTW	=	*A Bed by the Window: A Novel of Mystery and Redemption* (New York: Bantam Books, 1990)
WRCIM	=	*What Return Can I Make? Dimensions of the Christian Experience* (with Marilyn von Waldner and Patricia Kay) (New York: Simon & Schuster, 1985)
GFTJ	=	*Gifts for the Journey: Treasures of the Christian Life* (formerly titled *What Return Can I Make?*) (San Francisco: HarperSanFrancisco, 1995)
ISOS	=	*In Search of Stones: A Pilgrimage of Faith, Reason and Discovery* (New York: Hyperion Books, 1995)
DOTS	=	*Denial of the Soul: Spiritual and Medical Perspectives on Euthanasia* (New York: Harmony Books, 1997)

CHAPTER 1: THINKING

PAGE

25   "It is not through": Leonard Hodgson, *The Doctrine of the Trinity* (London: Nisbet and Co., 1943), p. 138.

28   passive dependent personality: *TRLT,* p. 99.

32   "A lie which is half": from "The Grandmother" by Alfred, Lord Tennyson.

35   Such thinking may border on the irrational: POL, p. 212.

43   Now I have the illusion: *ISOS,* p. 149.

43   "Neurosis is always": *Collected Works of C. G. Jung,* Bollingen Series, No. 20, *Psychology and Religion: West and East,* R. F. C. Hull, transl. (2nd ed.; Princeton, N.J.: Princeton University Press, 1973), vol. 2, p. 75.

44   "True to form": *TRLT,* p. 17.

50   An industrial psychologist once pointed out: See *TRLT,* p. 121.

51   the will to extend oneself for mutual growth: See *TRLT,* pp. 81–84.

55   "a radical response": Matthew Fox, *On Becoming a Musical Mystical Bear* (Mahwah, N.J. Paulist Press, 1976).

57   a conversation I had with a wealthy white stockbroker: *ISOS,* pp. 9–10.

58   Sunday morning Christian: *DD,* pp. 234–35; *ISOS,* p. 367.

59   what the patient does *not* say: *DD,* p. 237.

CHAPTER 2: CONSCIOUSNESS

PAGE

63   In *In Search of Stones,* I wrote: *ISOS,* pp. 348–49.

67   This loss is symbolized: *FARLT,* pp. 18–19.

68   In contrast, the impulse to do evil: See *FARLT,* p. 109.

70   I wrote in *People of the Lie: POL,* pp. 67–68.

72   The case of Bobby and his parents: ibid., pp. 47–61.

74   The Shadow: The term implies our "dark" side. I place quote marks around the word "dark" here because as I've become increasingly conscious of our cultural tendency to distort language, I take care to avoid stereotyping on the basis of color and racial connotations. Thus readers should view the word here symbolically, not literally.

75   It is our most effective safeguard: *WRCIM,* pp. 60–62.

CHAPTER 3: LEARNING AND GROWTH

PAGE

CHAPTER 4: PERSONAL LIFE CHOICES

CHAPTER 5: ORGANIZATIONAL LIFE CHOICES

183   Employees often suffer grievously: The anecdote that follows also appears in *WWTBB*, pp. 36–39.

187   The work at FCE: *WWTBB*, pp. 332–36.

187   As I noted in *The Road Less Traveled: TRLT*, pp. 65–66.

191   "What happens when": *WRCIM*, p. 152.

192   *The Wounded Healer* (New York: Doubleday, 1979).

194   The spirit of "dirty tricks" was virtually everywhere: *WWTBB*, p. 258.

CHAPTER 6: CHOICES ABOUT SOCIETY

PAGES

205   as I made quite clear in *People of the Lie: POL*, p. 211.

205   Using My Lai as a case study: *POL*, pp. 217–18.

206   When any institution becomes: *FARLT*, p. 180; *DD*, p. 251.

212   Whenever someone is bold enough to ask me: *FARLT*, p. 115.

214   "The truth will set you free . . ." . . . our glory as human beings: *DD*, pp. 178–84.

217   Perhaps no pitfall is more dangerous: The sense of entitlement to peace is discussed in *ISOS*, pp. 254–56.

217   the Prince of Peace: *ISOS*, p. 260.

226   It's just that as a Depression baby: *ISOS*, pp. 176–78.

232   "It is almost always easier": quoted in *Smithsonian*, v. 26, no. 12 (March 1996), p. 56.

232   Yet its influence is greater than ever: *ISOS*, pp. 172–73.

233   We were able to meet: *ISOS*, pp. 276–77.

233   In *A World Waiting to Be Born: WWTBB*, p. 222.

235   "Now there are diversities of gifts": I Corinthians 12:4–26.

236   what a wonderfully variegated fabric we are: *WWTBB*, pp. 223–24.

CHAPTER 7: THE "SCIENCE" OF GOD

PAGES

243   The use of measurement: *TRLT*, p. 226.

243   "To what appear to be": quoted in *TRLT*, p. 227. Originally in *Science and the Common Understanding* (New York: Simon & Schuster, 1953), p. 40.

244   the sacred consciousness and the secular consciousness: *Ascent of the Mountain, Flight of the Dove* (New York: Harper & Row, 1978).

246   *Stages of Faith* (New York: Harper & Row, 1981).

248   "My Name is Legion": *Masterpieces of Religious Verse* (New York: Harper & Row, 1948), p. 274.

249   "Henceforth you will be called Israel": Genesis 32:22–32; I am indebted to Frederick Buechner for bringing the meaning of this story home to me in his superb book of sermons, appropriately named after this great myth: *The Magnificent Defeat* (New York: Seabury, 1968).

250   We are all Israel: *DD,* pp. 206–208.

251   Since natural knowledge became: *FARLT,* p. 236.

251   This unwritten social contract is tearing us apart: *FARLT,* pp. 179–80.

256   The Holy Conjunction is the conjunction of integrity: *ISOS,* pp. 368–69.

258   we fail to take full advantage of them: *TRLT,* pp. 257–58.

258   The indications of grace and/or serendipity: *TRLT,* p. 260.

265   We must let them be true gifts: *TRLT,* pp. 309–10.

269   nowhere else on earth: *POL,* p. 264.

270   The deepest healing: *WRCIM,* p. 14.

273   And the most common emotional response: *DD,* pp. 86–105.

280   In *A World Waiting to Be Born: WWTBB,* p. 360.

283   Indeed, we might think on our more optimistic days: *WWTBB,* pp. 359–63.

283   And there are also many other things: John 21:25.

284   *The Weight of Glory & Other Addresses* (New York: Macmillan, 1980).

286   "It is a terrifying thing": *FARLT,* p. 234.

About the Author

·❈·

M. Scott Peck, M.D., is a psychiatrist and best-selling author of many books. Educated at Harvard (B.A.) and Case Western Reserve (M.D.), Dr. Peck served in administrative posts in the government during his career in the Army Medical Corps, and was then a psychiatrist in private practice from 1972 to 1984. For the past thirteen years, he has devoted much of his time and financial resources to the work of the Foundation for Community Encouragement, a nonprofit organization that he and his wife, Lily, helped found in 1984. He lives in northwest Connecticut.

❖

All who wish to explore FCE's services
or support its mission
are welcome to write or call

The Foundation for Community Encouragement
P.O. Box 449
Ridgefield, Connecticut 06877

Phone: (203) 431-9484
FAX: (203) 431-9349